D1558889

12/11/74

POWER
STRUGGLE

POWER STRUGGLE

RICHARD L. RUBENSTEIN

CHARLES SCRIBNER'S SONS
NEW YORK

Copyright © 1974 Richard L. Rubenstein

Library of Congress Cataloging in Publication Data

Rubenstein, Richard L
    Power struggle.
    Autobiographical.
    Bibliography: p.
    1. Rubenstein, Richard L.   I.   Title.
BM755.R83A36   296.3′092′4 [B]   73-1354
ISBN 0-684-13757-7

1 3 5 7 9 11 13 15 17 19 c/c 20 18 16 14 12 10 8 6 4 2

Printed in the United States of America

TO MY SISTER, ROBERTA SPOHN

CONTENTS

PREFACE

The story I have to tell is how a deeply disturbed individual was moved by his dis-ease to become a religious leader. I am that individual. This is the story of my dis-ease. It is also the story of my quest for healing and wholeness, for my dis-ease was always a painful search after health. In the course of that quest, I have turned for help and guidance to both traditional religion and psychoanalysis. As a result of psychoanalysis I was able to understand the extent to which my religious vocation was an expression of my profoundly disturbed emotions. Nevertheless, to the extent that I have found any degree of personal wholeness, my religious life has been at least as important as my psychoanalytic probing. If religion has been a dis-ease, it has in the long run been a healing dis-ease. Had I been healthier and better "adjusted" as a child and young man, I might never have turned to religion. I might have rested content with a mono-dimensional existence as a well-functioning cog in some corporate or institutional bureaucracy. Without my religious involvement, it is doubtful that I would have ever felt compelled to integrate my childhood with my adult experiences, my depth with my surface emotions, and the ancestral wisdom and experience of the race with the technological competences of the present age. Obviously, the quest for wholeness is never complete. Nevertheless, if religion was my illness, it also was and is my road to health.

Much of this book was written in Florence, Italy, where I spent part of 1972 teaching at Florida State University's Study Center. I cannot think of the hours I spent working on the book in Florence without conjuring up the image of the stones of Florence. They were a living presence that helped to make this book possible.

I am grateful to Miss Kathy Siriani who assisted me with the typing in Florence and to Miss Janice Donahoe who helped me in the same capacity in Tallahassee. I am indebted to Professors John Carey and Lawrence Cunningham of the Department of Religion of Florida State University for reading parts of the manuscript and offering their helpful comments. Because of the very personal nature of this book, I am especially grateful to my wife Betty for her help at every stage of writing and editing. Above all, I am indebted to my editor, Norman Kotker, whose assistance and counsel were indispensable and invaluable.

Tallahassee, Florida
November 7, 1973

POWER
STRUGGLE

1

THE SCREECH OWL

When a theologian discusses his religious commitments, especially in scholarly writing, his readers seldom catch a glimpse of the anguish that moved him. What is affirmed often appears bloodless, as if arising out of intellectual reflection rather than experience. Nevertheless, every theologian has a story to tell. Good theology is always *embodied* theology. It arises out of and reflects life. And, in life, we are more often instructed by heartbreak and failure than by success. This book tells the story of my instruction.

Today, I am professor of religion at Florida State University. I first came to Tallahassee in March 1970 as a visiting professor for one term. I had been a rabbi at the University of Pittsburgh for twelve years, serving as director of the B'nai B'rith Hillel Foundation and Chaplain to Jewish Students. I had been entitled to a sabbatical leave for several years. When Florida State's invitation came, I decided to take the overdue sabbatical. I expected to return to Pittsburgh the following fall. I never did.

For reasons that will be made evident, I am a theologian committed to academic service in a secular university. I no longer have any interest in professional employment within the Jewish community, although at one

1

time I wanted to serve the Jewish people both as a rabbi and a theologian. Theology has been my principal concern for years. However, the theological position at which I arrived inescapably involved my estrangement from the American Jewish community, an estrangement that is intellectual, spiritual, and geographical. The roots and dimensions of that estrangement will be explored in the pages that follow.

I first met the men who were to invite me to Tallahassee in Atlanta, Georgia in the fall of 1965. I had been asked to participate in a conference on "America and the Future of Theology" at Emory University as one of the respondents to a paper by Thomas J. J. Altizer. Altizer was then a professor at Emory. He was and is one of America's most famous 'death-of-God' theologians. Altizer's other respondent was Professor Charles Long, a distinguished black historian of religion at the University of Chicago. I was puzzled by the invitation. I had not previously heard of Altizer. I had no idea of why anybody would want me to respond to him. At the time, the 'death-of-God' controversy was receiving its most intense coverage from the news media but I was paying little attention.

When Altizer read his paper practically every seat in Emory's Glenn Memorial Church was taken. Because of the excitement generated by the 'death-of-God' controversy, a disproportionately large number of the academic teachers of religion and their graduate students throughout the South were present. They had come to hear Altizer. Hardly anyone at the conference, save the planners, had ever heard of me. I had no academic position. I had published no books. I had, however, published a number of articles expressing involvement in the problem of the 'death of God.'

It is difficult briefly to do justice to Altizer's brilliant conference paper. However, a few words are sufficient to indicate where we agreed and disagreed. One of Altizer's books is entitled *The Gospel of Christian Atheism*, that is the *good news* of Christian atheism. For Altizer the 'death of God' has always been an enormously liberating event. Seldom has Altizer been as insistent in his optimism as he was that day in Atlanta. In his presentation, he insisted that the 'death of God' was a redemptive event which fulfilled the true meaning of Christianity: The 'death of God' finally permitted men to be truly free and fully human in Christ for the first time.

In my response, I agreed that "we live in the time of the death of God." I hesitated then as I hesitate to this day to use the phrase "God is dead." I explained that I used the phrase the "time of the death of God" to indicate my conviction that "radical cognition of God's absence as a cultural fact offers the only basis for theological speculation in our times." I was not then nor am I now an atheist. Nevertheless, by agreeing with Altizer, I had publicly rejected the normative, biblical-rabbinic conception of God in Judaism. That rejection was to have far-reaching consequences in the years that followed. At the time, however, I gave little thought to the consequences although I can honestly say that I would not have altered a single word had I foreseen all of the ramifications of my stand.

I did part company with Altizer on the enthusiasm with which he greeted the contemporary collapse of faith. The event struck me with sadness rather than enthusiasm. I believe that men are irretrievably locked in the biological world of growth, decay, and mortality with no hope of escape. I was, however, deeply skeptical of the capacity of most men to look upon their common condition without illusion. There is, in Sartre's phrase, "No Exit" from these primordial limitations of the condition of mankind. Unlike Altizer I saw no redemptive significance in the world both of us agreed we were confronting. Nor did I look forward to the future with his hopefulness. I expressed my apprehension:

> Who knows what forms of secular tyranny and security America may choose rather than endure the awesome anxiety of a hopeless and meaningless cosmos? Dostoievsky saw this in the legend of the Grand Inquisitor. The sad few who acknowledge the truth [of the 'death of God'] will not rejoice in it.

I spoke also of my own religious faith in the "time of the death of God," a faith that partook of ultimate resignation in the inevitable disappearance of all things human. Trained a rabbi, I had become a thoroughly convinced pagan without ceasing to be Jewish. My deepest conviction, then as now, was that we are of earth, that we were destined to return to earth, and that the joys available to us as men are earthly joys and celebrations.

My pagan faith was one that the conservative southern Protestants at the conference were unable to share. Nevertheless, they understood my theological pessimism in the face of the 'death of God.' I had the distinct feeling that many of those present recognized my position as one to which they might be drawn were they ever to lose their Christian faith.

There was another element in my response that was apparently understood. Where Altizer rejoiced at the redemptive possibilities of the 'death of God,' I looked upon Auschwitz as a paradigmatic expression of that event. In a technologically sophisticated world in which men are restrained only by the limitations of their own power, nothing can prevent the mass annihilation of millions if the perpetrators of such projects have the competence and the will to carry them out.

When I completed my response I understood immediately that, though I had not found agreement, I had been taken seriously. Dean Roger Shinn of New York's Union Theological Seminary has described the confrontation in his book *Man: The New Humanism*:

> At Emory University's convocation on "America and the Future of Theology" in November of 1965, a dramatic confrontation . . . took place. Thomas Altizer expressed his jubilation in American messianism and the coming of the new age. Then Rabbi Richard L. Rubenstein, replying, said that he missed the needed note of anguish. He agreed with Altizer about "the death of God as a cultural event." But he rejected "too quick a dance of joy at the great funeral." Then the rabbi reminded the Christian of "the old Augustinian-Calvinist notion of original sin," describing it as a theological insight "on target." Throughout two days Rabbi Rubenstein impressed the predominantly Christian gathering with the facts of the concentration camps of the twentieth century and the vicious nature of the human sin that is sometimes subdued but never eliminated from life.

When the session was over, a small group gathered around me to ask further questions. A young man introduced himself as Edward Fiske of the *New York Times*. He asked me to discuss some of my ideas with him at lunch. Fiske is theologically trained and reports on religion for the *Times*. The next day the *Times* carried a story with a four column headline on my talk and Fiske's subsequent interview. I had irrevocably crossed a point of no return. Henceforth, my theological views, which received wide publicity, would be unacceptable to most of my fellow Jewish thinkers.

Shortly after the Atlanta conference, I received a letter from Lawrence Grow, then an editor at Bobbs-Merrill, expressing interest in publishing a book on my theological views.

I had been approached by a number of publishers in previous years about the possibility of doing a book for them. I had not felt ready. When Grow wrote to me, I did feel ready to offer a serious statement of my views. As a result of the Atlanta conference I had achieved instantaneous visibility in theological circles, but I was determined not to become a

4

creature of the media. I had trained too long and had developed my position out of too much personal anguish to rest content with having my theology communicated primarily by the news media, with the inevitable leveling and distorting process that attends the translation of complex ideas into notions a mass audience can grasp. The spectacle of a rabbi taking a controversial theological position had a certain news value. That was not the foundation upon which I wanted to build my career as a theologian. I welcomed Grow's invitation because it afforded me the opportunity to state my convictions in my own way and in my own words. My first book, *After Auschwitz*, appeared toward the end of 1966.

The title *After Auschwitz* was meant to pose an obvious question, *"What kind of God can Jews believe in after the death camps?"* *After Auschwitz* expressed a distinctively Jewish involvement with the theme of the 'death of God,' a theme with which I had become increasingly preoccupied over the years.

My involvement was largely rooted in the awesome encounter of German and Jew in the twentieth century. My first wife was a Dutch Jewish woman whose family had escaped from Holland immediately after the Nazis began their invasion in May 1940. When the invasion suddenly began, Max van der Veen, Elly's father, clearly understood the danger. He abandoned his beautiful home in Aerdenhout and, without money or passports, made his way to the harbor at Ijmuiden where he, his wife Lucy, and their family were taken to safety in England by a British mine sweeper. One day the van der Veens lived in an elegant three story home in a wooded area of Aerdenhout, an upper-middle-class community; the next they were among the lucky few who were penniless refugees. Most Dutch Jews were not so lucky. They were to be funneled through Westerbroek concentration camp to their final destination at Auschwitz.

Like Anne Frank, Elly was twelve in May 1940. In addition to the transitions of normal adolescence, Elly had to cope with the totally unanticipated transition from one country and language to another. I met the van der Veens in Cincinnati, Ohio, where Max eventually found work as a greeting card salesman. Unlike Anne Frank, Elly did not have to spend her adolescent years hiding in the *achterhuis*. She escaped but the narrow escape became part of the psychic fibre of our family.

In the summer of 1960, immediately after receiving my doctorate, I spent three months in Holland with Elly and our three children, Aaron,

Hannah, and Jeremy. At the time the children were eleven, nine, and two respectively. One day I was walking on Amsterdam's Leidsestraat and met nine-year-old Hannah. She was reading a book she had just purchased and was oblivious to what was going on around her. I stopped her and noticed that the book was *Anne Frank: The Diary of a Young Girl*. Even at nine Hannah read *Anne Frank* with a very different kind of involvement than most American girls. As she walked safely through the streets of her mother's birthplace, American-born Hannah knew that she was almost miraculously one of the survivors of the extermination of Europe's Jews.

It was almost a miracle but not quite. Nobody in Max van der Veen's circle of friends expected the Nazi invasion. They were all upper-class Jews. Their families had lived in Holland for over three hundred years. One of Max's forebears laid the cornerstone of the first Ashkenazic synagogue in Amsterdam. (There were two Jewish communities in Holland, the Sephardim who came originally from Spain and Portugal, and the Ashkenazim who came primarily from Rhineland Germany.) The first night of the German invasion, Max gathered together with a group of friends and relatives to talk over the situation. The group consisted of stockbrokers, bankers, and prosperous businessmen. Judaism had only a vestigial significance to them. Rabbis were called in for weddings and funerals, if at all. At best, these highly successful men regarded Jewishness as an incurable hereditary disease. Yet they were believers. They believed in the stability and predictability of their enclosed, comfortable bourgeois world. Even the initial shock of the invasion did not dislodge their faith in that world. Max was the only unbeliever among them. He had used his private resources to help German Jews escape. At the time of the invasion there was a German Jewish family living with the van der Veens. Max had no illusions about what was coming, and wanted to flee immediately. One of his friends said he would remain until the banks reopened so that he could withdraw sufficient funds with which to flee. Another wanted to revalidate his passport before taking action. Everybody except Max had the best of reasons for doing nothing.

Most of the men were totally oblivious of the extent to which they resembled chieftains and warriors of African tribes immediately after their capture by slave traders. They did not comprehend that the social structures which had given their lives a semblance of order had instantaneously succumbed to total collapse. The comfortable world of banks, bourses, business, and bureaucracies no longer facilitated human intercourse for them. These conservative, law-abiding men had no idea of

6

how thoroughly their world had been destroyed by the invaders. In the days that followed there would still be business, banks, and bureaucracies but, for Holland's Jews, these institutions would become instruments of extermination.

Executions are important human events. They ought to be taken seriously. Animals know nothing of executions. When an animal is cornered, it is likely to become more rather than less dangerous. All of its vital instincts struggle for the sake of life. Animals may die of fright but only human beings willingly consent to their own undoing when cornered. Why should a victim at a hanging or a beheading die with dignity? Why does he not scream, kick, bite, defecate, injure, or perhaps kill those who seek to destroy him? Why does he offer even the slightest cooperation to his executioners? Is it that men are so terrified at the prospect of being expelled from the human world, that they willingly play their assigned roles, even when the role is victim at a beheading? At an execution culture triumphs over nature. Most men fear expulsion from the human world more than death.

Max's friends did not yet know that they had been condemned to elimination. They were destined to play out their part at history's greatest execution, but they still believed in laws and authority, even when the authorities had become their executioners. A few miles away in Bossum near Utrecht, Lucy van der Veen's sister, Ida van Sohn, was taking stock of her family's situation. In addition to her children, widowed Ida had an adolescent foster son who had no illusions about the new "authorities." He was born in Vienna and lived there until the *Anschluss*. His parents thought they had sent him to safety in Holland. His name was Jakov Lind. Today he is a distinguished writer. (Jakov has told the story of his escape in his memoir, *Counting My Steps*.) In May 1940 he was a teenager who understood what most of Holland's Jews were not to understand until it was too late, that the twentieth century's really dangerous criminals were often to be found at the heads of government bureaus rather than in the underworld. Every layer of European society contained men and women who were ready to render the ruling criminals their homage. Jakov understood that survival depended upon an attitude of almost universal distrust and deception. He could trust neither the Nazis nor their Dutch puppets. Nor could he trust the *Joodsche Raad,* in German, the *Jüdenräte,* the Jewish communal authorities the Nazis permitted to function in order to facilitate the executions they had planned.

Jakov survived by disbelief, disguise, and incredible cunning. He was more like a cornered animal than the human victim who dies "a good death." He acquired false papers and, disguised as a non-Jew, went into hiding in the "eye of the hurricane," in Nazi Germany itself!

Jakov's solution was impossible for Max and his family. Max instinctively understood that his world had collapsed and that the "new order" offered his family only death. What does one do in a world in which the forces of "law and order" take you away to be starved, dehumanized and then gassed, when the police may assign your daughter the role of *Feldhure*, a compulsory prostitute in a *Wehrmacht* brothel, until, broken and used up, they exterminate her? In what does sanity consist? Does it consist in adjustment to society? Is it sane to be well-adjusted at one's own beheading? Does sanity consist in trusting Jews and mistrusting non-Jews when even the Jewish community's "leaders" cooperated with the Nazis by registering their own people and selecting those who were first to fill the deportation quotas for "labor service" in the East? Of course, the Jewish "leaders" had reasons for acting as they did: Things might have been worse, they argued, if they had not cooperated. The same argument was offered by church authorities to defend Pope Pius XII's refusal publicly to condemn the death camps. Who could one trust? The Jewish leaders? The Nazis? The Pope? Was Jakov Lind insane in his total distrust of everybody, Jew and gentile alike, and in his clawing resolve to survive under all circumstances?

In what does morality consist in a topsy-turvy world? Is it wrong to "do it in the road," to use the Beatle's phrase, or to take part in perverse orgies, but right to become a *Feldhure* because that is the role the forces of "law and order" often assigned to young, physically attractive Jewish women in Nazi Europe? Is a single privately motivated killing wrong while the killing of thousands at mass graves was right because the order was given?

For Max there was a way out—escape to England and thence to America. Fortunately, like Jakov Lind, he had no illusions. *Those who believed too much perished.* Max never had a God to believe in. He was never compelled to endure a 'death-of-God' experience, but before May 10, 1940, there was much that Max trusted and in which he believed. He survived because, unlike his friends, he did not deceive himself. After May 10, 1940, he knew he could no longer trust the men and the public institutions that had hitherto comprised his world.

The 'death-of-God' is a theological code word for *the collapse of authority*, political authority, moral authority, social authority and religious authority. It is a worldwide phenomenon that has many roots. Perhaps the deepest root has been the intuitive recognition that all men are caught in a seemingly tragic dilemma: They cannot do without social structures and their legitimating ideologies, yet these structures have had an increasingly pathogenic effect upon them as individuals. To trust too willingly those in authority, whether that authority is political or religious, often results in condemning oneself to illness and even death; to reject all authority is to condemn oneself to suicidal anarchy.

My own preoccupation with the 'death of God' had many roots. Max van der Veen's refusal to deceive himself about the total collapse of his society was especially important. There were also intellectual roots: While a graduate student at Harvard in the fifties I was deeply influenced by Paul Johannes Tillich, whom Thomas Altizer and William Hamilton have rightly called "the father of radical theology." Tillich's course on "Classical German Philosophy" in which he discussed Kant, Fichte, Schelling, Hegel, Kierkegaard, Marx, and Nietzsche had a profound effect upon me. More than any other teacher, the lectures of this great Protestant thinker helped me to understand that the crisis of faith confronting contemporary Judaism and Christianity had its origins in the titanic social and technological transformations of the nineteenth and twentieth centuries.

My encounter with psychoanalysis and psychotherapy was another source of my involvement in the problem of the 'death of God.' I entered psychoanalytic psychotherapy in 1953, a year after my rabbinic ordination. At the time, I was the rabbi of a small middle-class congregation in Brockton, Massachusetts. For several years, I had suspected that there was much emotional illness in my ambition to become a rabbi. When I think of my early years as a rabbi, I am reminded of a painting in the Capodimonte Museum of Naples, Italy, Pieter Brueghel's "The Blind Leading the Blind." The crisis that finally moved me to seek help was the realization that the most important single adult relationship in my life at the time, my marriage, had collapsed almost entirely.

There was much irony in my resort to psychoanalysis. Every Sabbath members of my congregation would gather to hear me interpret Judaism's ancient wisdom so that it could help them in the conduct of their lives. Like most members of the American middle class, they were doing the best they could to cope with the problems of marriage, childrearing and breadwinning. They would often turn to me for counseling when day-to-day living became too difficult to manage. Yet, I was perhaps in greater need of help than they!

One of the many hopes with which I entered rabbinical studies was that normative Judaism might contain the wisdom out of which I could construct a fulfilling life. Normative Judaism had given millions of mén such guidance for thousands of years. As a rabbi, I was supposed to interpret Judaism's wisdom so that it might serve as a guide to my community. Had I been capable of ameliorating the anguish of my life as man, husband, and father by living in accordance with traditional belief and practice, I would not have turned to psychoanalysis. Initially, I felt extremely guilty; I was convinced that there was something terribly wrong with me that made me incapable of being nurtured by my ancestral faith. Very slowly, painfully, and hesitantly, I came to understand that the wisdom of the past could not have anticipated the personal and social disorders of the topsy-turvy world of the twentieth century.

Tillich and psychoanalysis contributed to my concern with the collapse of faith. A dramatic confrontation on August 17, 1961, in West Berlin brought the issue to a head. I have told the story of that encounter in *After Auschwitz*. A part of that story must be retold here.

I was scheduled to enter Germany from Holland on August 13, 1961 for a two week fact-finding tour that had been arranged for me by the *Bundespresseamt*, the Press and Information Office of the West German Federal Republic. August 13 turned out to be the day the Berlin Wall was suddenly erected. I delayed my trip for two days because of the crisis. When I arrived in Bonn, the representatives of the *Bundespresseamt* encouraged me to fly directly to West Berlin and concentrate on what was taking place there. The atmosphere in Germany was apocalyptic. No one knew whether or not the crisis would lead to a nuclear war between the great powers. It was not at all certain that those who entered Berlin would ever leave it.

When I arrived in Berlin, the *Bundespresseamt* arranged an interview for me with Dean Heinrich Grueber of the Evangelical Church in East and West Berlin. As long as I live, I shall never forget one comment made by the dean in our conversation. Referring to Auschwitz, Dean Grueber insisted, "For some reason, it was part of God's plan that the Jews died. God demands our death daily. He is the Lord, He is the Master, all is in His keeping and ordering."

The dean went on to liken Hitler to Nebuchadnezzar and other "rods

10

of God's anger." Hitler was just a latter-day "whip" God had used against "his own people." The dean's conviction that Hitler had been the "rod" with which God had smitten Israel was not the expression of an anti-Semite. Grueber had almost lost his life in the concentration camp at Dachau. He was the only German voluntarily to go to Jerusalem to testify at the trial of Adolf Eichmann. Dean Grueber was a man of impeccable honesty, courage, and religious faith. Furthermore, his insistence that even in the death camps, God was responsible for the destiny of Israel as his chosen people was fully consistent with normative Jewish faith. In the face of every major disaster in Israel's history, her religious leaders have always discerned the hand of a just and all-powerful God. There are today Orthodox Jews who do not shy away from the dean's conclusion. They would, of course, add that the God who had destroyed his people at Auschwitz was the same God who was to bless them with the land of Israel and Jerusalem within less than a generation.

In the atmosphere of crisis-laden Berlin, the unambiguous declaration by a leading German clergyman that God had sent Adolf Hitler to exterminate the Jews unified the intellectual and experiential roots of my growing collapse of faith. It finally brought to expression a thorough-going rejection of the biblical God on my part. If indeed such a God holds the destiny of mankind in his power, his resort to death camps to bring about his ends is so obscene that I would rather spend my life in perpetual revolt than render him even the slightest homage. For millennia men have insisted on the poverty of human knowledge before the infinite wisdom of the Divine. Most men have followed Job's example and silenced their bitter complaints. If this God, the God of Auschwitz exists, I could not silence mine.

In actuality, Dean Grueber's insistence that Hitler was God's tool was indicative of the incredible extremes to which men are driven when they try to make sense of the surrealistic world of the twentieth century in pre-twentieth century terms. Most men find the loss of meaning exceedingly difficult to bear. Durkheim called the absence of meaning and structure *anomie*. He regarded mankind's social world as a fictitious but nevertheless potent defense against anomie. In the twentieth century, human society is no longer a defense against anomie. Society itself has become the source of *rationalized meaninglessness* for countless millions. Yet, so great is the threat of worldlessness, the fear of being without a place in the human world, that even when society's role is that of impersonal executioner, the victims desperately seek meaning and purpose

11

in their own execution. Some very religious Jews agree with Dean Grueber because they share with him a terror of a totally anomic world. If Hitler had been doing God's work, they could at least believe that their agony had some ultimate reason behind it. If Hitler was simply an extraordinarily capable criminal who had successfully wreaked havoc on half a planet, the experience of the victims had neither meaning nor purpose. It was simply their pathetic destiny to be born to the losing side and never, never, never would the scales of vindication be balanced.

For more than two thousand years most Jews had no choice but to believe that they were the elect of God and that God was ultimately responsible for whatever happened to them. Living as they did, as powerless outsiders, only the conviction that their destiny was in the hands of a king more powerful than any earthly king could give any sense of cosmic dignity and security to their radically insecure lives. Even the shock of Auschwitz was not potent enough to disillusion them.

When Dean Grueber spoke to me I realized that I could evade the question of God and the death camps no longer. The components of my world could no longer neatly fit together. As a rabbi I was obliged to defend Israel's sacred traditions. No doctrine was as central to normative Judaism as the doctrine of Israel's election by a just God who guided her destiny. Yet, I could only defend that doctrine by agreeing with Dean Grueber.

My crisis of belief had been building up for years. I had good reason for seeking to avoid it. Hitler had almost succeeded in destroying Judaism completely. In the face of so catastrophic an assault, the natural instinct of any Jew with a particle of loyalty was to defend the pathetic remnant of the religious tradition the Nazis had almost completely annihilated. When I entered the Jewish Theological Seminary in 1948, only three years after the ovens had been stopped, I was determined to do what I could to help heal the wounds of my people. I had absolutely no desire to express serious doubts about a religious tradition which had almost succumbed to the worst assault ever mounted against it. I understood that the loss of the great centers of Jewish learning in Eastern Europe was a disaster of millennial proportions. The Eastern European centers were the custodians and the authentic transmitters of the traditions of the Jewish past. As long as these centers flourished, the link between the Jewish past and the present had been alive. The Germans smashed irretrievably a European Jewish culture which had proven viable for almost two thousand years.

In 1948 those of us who entered the Jewish Theological Seminary were unknowingly far more like young Sioux or Cherokee warriors after the defeat of their people than we could possibly have imagined. Triumphant white men had smashed the Indians' native cultures. Others had smashed ours far more thoroughly than we knew. In retrospect, that too was part of what the 'death of God' meant to me. I was the heir of a native culture that had begun to decay in the eighteenth century when some of my ancestors were "emancipated" from the world that had given structure and integrity to their lives. The process of emancipation was brought to completion at Auschwitz. No matter how resolved we were in 1948 as rabbinical students to restore our tribal culture and its gods or to synthesize it with twentieth-century America, the task was beyond our capacities. There are today centers of traditional Judaism in both Israel and America but they cannot begin to replace what was lost.

When Dean Grueber spoke to me of Adolf Hitler as God's tool, my immediate response was to declare, "I'd rather be an atheist than believe in such a God."

He responded, "Dr. Rubenstein, how can you be a rabbi and say such a thing?"

"There is one thing I need more than God to be a rabbi—a few live Jews," I replied. "If I believed in your God I'd have to believe that the victims of the camps received from their God no more than what they deserved."

The question, "How is it possible to believe in a just, all-powerful God after Auschwitz?" is so immediately obvious that any child might ask it. Nevertheless, for almost twenty years after World War II hardly any Jewish religious thinker save Martin Buber dared to give expression to it in print. Undoubtedly, the wound was too painful. There were also overwhelmingly important practical problems to be dealt with. The displaced persons camps of Europe had to be emptied. The Jews of Israel had to find a way to secure their settlement and establish their state.

It was never certain that Israel would survive. To this day no Jew can ever be free of the fear that Auschwitz may someday be repeated. In a period when survival and reconstruction took absolute priority, radical questioning of the cornerstone of Jewish faith had to be avoided at all costs.

Nevertheless, there is a certain strangeness to the silence about Auschwitz in Jewish religious writing from 1945 to 1965, with the possible exception of Martin Buber's *Eclipse of God*. One theologian of Hasidic origin wrote nostalgic recollections of life in Eastern Europe; other scholars began to discuss Kierkegaard's "leap of faith"; another leading thinker optimistically described God as "the power that makes for salvation in the world," but nothing was written that might have indicated that the writers lived in the same century as Auschwitz and the birth of Israel.

In recent years a prominent Jewish thinker has taught that God speaks to Israel out of Auschwitz in a "commanding voice" which forbids his people "to deny or despair of God" lest, by their denial, they give Hitler "yet another posthumous victory." I can respect the loyalty that moves this man to attempt to replicate the faith of those whose culture was extinguished with their lives in the death camps. It is my conviction that what he proposes is futile. Nevertheless, the same resolve to be faithful to the memory and the God of the victims was one of the healthier elements in my choice of a rabbinic rather than a secular career. Unfortunately, I could not affirm both the justice of God and the innocence of the victims.

That same writer, who today speaks of God's "commanding voice" at Auschwitz, has confessed that for years he believed that historical events such as the extermination camps were utterly irrelevant to Israel's faith in God! His attention was so exclusively focused on a sovereign and omnipotent God that the extermination of Europe's Jews was a datum of no consequence to his Jewish theology.

According to Anna Freud, the ego often defends itself against unwanted pain by what she calls "denial in fantasy." Though one part of the ego knows the truth, the subject resorts to wish-fulfilling daydreams to deny it. It is not surprising that Jewish religious thinkers avoided the subject of Auschwitz for as long as they did. The very magnitude of the catastrophe, as well as its radical novelty, had an understandably paralyzing effect upon them. Only the Israelis were denied the luxury of denial. They may not have taken Auschwitz seriously as a religious problem; they certainly understood the threat it implied to their survival. For the Israelis, Auschwitz had a simple lesson: If they possessed the resources and the resolve to defend themselves, they and their community would survive; if they failed of either resource or resolve no power would or could prevent a second Auschwitz. There was little religious faith in Israel; there was animal health. The Israelis had no intention of consenting to their own execution.

In the midst of catastrophe the expression of radical theological doubt is a luxury. I was ordained less than ten years after the war ended. For nine years I fought an increasingly difficult fight with myself. I wanted to believe in my ancestral faith. Tillich, psychoanalysis, and the gut-perception of my own animal vitality finally forced me to a posture of radical questioning. The overwhelming travail of my people restrained me. After meeting Dean Grueber, nothing could hold me back any longer.

Shortly after the publication of my first book, Tom Altizer told me he expected that my writings would be better received among Christians than Jews. In the past eight years Altizer's prediction has proven essentially correct. When *After Auschwitz* first appeared it was reviewed favorably in *Christian Century*, *Commonweal*, and in a few Jewish publications. However, the establishment Jewish publications largely ignored it. To this day the official journal of the Rabbinical Assembly of America, the national rabbinical organization in which I remain a member in good standing, has yet to review any of my books.

The public ignoring of my books was one response—and a relatively kind one. Beneath it lay another response: anger. Recently, Professor Jacob Neusner wrote of mainstream Jewish reaction to my writings: "The consequence [of the writings] has been an unprecedented torrent of personal abuse, so that he has been nearly driven out of Jewish public life." * Neusner generously regards the abuse as "the highest possible tribute . . . to the compelling importance of his contribution." I regard the response as entirely predictable. Social scientists note that groups tend violently to reject negations of beliefs that have been "held with deep conviction" and that have "some relevance to action." They also tend to react with great hostility to those who come forward with such negations. For thousands of years, Jews have drawn strength, pride, and dignity from the belief that they were the community of the elect. They could hardly be expected to react with dispassionate calm when one of their own rabbis asserted publicly that the bitterest tragedy in their entire history empirically disproved their most deeply held belief about themselves.

One of the most thoroughly modern responses to my writings was *bureaucratic excommunication*. A leading executive of a major Jewish organization, who was not without experience in the ways of religious bureaucracies, once told me:

Dick, you have been subjected to bureaucratic excommunication. You will not be dropped officially, but you have already been dropped

* Jacob Neusner, "Implications of the Holocaust for Jewish Theology," *The Jewish Advocate* (April 30, 1972).

from every establishment committee. Every attempt will be made to isolate you. Formal expulsion would run the risk of a story in the *New York Times* or *Time*. Heresy trials have gone out of fashion. There is something ugly about inquisitions. Besides, they are unnecessary. The same result can be accomplished without publicity and without allowing you a chance to defend yourself, something your "friends" in the establishment would hardly welcome. They have for all practical purposes excommunicated you without doing anything publicly that might embarrass them.

At the time, I found those observations hard to accept. One might expect that kind of Kafkaesque response from a Stalinist apparatus. Initially, it seemed implausible that this was happening to me in a religious community which stressed "unity in diversity." I no longer doubt the accuracy of his observation. Nor is there anything unique about my experience. Contemporary religious communities are as subject to the processes of routinization, rationalization, and bureaucratization as any governmental or corporate organization. Bureaucratic excommunication is a very effective contemporary means of dealing with heterodox thinkers. It is fully consistent with strategies used in government and business. Religious bureaucracies are as likely to have their enemies lists as government bureaucracies. Thousands of men have lost their positions, failed of promotion, or have been consigned to professional limbo by anonymous bureaucrats whose decisions are subject to review only by their fellow bureaucrats.

As my publications became better known, it became increasingly difficult for me to secure any position within the Jewish community. When I sought to be considered for specific rabbinic positions, it was somehow impossible for me even to be interviewed by the congregations. Of far greater importance, I found it impossible to secure a full-time academic post for ten years after receiving my Ph.D. at Harvard in a period of the greatest prosperity the American academic community had ever enjoyed.

Most religion departments that hire Jews depend upon Jewish money to pay for the appointment. In private universities there is a measure of justice in this arrangement. Most private universities still retain very strong ties to Protestantism. Even when these institutions become nonsectarian, the social, religious, and historical links to Protestantism remain very potent. When Jewish studies are introduced, it is normal for these institutions to seek financial support for the project from wealthy Jews or from the established Jewish community.

I was apparently considered by a number of universities after the publication of *After Auschwitz* and my second book, *The Religious Imagination*, but no position was ever offered. After I became a professor at Florida State University, a number of professors at religion departments at other universities volunteered the same story: They had wanted to invite me to their university, but the appointment of a Jewish professor of religion could not be made without the approval of the Jewish family or the local federation of Jewish philanthropies that was providing the funds for the project. In each instance, the department was informed that I was too "controversial" to be approved by the Jewish leaders of the community.

In contemporary society, instantaneous electronic communication and computer technology make every person's dossier readily available. In the Jewish community, the process of getting a line on an individual is relatively simple. Directors of charitable federations get to know each other at conventions of their professional organizations. Well-to-do, lay leaders frequent the same winter resorts and are likely to meet their opposite numbers from other large cities. Reputations are made and broken over the long distance lines connecting Los Angeles, Pittsburgh, Dallas, Atlanta, Boston, and Miami.

When I wrote *After Auschwitz* I did not fully comprehend how effective the new system had become. Nevertheless, I was fortunate. The system may have added obstacles to my career. It was not able to prevent me from writing and teaching. America is simply too diversified socially, culturally, and religiously for any voluntary group to control the destiny of any man who is willing to take the risk of finding a place for himself. After I came to understand that I would be confronted with the hostility of men of great power within the Jewish community, I realized that it would be wise to find a position that would be free of such pressure. It was not easy to uproot myself and my family and move to a community in which there were very few Jews. Nevertheless, after writing *After Auschwitz* I could only pursue my career as a theologian in such a community! When Tom Altizer told me that my work was more likely to be taken seriously by Christian than by Jewish thinkers, I did not anticipate that I would be compelled literally to become an exile from my own people in order to interpret their religious existence in freedom. In

17

fairness, the estrangement has had as much to do with my inner dynamics as the community's.

Naturally, it is easier for reflective Christians to face the problem of God after Auschwitz than it is for Jews. Their history, their lives, are less involved. Their theological foundations are less likely to be shattered by the holocaust. A conservative Christian might interpret Auschwitz as further proof that God has rejected Israel for having denied Christ. Immediately after World War II, a number of Christian groups did profess to see the hand of God in Auschwitz. When I spoke at Emory in 1965, I was not really challenging the faith of most of the Christians at the conference. On the contrary, I was confirming it in at least two distinctive ways: I reminded them of the anthropological and psychological relevance of one of the most fundamental Christian doctrines, original sin and the fallen condition of mankind; I also gave them a glimpse of what it would *really* be like to give up the biblical God of history. When I raised with Jews the issue of God and the death camps, I was focusing on an area of maximum pain; when I raised the same issue with Christians, I was helping to sharpen their perceptions of where they stood as Christians. It is not surprising that Christians were less disturbed by what I said and wrote than were Jews.

There were moments when silence about God and Auschwitz seemed the wiser, certainly the more practical, course, yet I could not consent to be silent. An unacknowledged psychic wound ultimately does far more harm than a wound one probes in spite of its excruciating pain.

Herbert Marcuse is responsible for the conception of "surplus repression." A certain amount of repression is necessary for the functioning of society. Marcuse has designated this necessary repression as "basic repression." Surplus repression arises from the *additional* restraints required by "institutions of domination to maintain their hold over men." In my opinion, the massive presence of surplus repression in mainstream Judaism is indisputable. My own refusal to remain silent about God and Auschwitz paralleled my growing realization of the life-destroying character of the repression that characterized my personal life. Yet, as I began to reject the traditional interpretation of Jewish existence before God, my ability to affirm my own identity as a Jew became *less* problematic. I no longer needed the myth of God's election to render acceptable my religious identity. Slowly, in the aesthetic, sexual, and religious areas of life, I was learning to accept and be grateful for the sheer givenness of my own being.

I shall never forget the first breakfast I had in my new home in Tallahassee. As I sat down, I mentioned to my wife that a girl at the university had brought a copy of "The Owl of Minerva" to my office the day before. The "Owl" is the four page quarterly published by the Hegel Society of America to keep its members abreast of Hegelian studies and research. I reminded Betty of Hegel's remark at the end of the preface to the *Philosophy of Right*:

> When philosophy paints its grey in grey, then has a shape of life grown old. By philosophy's grey in grey it cannot be rejuvenated but only understood. The owl of Minerva spreads it wings only with the falling of the dusk.

It was ten minutes after seven in the morning. I looked up and was startled to notice a screech owl perched on the huge live oak directly behind our house. The owl stared at me through the window. We maintained a kind of hypnotic eye contact for over a minute. Dawn was breaking rather than dusk falling. Somehow, at that instant, the bird symbolized Minerva's owl to me. Dusk had fallen on the proud and venerable faith that had guided my people. Today it can only be understood; it cannot be rejuvenated. I am by no means the only rabbi for whom the majestic tradition has lost its ancient meaning. I am one of the few who is willing to declare openly what many feel but cannot say. If the questions I have been asking and the views I have been propounding were really without substance, they would not have evoked so much anger.

The shape of that venerable tradition has grown old. The embattled history of the State of Israel has done as much as the European tragedy to hasten its senescence. Today it can be maintained only by a strategy of withdrawal and isolation from the larger world. This is very difficult in the century of electronic communication. In the past, religious Jews could usually lock the world out by closing their doors and turning to their sacred books. Today, the larger world invades their homes and their consciousness through radio, television, mass publications, and phonograph records. Whoever invented the phonograph was unknowingly in the service of *Dionysus redivivus*.

Yet if my screech owl reminded me of Minerva's owl at dusk, I take it as most significant that the bird appeared to me at *dawn*. Old forms of religious consciousness are dying because they no longer serve life, as once they did. After they pass on, life will be served by other modes of personal

19

and religious consciousness which have, happily, yet to be institutional-
ized. This book tells the story of one man's journey out of the graveyard of
a senescent tradition into the seedling ground of his own exilic consciousness. The new modes of consciousness, now arising to enjoy their hour,
will eventually atrophy, become senescent, and perish when they are no
longer in the service of life. Yet, in the world of the spirit, the death of the
old is ever pregnant with the birth of the new. My owl spread its wings at
dawn.

2

VOCATION FOR
THE SUMMIT

My father, Jesse George Rubenstein, was born in New York City in 1897. He died there in 1954. He was a handsome, slightly stocky man who measured five feet seven inches tall. He had blue-gray eyes and wavy, dark brown hair which he parted in the middle. He was more inclined to physical than intellectual work. During World War I he served as a seaman in the Navy and competed successfully in the amateur boxing contests the Navy organized for sailors. He did not go to college; his wife did. The difference in educational background and cultural interests was a perennial source of tension within our family. Yet, as far as I know, there was only one woman in his life, my mother, Sara Fine, who was also his second cousin. Jesse acquired his job-training as an apprentice to his father, Nathan Rubenstein. Nathan had built up a business largely connected with the installation of steam equipment for New York's clothing industry. He had invented a number of steam devices, including an iron and a pressing machine. He also designed a floating airport to be placed in mid-ocean to facilitate transcontinental flights. The floating airport was featured on the cover of a 1917 issue of *Popular Science*. According to family lore, other men reaped the benefits of his inventive-

21

ness more than he. He prospered until the Great Depression when his business and his health declined. He died in 1932. Jesse and his brother Marcy inherited the remnants of the family business. Their partnership dissolved soon thereafter and my father was left with a rapidly deteriorating business in the midst of the Great Depression. He was trapped by titanic economic and social forces he was incapable of mastering or even comprehending.

As the thirties wore on, we were evicted several times for nonpayment of rent. During the bleakest times, my father would often come home at the end of a day with no money for food but with inflated and unrealistic promises about the big deals he had made or was about to make. He kept on telling us things were about to get better. Inevitably, they got worse. My father believed his own dreams; he had to in order to keep going. I believed them too. I went through a repeating cycle of hopeful expectation and disappointment until I finally despaired of his or anybody else's well-meant promises. I was disappointed so often that it became impossible for me ever to be overly optimistic about the future. I came to prefer a skepticism that left me immune to the disappointments that had been so much a part of my childhood. That skepticism was to have a decisive influence on my adult political and religious views. While yet a child I developed an aversion to men, institutions, and causes that promised more than they could deliver.

I was not privy to the details of how my father's business failed, but I was painfully aware of the effect of business failure on him. He defined himself in terms of his work. He saw it as a test of masculinity. He had grown up in a world that measured a man's worth in terms of financial success. He probably knew better, but he could not prevent himself from applying the same measure to himself.

During the early part of the thirties we lived in Long Beach, an upper-middle-class suburb of New York. In 1936 we moved into the city, eventually settling in a brownstone walk-up in Manhattan's Upper East Side. The choice of neighborhoods was my mother's and expressed her social aspirations. She graduated from New York University in 1920, a time when few women entered college, and continued to develop her intellectual interests in later years. Wherever we lived she was always one of the best-educated women. She was also one of the poorest. Our financial condition deprived her of the status to which she felt entitled by virtue of her learning.

22

Millions of people were without resources during the Great Depression. There was nothing exceptional in our predicament, save that our aspirations prevented us from living among people whose situation was like our own. We could have afforded to live in one of the lower-middle-class Jewish neighborhoods of the East Bronx or Brooklyn, but my mother spoke with disdain of the "uncultured" people who lived there. Instead, we lived where we didn't belong and where people who knew us tended to look upon us as outsiders.

Surrounded by evidence of wealth he could not provide, my father blamed himself. His self-reproach was aggravated by the fact that my mother's brother, Abraham Fine, carried on his father's wholesale produce business with considerable success. Abe left school at a very early age. He did not possess book learning, but he did know how to succeed in business even in difficult times.

My feelings about my father were highly conflicted. We had some very good times together, especially in Long Beach. I loved the water. So did he. He used to take me fishing in Long Beach bay on weekends. When he had money, we would rent a boat and row out to the center of the bay. We would sit for hours talking and waiting for the fish to bite. It was especially pleasant to fish on a clear, crisp fall day. When he lacked the coin, we fished off the pier. Either way, it was fun for me.

Part of me always wanted to be like my father. Yet it was too threatening. To be like him meant condemnation to a life of poverty in the midst of wealth, the derision of relatives, and the bitter outbursts that often characterized my parents' relationship when the stress became too great. My father seemed to be a beaten man. I was desperately afraid that I too would be defeated. I vacillated between my mother's ambivalent insistence that somehow we were better than other people and her unexpressed conviction that there was something extremely shameful about our lack of means.

I came to experience that shame through the pores of my skin. In grade school I attempted to defend myself against it by trying to prove that I was a better student than the other children. My attempts to prove that I was smarter did not make me very popular. On one occasion some Jewish boys invited me to a party. It was a party for them but not for me. When I got into the house, they pounced on me and gave me a thorough beating. They then told me that they expected me to become "one of the fellows." The trickery and the beating only increased the distance between

23

us. I felt even more like an outsider. My fury was aggravated by the fact that the father of the host was present and was not man enough to put a stop to his son's games.

My mother encouraged my isolation. She told me that some of the other children's mothers were uneducated women, secretaries who had married their wealthy employers. She made me feel that I was superior to the other children because she was intellectually superior to their mothers. As far back as the third grade, I sought to compensate for the feeling that I was an outsider by relating to my peers as she related to hers. Before I was ten, I had learned to use my mind in all-out rivalry with my classmates.

If becoming like my father meant failure, there seemed to be only one other option. I could become worthy of my extraordinary mother by becoming like her. Her values became my values. Her ways of relating to the world became mine. Years later, when I became a rabbi, I found that I was expected to give more than a surface deference to the rich and prosperous leaders of the Jewish community. Usually these men had more money than learning. The situation I faced as a rabbi replicated some of the situations of my childhood. I was truly my mother's son in my unwillingness to render these men and women the deference the community expected from a financially dependent rabbi. An old familial will to power asserted itself. Just as I had learned as a child to pit my mind against my classmates' in grammar school, so as a rabbi I often used my learning to prevent people from challenging me.

In becoming a rabbi, I also acquired another weapon, the priestly office itself. According to Jewish tradition, the rabbi is not a priest but a learned layman. No matter. Over the centuries he has acquired what Max Weber has called the "charisma of office." The most skeptical Jew can never be entirely certain that the rabbi does not possess the magic power common to all priesthoods. Some corner of his being is almost always fearful of the rabbi as priest.

And with good reason. For the angry rabbi or priest may be tempted to use the power he wields. During the years I served as a rabbi in Pittsburgh, I developed a strong dislike for one of the most powerful leaders of the community. My aversion was rooted in my own fear. He could without difficulty have had me dismissed at any time during my twelve year tenure. No overt struggle ever developed between us. We elected a surface cordiality in our dealings with each other. I could never accept a situation that permanently subordinated me to this man, yet he had power over me in almost every situation that counted. Fortunately, he

24

seldom sought to exercise it. In spite of his power, there was one realm in which my power might exceed his. He came from a traditional Jewish background. He could never obliterate its impact upon him.

Whenever I became really furious with him, I would daydream that I would use my priestly magic to undo him: During the Pittsburgh years I led services on Yom Kippur for over two thousand people in one of the city's leading synagogues. I would often imagine myself ascending the pulpit at the height of that service, at the moment of the recitation of the prayer "On Rosh Hashanah it is written and on Yom Kippur it is sealed: Who shall live and who shall die . . ." I imagined that while awesomely dressed in white robes, I would solemnly declare to the congregation: "By the authority vested in me as a rabbi in Israel, I call God's most terrible curse down upon one of his most unworthy sons, Sammy Silverman.* May he perish miserably during the coming year for his sins. . . ." Silverman was not a member of the congregation, but he would have learned of my malediction within a very short time. I was convinced that the curse would work although I could never have permitted myself the luxury of such priestly wrath. Yet, when I read Friedrich Nietzsche's description of the ancient struggle for power between the priests and the knightly aristocracy, I easily recognized myself as one of the priests.

I also recognized myself in the interview in James Joyce's *Portrait of the Artist As a Young Man* between young Stephen Daedalus and the priest who seeks to persuade him to elect the priesthood as his vocation. The priest tells Stephen:

> No king or emperor on this earth has the *power* of the priest of God. No angel or archangel in heaven, no saint, not even the Blessed Virgin herself has the *power* of a priest of God; the *power* of the keys; the *power* to bind and to loose from sin, the *power* of exorcism, the *power* to cast out from the creatures of God the evil spirits that have power over them, the *power,* the *authority,* to make the great God of Heaven come down upon the altar and take the form of bread and wine. What an awful *power,* Stephen!

Joyce described the lure of sacerdotal power offered to a potential candidate for the Roman Catholic priesthood. The same lure is present whenever a young man embarks upon a sacred vocation. There were, of

* Silverman is, of course, a pseudonym.

25

course, other, more constructive reasons for my choice of vocation. Nevertheless, I cannot pretend that in becoming a rabbi, I was not driven by a darkling will to power rooted in the insecurities of earliest childhood.

My fierce competitiveness with peers had even earlier roots. I was the firstborn. My sister Roberta was born when I was three. We scrapped almost from the start, but we managed to get along. She was a girl. She was like Mother, but I wasn't afraid of her as I was of Mother. To this day, our relationship is close.

I was six years old when my brother Clifford was born. I thought I loved my baby brother. Actually, I resented him far more deeply than I could acknowledge. Above all, I was determined that he would not take my place with my mother. My later struggles with peers were undoubtedly rooted in the painful fact of his arrival. Fraternal rivalry was to remain one of my most potent motivations throughout life. Over and over again, I utilized the same strategy in a repetitive struggle for power for a never-changing prize. I was more intellectually inclined than Clifford. That made me more like my mother and gave me the hope that she would favor me. For years I was to use my mind as a weapon against latter-day stand-ins for my brother. Like Jean-Baptiste Clamence in Albert Camus's *The Fall*, I have been afflicted with an unquenchable "vocation for the summit."

There was a double urgency to my concentration on learning and inquiry. It was, as I have suggested, an extension of my oldest rivalry with Clifford. It was also related to my body image and my intense feelings of shame. It was through learning that I hoped to extricate myself from an existence I regarded as shameful for almost as long as I can remember. Where do the boundaries of the self begin? Are clothes a part of the self? Mine were a part of the way I presented myself to others. In the thirties, boys in Long Beach usually wore knickers to school. Unfortunately, knickers were impractical for an active boy from a depression-beset family. Blue jeans would have been more practical. My son Jeremy hardly ever wears anything else. Patches never disturb him, but he has a choice of what he wears. There was nothing stylish about patches in the thirties. Knickers tended to wear out at the knees before they wore out elsewhere. It was impossible for my parents to buy new clothes for me every time the old ones wore out. As the unpatched knickers grew thinner my knees would show through. I felt even more ashamed when I wore patched pants and frayed shirts to school. I seemed to be the only child who did. I imagined people could see my shameful secret. I had no idea of what that

26

secret might be, save that we were very poor. I felt the shame in my flesh more than in my frayed clothes. I didn't want people to come close to me lest they notice my disgrace. I wanted a high fence to keep people away.

Could it be that my decision to become a preacher was partly rooted in the desire to compel people to look at me in a way *I* could control? I never used notes when I preached. I could always feel my domination of the congregation. Over the years I developed the ability almost to hypnotize my listeners. Could it be that, in addition to my profound need to dominate my peers, I had a related motive for becoming a preacher, the need for a way safely, perhaps even defiantly, to exhibit the very same self I had experienced as both repugnant and exceptional since childhood? And isn't it also possible that the confessional elements in my theological writings have arisen in part from the same motives, the desire both to be seen and control the way people regarded me?

As a rabbi, my favorite robe was my crimson Harvard doctor's robe and hood. I could not normally use it when preaching but I could safely permit people to look at me when I did wear it. I often wore it when conducting weddings. There were no longer any poor boy's frayed shirts or patched knickers. The Harvard robe satisfied, at least momentarily, the "vocation for the summit" as well as my need to control the way people looked at me.

I know a bishop who became a Prince of the Church. I was at a small private reception in his honor shortly after his elevation. As he received well-wishers, he seemed to take an almost sensuous delight in his newly acquired cardinal's robes. I identified with him in his moment of triumph. He too had started out as a poor boy. My reaction was instinctive. I thought to myself: "Good for you! You've wanted this all your life. You've worked for it ever since you were a seminarian. I understand you. We have been driven to the service of God by the same demon."

There is absolutely no evidence that my thoughts about the cardinal were other than my own private projection, yet I instinctively empathized with him in his obvious triumph as I have with few other men.

In the pulpit and on the lecture platform, I always sought to be properly dressed, yet something of the child's sense of shame seemed forever to pursue me. In my preaching and lecturing, the will to dominate and to enchant were equally operative. These impulses were never more manifest than when I stood before the congregation on Yom Kippur, resplendent in white robes and proudly called upon them to repent their sins and submit to their God.

In grade school, my ambitions were more modest. Had I been less caught up in the need to compete with the boys, I might have been more responsive to the lovely young girls in the class. I was smitten in turn by Joan, Sherry, Pearl, June, and Marion, but they never knew. I was especially awkward with the girls I found attractive. I felt it was a sign of some kind of masculine strength to hide the tender feelings I felt toward them. Although I was often told I was not bad-looking, I thought of myself as ugly and unattractive. Above all, I never wanted people to see me at close range.

When I was in the sixth grade, I was invited to a party at which spin-the-bottle, a kissing game, was played. On Pearl's throw, the bottle pointed to me. We were directed to a room where I was supposed to kiss her. She was diminutive and pretty. I wanted to kiss her but I was too afraid. She urged me but I couldn't let another person get that close to me. For about fifteen minutes she encouraged me while I refused. Finally, she gave up in disgust. She did not mention the incident again, but I was never invited to another party. The girls were lovely; undoubtedly, Marvin, Robert, Bert, and the other boys look back today on those parties with a wistful thankfulness. I remember those days as a time of building high walls to keep people away from me.

We were evicted from our home in Long Beach shortly after the party. We were compelled to move to New York City. For a brief period we rented an apartment in a working-class neighborhood in the East Bronx. If my classmates in Long Beach seemed too rich, our Bronx neighbors seemed too poor. My mother hated living there. So did I. She disliked living anywhere in the Bronx, which was then largely a Jewish bedroom community.

We did not remain in the Bronx. Within a few months we moved to New York's Upper East Side. We could not afford to live in one of the East Side's high rise apartments where people paid more for rent than my father earned. "Railroad flats" were available in the older, brownstone walk-ups in the same neighborhood. They were called "railroad flats" because the rooms adjoined each other like the cars of a train. Apart from the roaches, which were endemic to those ancient buildings, and the lack of privacy, our apartment wasn't at all unpleasant. Nevertheless, living amidst great wealth in a situation of almost catastrophic financial insecurity produced further conflict and fear in me. My "vocation" was further heightened by where we lived. I wanted a power that would be

28

greater than the financial power of my neighbors. I was desperately afraid that I would become an anonymous loser.

Of course, it would not have mattered where we lived. I did not invent my "vocation." It was our family's response to social and economic marginality. It was our private equivalent of the doctrine of the Chosen People. Had my parents been religious, they might have rested content with mythic assurances of their superlative worth. Religious belief and practice had disappeared in our household, but not the need for assurance of exceptional worth in the face of marginality and radical insecurity.

I did not change schools after moving to Manhattan. I remained at the Junior High School in the East Bronx. I had an exceptionally able homeroom teacher, Dr. Platt. Because of the depression many talented men and women sought job security as teachers. Dr. Platt was a *doctor juris*. He practiced law as best he could after school hours. He could be sour and harsh but he was basically ambitious for "his boys," and he wanted them to succeed and did what he could to motivate them. His ambitions were consistent with my own ambitions for myself.

Dr. Platt encouraged me to take the entrance examinations for Townsend Harris High School, the preparatory school of City College. It was New York's equivalent of the Boston Latin School. It was not part of the regular high school system, but was run administratively by City College and housed in the building of the City College Business School on East Twenty-third Street. Admission was by competitive examination.

Year in and year out, Townsend Harris managed to be the top school in practically every statewide regents' examination. Students were expected to complete the regular course in three years rather than the usual four. Graduation entitled its alumni to admission to the freshman class at City College. During the depression competition for admission to the then tuition-free college was especially severe.

Given my inclinations and the family's resources, Townsend Harris was an ideal school—it was an achievement-oriented all-boys school. Only two boys from my junior high school passed the entrance examinations. It was a hard school to enter and even harder to complete, but it was unquestionably the best public high school in New York State and one of the very best in the country.

There were, of course, drawbacks. The student body was overwhelmingly Jewish. This gave us a distorted view of American social reality. Since the entrance exams stressed intellectual ability, the school attracted boys who were far more like me than I realized. As a group, we were more timid with girls than students at coed high schools. We were constantly reminded by a highly motivated, all-male faculty that we were an élite group; we were also ceaselessly urged to be worthy of the distinction that had been conferred upon us. We were book- rather than people-oriented to begin with; Townsend Harris encouraged this tendency.

The emphasis on books was realistic. The school had gathered together a group of ambitious young men, most of whom came from families that had been hurt by the depression. The most likely avenue to advancement for us was through academic achievement. Had we come from better established families, we might have cultivated the social and athletic side of our natures. If today many of my high school classmates are able to enjoy the kind of life we hoped for but feared would never be ours, it was largely because of the training we received at Townsend Harris.

At the beginning of my freshman year in 1937, a German boy who was a senior at the school got his girl friend pregnant. The couple became desperate. They made a suicide pact. He was supposed to kill her and then kill himself. The young man slew the girl but then lost his nerve. What was supposed to have been a *Liebestodt* became murder.

The *New York Daily News* featured the story with huge black headlines for several days. I didn't know how babies were born. As a result of the story I became frightened that I might inadvertently do something to a girl, perhaps by touching her arm or by a kiss, and find myself in a predicament not unlike the German boy's.

The year of the love murder was also the year I became thirteen. I was puzzled by the pubic and facial hair which was appearing on my body. Since leaving Long Beach I had had practically no opportunity to meet girls outside of the family. I had no understanding of the turbulent emotions that were awakening within me. The murder was a brutal shock. Even before it occurred I regarded encounters with girls as mysterious and potentially dangerous. Afterward, I was terrified by the thought that a man might be driven to kill the woman he loved.

I felt that there was no one with whom I could talk things over. We changed neighborhoods too often for me to make friends my own age. Unable to share my feelings, I was under the impression that they were somehow perverse. I thought that I wanted to do "dirty" things to women. I only wanted to make love, but I had no way of knowing that what I wanted could give a woman as much pleasure as it could give me. I felt that there was something very evil about my yearning for bodily delight.

Our home was rigidly puritanical. There was never any sex talk. About a year after the murder, my sophomore year in high school, I enrolled in an afternoon painting and drawing class sponsored by the WPA. The class was an effort by the federal government to provide employment for artists who had been impoverished by the depression.

The program provided an opportunity for serious training by excellent teachers. One of the most interesting teachers was Sammy "Zero" Mostel. He was a brilliant wit who later exchanged an impecunious career as an artist for a spectacular career as a comedian.

At first the models wore bathing suits. Then one day the model was nude. She was the first unclothed woman I had ever seen. She was very beautiful. It was delightful just to look at her. It was very difficult for me to concentrate on drawing that afternoon. The uncovering was unsettling. As I drew the models in their bathing suits, I used to imagine them nude. Now I no longer had to use my imagination. Femininity had been a tantalizing, frightening mystery. Now something of the mystery had been happily unveiled. In the ensuing weeks my work became increasingly skillful. My drawings were both warm and accurate. My teacher praised my work and encouraged me to go on. I decided to bring some of the drawings home.

When my mother saw the drawings, she reacted angrily: "No son of mine is going to spend his afternoons drawing naked women! You're never going back to that place!"

I dared not oppose her. My interest in drawing and painting and the sexual curiosity that lay beneath it were thwarted. I drew the conclusion that any overt expression of sexual interest on my part would meet with the strongest maternal disapproval.

There may have been yet another reason for my mother's insistence that I quit. My father was artistically inclined. He was always able to relax by sketching and by creating sculptured figures out of soap bars. His work was excellent. He worked with his hands; he also relaxed with them. Most of his sketches were facial studies. A few were nudes drawn from magazines devoted to art studies. I was not supposed to see his nude studies, but a boy with normal curiosity was bound to discover such things.

The art classes offered me a safe way of identifying with my father. I dared not become like him as a breadwinner. There was less hazard in being like him at play. I could behold woman's beauty and be an artist

31

like my father. I might perhaps even outdo him. He took his models from a magazine; I drew mine from life.

When my mother demanded that I quit, I interpreted her real message to be, "Don't dare become like your father either at work or at play." Nor did my father object. My mother was always the final authority within the family. He remained passively in the background.

There was, of course, yet another way I could become like my father. I could sire children. While the excitement over the high school love-murder was at its height, my father called me aside for a talk.

"Don't do anything foolish if you ever get into a jam with a girl," he said. "If you need help, I'll be there."

His well-meant words only added to my fright. He thought I could get a girl pregnant! I didn't know how. I was too frightened to ask him. I was also too proud. To have asked him about sex would have been to have asked my progenitor about the mystery of my origin, of how he had gotten my mother with child and brought me into the world. I was unable to acknowledge so extraordinary a measure of dependence upon any power outside of myself. I could not acknowledge that I enjoyed life because of my father's desire for my mother. Such humbling realism would have contradicted the hidden yearnings for omnipotence which had possessed me for as long as I could remember. Later this same refusal was to manifest itself in my refusal to humble myself before my people's ancestral Father-God.

Instead of asking my father about sex, I went to the public library. I started by looking up words like coitus in the *Oxford English Dictionary*. By cross-referencing articles in the *Encyclopedia Britannica*, I arrived at a fairly accurate idea of what was physiologically involved in normal sexual intercourse. I was aided in this by one of the first books I ever purchased, the Modern Library edition of *The Basic Writings of Sigmund Freud*. When I entered high school as a twelve year old, my paternal grandmother bought me a wool scarf as a present. The scarf cost four dollars. I exchanged it for four Modern Library volumes, Freud, Marx's *Das Kapital*, and the two volume edition of Gibbon's *Decline and Fall of the Roman Empire*. My first book purchases proved an accurate index of my life-long interests. Although I was becoming conversant with the ancient theological controversies of Arius and Athanasius, and was attempting to uncover the depths of the unconscious by reading Freud, the elementary information about sex that most adolescent boys pick up from peers or from obliging young ladies came to me in the public library.

32

As a result of my library research, I came to understand the mechanics, but remained ignorant of the profound emotions that attend the act of love. I also had an intuition that my own emotional development had been somewhat disordered. I turned to Freud for help in the hope of somehow healing myself. In addition, I hoped to find a tool which might gratify my troubled but exceedingly potent will-to-power. I decided to become a psychoanalyst. I was, of course, ill-prepared to comprehend most of what I read but I did grasp that there was power in understanding why people are driven to behave as they do.

I had a further reason for becoming interested in psychoanalysis. It was somehow possible for my mother to see an analyst on a regular basis. The stress in her life was becoming increasingly severe. The conflict between her elevated self-image and our actual circumstances must have been a source of constant distress. In addition, there must have been older conflicts which had remained unresolved throughout her adult years. I have no way of knowing what they were. She has told me that when her father died, she had what was then called a "nervous breakdown." As early as 1926, she consulted one of Freud's disciples on a regular basis. My father's difficulties during the depression undoubtedly affected the emotional balance between them. In the late thirties, she felt compelled to seek analytic help once again.

I wanted to become the analyst who would cure my mother, hoping to do for her what neither my father nor her analyst seemed able to do. In the process I imagined that I would outdo both my father and the analyst. At the deepest level, the desire to become an analyst must, it's apparent now, have been the wish both to marry my mother and to be my own father.

The desire to become an analyst was also an attempt to master my acute sense of shame by controlling the way people saw me. I sensed intuitively that patients had a difficult time challenging their analysts. The advantage lay on the side of the possessor of the analytic magic. I wanted to possess that magic. Later, I chose what I thought was the apparently greater magic of the psychoanalytically oriented priest.

My ambitions vaulted upwards, but our actual circumstances became ever more precarious. There were times when my mother sent me to "borrow" five dollars for food from her mother, Anna Fine. I remember one such borrowing expedition with especial pain. My grandmother had remained strictly orthodox all of her life. She never learned how to speak English and never moved out of the immigrant Jewish quarter of New

York's Lower East Side. The rhythm of her life was not very different from what it might have been if she had remained in her native city, Vilna, Lithuania. It was late Friday afternoon when I set out. The Sabbath commenced at sundown. It was already dark when I arrived at her flat on Ludlow Street. The downstairs neighbors told me that she had gone to the Norfolk Street Synagogue for evening services. I did not want to disturb her at prayer, yet I could not return home empty-handed. I went to the synagogue which had originally been a Gothic-style Protestant church. I climbed the stairs to the women's gallery. The cantor was chanting the *L'cha Dodi*, the prayer of welcome to the Sabbath, Queen of the Days. There was not a sound among the sombre, old-world matriarchs who crowded the gallery. Their gray heads were covered, peasant style, with simple scarfs. They followed prayers that had been dear to them since childhood and that women like them had recited for almost two millennia. The Sabbath was their haven in time. When all other havens failed, it continued to succor them.

I tapped my grandmother on the shoulder. She knew something was wrong. I thought I detected a flash of anger as she looked at me. I tried to make myself understood. Again, there was the meeting of alien worlds. She spoke no English, I no Yiddish. All of her resentment at my mother's departure from her way of life and my father's failure as a breadwinner seemed to well up in that instant, but kinship constituted an even more urgent claim. She quickly suppressed her fury. Silently, she left the synagogue and took me to her apartment. Although it is a violation of Orthodox Judaism to touch money on the Sabbath, she went to a bowl in which she kept money and without a word handed me a five dollar bill.

With all of our pretensions to modernity and culture, we would have starved had it not been for my grandmother. Although she had never left the confines of her ancient Jewish world, she felt compelled to violate one of its most stringent prohibitions to protect her daughter and grandchildren.

We also had our own form of care packages. There was a period when I was sent down to the Washington Street wholesale market every week or two to get a huge package of fruits, vegetables, and eggs from my Uncle Abe. The packages made the difference between eating and starving or what would have been the ultimate disgrace, going on what was called "relief."

My mother had a host of bodily complaints. My father and sister did

34

most of the housework. Sparing his wife the agonies of housework was one of the ways he expressed his love. Nevertheless, although my mother lacked energy for housework, she had almost inexhaustible energy for the typewriter. My most constant childhood memory is of my mother at the typewriter. She wanted to be a writer. Over the years her interest shifted from fiction to nonfiction involving scholarly research. She had an incredible capacity for searching out the most minute details of her subject matter. I have read some of her studies recently. They are psychoanalytic studies of Emanuel Swedenborg, the Swedish mystic, and Henry James the Elder, who was also a mystic. I was both shocked and amazed to discover how very similar they are to my own writing, although we never discussed the psychoanalytic interpretation of religion. Apparently, she had a potent though unconscious influence on the way I understood the phenomenon of religion.

Her writing kept her going although she never published anything. She took some comfort in the more encouraging rejection slips. When I finally turned to writing and research as a career it was with intense conflict. To be a writer meant that I had chosen my mother rather than my father as my parental model, with all of the underlying confusion of sexual identity such a choice involved. To become a published writer meant to outdo her. Before I could turn seriously to writing, I was compelled to face the emotional issue that becoming a published writer might have been for me an act of symbolic matricide.

There were times when my behavior enraged her. She would insist that my father take me into the bedroom and "whip the boy within an inch of his life." Occasionally he did administer the beatings. More often, he was caught between his inability openly to oppose his wife and his own sense of what was appropriate. When the bedroom door was shut behind us, he would loudly beat on a pillow while whispering to me to cry out every time he hit the pillow. I was always far more afraid of my mother and her emotional stand-ins than of my father and his stand-ins. Although I regarded my father's refusal to carry out my mother's orders as a victory, his inability to take his own stand gave me more problems in the long run than the pain I was spared. I saw the woman as inevitably dominant within the family constellation. This affected disastrously my own perceptions when I became a husband and father. There were times when I was as unable openly to oppose my first wife's insistence that our children be punished as my father had been. When I felt that her demands were unjustified, I repeated my father's method of coping with the situation with my own children, thereby visiting upon them the same confusions I had had to resolve.

As my father's financial situation worsened, he became ever more ambitious for me. I had to succeed for both of us. In spite of our grinding insecurity, there was never any question in his mind that I would go to college. He insisted that somehow he would support me until I earned the Ph.D. He told me he wanted me to become "a great scientist." He wanted me to have the kind of professional education that would free me from day-to-day worry about the next dollar. If I wanted to outdo my father, it was with his blessing. Had he discouraged me, I might have been condemned to repeat in my own way the frustrations and disappointments which had beset him.

During my twelfth year a family quarrel erupted over whether I would have a bar mitzvah when I became thirteen. I was the oldest male grandchild of Anna Fine, but my mother had so completely rejected her childhood religious background that she served us ham and bacon in the hope that Jewish ritual would have no hold on us. Long before we left Long Beach, my mother had taken me out of Hebrew lessons at the local synagogue. I shall never know how much her decision was influenced by her own rejection of traditional Judaism and how much by our difficult economic situation. To the extent that we were involved in the Jewish community of Long Beach, we were condemned to a position of social inferiority by our sparse means. My mother could not accept the inevitable social subordination involved in synagogue membership.

However, it was unthinkable for Anna Fine that her oldest grandson would not pass through the rite Jewish men entering puberty have always undergone. America might be different, but not that different. My mother and father were adamant in their refusal. Was it my mother's desire to liberate me from an irrational tradition she saw as little more than gross superstition? Was it the fact that we could afford a proper bar mitzvah only by borrowing money we could not repay? Was it in part my mother's attempt to define the boundaries of her personality so that she had a psychic life independent of the family matriarch? I am certain that my mother's complicated relations with her mother were somehow involved in the decision.

I wanted the ceremony badly. I didn't understand why. Of course, I wanted the presents and the attention that went with a bar mitzvah, but something deeper was operating. My body was changing, yet it was the same body that was the receptacle of my conflicting feelings of omnipotence, shame, and unworthiness. I had no idea of what to do with the masculine, physical, aggressive side of my nature. Nor was the question of a bar mitzvah unrelated to the problem of taking my father as a model. When the external trappings are stripped away, the ceremony fulfills the function of a tribal puberty rite. The young adolescent goes through the ordeal of chanting the Hebrew text of one of Israel's prophets. The exercise is usually mastered by rote memorization. No matter how badly the boy performs his task, he is heartily congratulated on his "achievement." He is the center of attention of a most significant family and clan occasion. Bar mitzvahs are usually followed by elaborate meals or receptions at which grandparents, uncles, aunts, cousins, and friends are present. He is welcomed into the society and fellowship of Israel's males. The ceremony confirms him in his sexual role and in his incipient adult, masculine identity. The ritual is also important as an occasion of reconciliation between father and son. By making the ceremony possible, the father accepts rather than challenges the son's new identity as an adult male. By following in the path the father had taken when he was thirteen, the son once again takes the father as a model. The identifications and reconciliations are achieved through the compelling drama of ritual rather than through the far less compelling method of discursive statement.

At least as important as the boy's relationship with his father is his new relationship with the other boys in the community. In most Jewish communities, boys who have just had their bar mitzvah constitute a fraternal unit. They attend each other's ceremonies and invite each other to their parties. Peer group ties are strengthened; a powerful bond develops. The process of growing up is a shared experience rather than an isolated terror as it was for me.

When it became apparent that I would not have a bar mitzvah I was greatly saddened. I did have a surprise party at a Rockefeller Center restaurant to which my cousins were invited, but it was only a consolation prize. Even the most elaborate party could not match the power of the archaic rite or perform the emotional work the rite automatically accomplishes.

In later years, when I was in psychoanalysis, I kept returning to an idea I had uncovered to my horror. I did not really believe I was a fully competent adult male. This idea was coupled with the strongest doubts about my being in any way sexually attractive to women. I was convinced that I had never really grown to a man's estate, in spite of the fact that I

37

was married and had three children. When the analyst encouraged me to probe the roots of my self-doubt, I finally said, "How could I be a man? I never had a bar mitzvah?" He found my response strange.

"But doesn't every bar mitzvah boy say 'Now I am a man'?" I continued.

An ancient tradition had revenged itself upon me for its neglect. For quite a while the favorite gift at bar mitzvahs was a fountain pen. It became a joke to say in place of "Now I am a man," "Now I am a fountain pen." The same basic idea was present. The fountain pen has sufficient phallic symbolism to make an excellent present at a male puberty rite. I equated the bar mitzvah ceremony with some kind of symbolic permission, without which I could never fully become a man. I was not consciously aware of the idea until at least two decades later. That did not prevent the equation from doing its psychic damage within me.

Not having a bar mitzvah also intensified my feeling that I was different from other Jewish boys. They belonged to a special fraternity; I was an uninitiated outsider. That feeling never left me. I also knew that I had been prevented from joining their fraternity because my father could not provide the means for the ceremony. This was not the only reason but it was there and I knew it. All of the violent competitiveness I felt toward Jewish peers was exaggerated by the fact that they had had something I badly wanted but did not have. Since I connected what they had with money, I became ever-more determined to find a non-monetary way to prove to myself my superiority.

If I had had a bar mitzvah, perhaps some of the worst edges of my adolescent crisis might have been moderated. Not only did I find myself more convinced than ever that I was "different," with no conscious awareness of how deeply my confidence in my own masculinity had been impaired, but one more opportunity to identify constructively with my father had been lost at the very moment when his problems were multiplying.

Shortly after the bar mitzvah crisis, my father finally went to work for Abe Fine, my mother's well-to-do brother. My father hated it, but the alternatives were public assistance or starvation. My mother's oldest brother, Robert, as well as her sister's husband were also compelled to go to work for Abe. They also hated it, but not the way my father did. They were never afflicted with the inflated pretense to uniqueness which beset us. No sibling of my mother had gone to college. Her sister and her oldest brother both lived in a predominantly Jewish part of the East Bronx. They were at home in traditonal Jewish folk culture. They knew no other. My uncles may have disliked working for Abe Fine but an ancient sense of family solidarity in time of need moderated their distress. Living in the elegant Upper East Side and aspiring to its economic and social status, my parents were the prisoners of their own deracination. Cast out of the mythic world of their folk inheritance, they were the victims of another, more savage mythology, the bourgeois conviction that a man's worth is established by business success. When my father went to work for his wife's brother, his pride and his self-image were injured almost beyond repair.

It was impossible for me to interpret my father's going to work for my uncle other than as he did. He saw it as a surrender. So did I. The surrender accentuated the bar mitzvah crisis. The interdict against becoming like my father was reinforced. Had our family been less deracinated, there would have been no question about whether I was to have a bar mitzvah. Bar mitzvah was never meant to be a ceremony for the rich. On the contrary, part of the majesty of traditional religion, both Jewish and Christian, is that it takes over and defines the individual precisely at those moments of extraordinary stress when he is incapable of self-definition. Had my parents been able to subordinate their problems to the intuitive psychological wisdom of tradition, I would have acted out an ancient role in which I would have automatically identified with and been at least partially reconciled to my father, no matter what his economic and social status might have been. After all, he was not the first poor Jew with an ambitious son. Furthermore, had my parents been less alienated from their tradition, they might have had a somewhat more compassionate view of what was happening to themselves, as well as to millions of other Americans. We would all have had very different self-images.

The failure to have a bar mitzvah had an even more catastrophic consequence. As a child, I was terrified by the thought that the day would come when I would be dissolved into nothingness and cease to be. In desperation I tried a number of strategies to overcome that fear. I tried, for example, to convince myself that the wonders of twentieth century science and technology were so extraordinary that, long before my time came to die, an antidote to dying would be found. Faith in science was, however, only the first of many strategies I employed to find a way out of dying. They were all destined to fail. One of the reasons I clung to the

39

illusion, perhaps still sometimes cling to it, that I might escape dying is that I repressed the knowledge that time was passing and that I was getting older, that is closer to death.

Had I had a bar mitzvah, I might have been dramatically reminded at an adolescent turning-point that time was passing and I was entering a new stage of life. I had, of course, no conscious knowledge of my deep and fearful resistance to the flow of time. Nevertheless, my personality, values, and, most especially, my sexual identity were profoundly affected by my unwillingness to grow up emotionally, love—and die. Everything that was happening to me was unknowingly thrusting me toward the choice of an omnipotent profession.

3

BREAD AND WINE

I made my first real friend my own age at Townsend Harris High School in 1937. Bob Abbott was a classmate. He was a tall, thin, light-skinned, freckled boy with sandy brown hair. Bob's father had died when he was an infant; his mother was an Irish matriarch who ran a rooming house on East Eighty-sixth Street between Second and Third avenues in Manhattan's Yorkville district. Mrs. Abbott spoke with a heavily accented Irish brogue. She came from peasant stock and had a large frame, gray hair, and the lined face of a woman who had struggled since girlhood for an existence almost totally devoid of ease. She was devoted to her church, although she would occasionally express vehement disapproval of a priest who failed to measure up to her severe standards. She lived by an invarying ancestral code. All sorts of people found her a good listener. It was as if her wisdom was not her own but the distillation of the experience of her race.

Yorkville was the German section of Manhattan and the Abbott rooming house was located above a German beer hall. Yorkville was overwhelmingly pro-Nazi and anti-Semitic. Most Yorkville Germans regarded Nazism merely as an expression of Teutonic national pride.

However, there was a fringe element that would have willingly constructed a death camp for Jews right on East Eighty-sixth Street.

I was constantly at the Abbott household. As a result, I was in almost daily contact with perhaps the most important German colony in North America. I became acquainted with several pro-Nazi German boys, including one, Henig, who was a good friend of Bob's. Henig also visited Bob regularly. We kept a hostile truce on the neutral ground of the Abbott household. Bob wanted both of us as his friends. Somehow, he managed to pull it off.

It was impossible to ignore the more sinister aspects of the Nazi presence in Yorkville. Hitler's American Storm Troopers, the German–American Bund, paraded, harangued, and promised death to the Jews. The swastika was visible in the German travel agencies, beer halls, and in some of the stores. In the evenings, the *Gemütlichkeit* of the beer halls was mingled with joyful anticipation of the day when *Deutschland* would be truly *über Alles*.

Because I lived in close proximity to Yorkville, the events that were taking place in Europe from 1937 to 1940 had an immediacy that they never would have had had I lived elsewhere. In 1938 I also began to meet Jewish refugees from Germany. Although only fourteen years old, I had few illusions concerning the Nazi program for the Jews. Though I regarded my Jewishness as a meaningless hereditary disease, there was little ambiguity in my perception of the Nazi threat; it was aimed at all Jews, and that included me.

There was also a flourishing Irish-Catholic anti-Semitic movement in New York, the Christian Front, led by Father Charles Coughlin, the radio preacher of Royal Oak, Michigan. The Christian Front was a more immediate threat to New York's Jews than the German–American Bund, because of the greater size and political influence of New York's Irish community.

One night, after a dance at the Ninety-second Street YMHA, as I was walking home, I heard three drunken Irishmen, yelling "God damned, dirty Jews." They were not yelling at me. I could have ignored them but I was too furious to be prudent. An instinctive aversion to passivity surfaced. I was not going to let them curse out the Jews. I yelled: "Shut your filthy mouths."

The three jumped me, pummeled me, knocked me down, kicked and beat me with their umbrellas. They left me badly hurt, lying on the sidewalk. After I hobbled home, my parents called the police. They were also Irish and made no attempt to disguise their hostility to Jews.

"What were you doing out so late?" one of them asked.

"Have you ever been in trouble with the police before?" the other joined in.

They wanted to turn the affair around. I was foolhardy for taking on three angry drunks, but the response of the police was uncalled for. When I understood what was happening I conceived a hatred for the Irish and a deep distrust of the police that, in spite of my friendship for Bob, was to last for years. I did not cease to hate the Irish until, as an adult, I came to understand some of the things the Irish have had to endure in their incredibly bitter history. I have never been able entirely to trust the police.

I was furious at my father. The police had insulted me and suggested that I was a delinquent in his home, and he had done nothing. The pain of the beating subsided quickly. The insults of the police and my father's passivity did not go away. Until that evening, I saw my father as a business failure. Failure now took on a new dimension. It meant powerlessness. He seemed incapable of doing anything in the face of the contempt the world might heap upon his family.

I also began to equate being Jewish with impotence. Nor could I divorce political impotence from its association with sexual impotence. Whoever has no power, I thought, is not a man. I understood instinctively the extremities to which Jewish impotence could and very shortly did lead. My whole perception of what it meant to be a Jew was radically altered. When measured against the degradation and extermination visited by the Nazis upon the Jews of Europe, I had scarcely been injured at all; nevertheless, the psychological effect was overwhelming. I understood why the Germans had chosen the Jews and why they felt free to play out their most obscene fantasies against them. There was simply nothing to stop them.

I resolved, if at all possible, never to put myself in a position where I was powerless to prevent people from doing what they wanted with me. My first reaction was flight: If being Jewish meant being impotent, I would give up Judaism. I returned to the library once again. I had already read extensively in Gibbon's *Decline and Fall of the Roman Empire* on the theological controversies of the late Roman Empire. I now began to read about Luther, Calvin, and the Protestant Reformation. In my flight from Jewish impotence, I was in search of a Christian denomination with which

I could affiliate without compromising my fundamental beliefs. This precluded accepting any tradition that affirmed the divinity of Jesus. Eventually, I came to feel that Unitarianism was the only Christian sect that I could join.

There was an imposing Unitarian church in the neighborhood, All Souls' Church at Eightieth Street and Lexington Avenue. The church was built in a simple but impressive red-brick, Georgian style. The spire rose above the nearby ten story apartment buildings. The sanctuary had a cool linear beauty; each white pew was outlined by a line of mahogany. The windows were of clear rather than stained glass. The entire sanctuary was dominated by the massive pulpit which gave expression to the centrality of word over sacrament in the life of the church.

With its simplicity, All Souls' possessed a measure of elegance and quiet dignity. Its founders had been men and women with roots in New England. Its minister, Minot Simons, had graduated from Harvard College and Harvard Divinity School. All Souls' was his final pulpit. The connection with New England was important to me. Although born in the United States, my mother had an immigrant's exaggerated respect for the formative institutions and personalities of American culture. She chose Lowell as my middle name after the poet James Russell Lowell. All Souls' Church seemed to offer me both a way out of Jewish impotence and a way into the world of New England Protestantism my mother admired so greatly.

I passed by the church at least a dozen times before daring to enter. I understood that entering that church meant crossing a formidable barrier. I talked things over with Bob. He had almost as many problems with his Irish Catholic background as I had with my Jewish background. Finally, we met with Miss Elizabeth Reed who was in charge of the church school and the Youth Group. She looked us over and decided to encourage us.

Both of us became active in the Youth Group. The group was very mixed. The youngest members were fifteen years old; some of the older members were over thirty. The format of the meetings was fairly typical. There was a short service, a church supper, often featuring macaroni and cheese, a discussion or lecture, and dancing. In spite of the confusion of identity and motive which brought me to the group, it was the first group in which I was made to feel at least somewhat at home.

Joining the Youth Group was the first step. Shortly thereafter I joined the church. Baptism was not required. I became a member of All Souls' by receiving the right hand of fellowship from the minister. I also joined the choir and took part in the Sunday services.

However, my flight from Judaism was by no means complete. I quickly decided to become a Unitarian minister. The decision had little to do with any desire to serve God. It is doubtful that I believed in him at the time. I saw the clerical office as a magic vocation and as a further defense against the curse of Jewishness and its impotence. I believed in the efficacy of the priest's magic. Although Unitarian ministers are perhaps the least priest-like of all clergymen, I was convinced that even they possessed that magic and I wanted it. In addition to controlling the way people would see the little boy in me who was still psychically clothed in tattered knickers, I imagined that I would prevent them from seeing the greater shame of my Jewishness. I wanted to neutralize their anti-Semitic hostility. There was, of course, a limit to the priestly power available to Unitarian ministers. They did not wear clerical garb. They stressed the non-priestly aspects of their work. Whenever I saw a priest or a minister in clerical garb, I envied him his costume. I was sorry that Unitarian ministers did not wear clerical garb, but I was unwilling to enter a theologically more demanding Christian community for the sake of the greater magic of the clerical garb.

The image of Jesus made no positive impression on me. On the contrary, Unitarianism was attractive because it seemed to offer the advantages of Christianity without Christ. I was actually somewhat repelled by Jesus. His crucifixion seemed to represent the ultimate expression of the very Jewish impotence I was attempting to flee. I had yet to understand the awesome power which informed both his career and his person.

Nevertheless, the Unitarianism of All Souls' Church was far more Christocentric than I initially realized. I attended church services every Sunday morning. One Sunday Holy Communion was offered. Dr. Simons used the age old formula of Christendom: "This is my body. . . . This is my blood. . . ." I looked at the bread and wine which were offered to me in my pew. It was only white bread and sweet wine, yet it was more. I was being called on to partake of the sacrifice of Christ's body. I did not fully understand the significance of the offering, but I did not want to take it. Had I declined, it would have concerned no one. Yet, the logic of my decision to flee Judaism seemed to force me literally to swallow both the bread and wine and my own objections to participation in the rite. It was far more difficult for me to partake of the bread and wine than it had been to accept the minister's right hand of fellowship.

45

There were other reminders of the historic connections of Unitarianism with Christendom. The choir rehearsed for weeks for the Christmas candlelight service. I invited my mother to attend the service. The church was magnificently lit by candlelight. "Silent Night" and "O Come All Ye Faithful" were sung. The children of the Sunday School offered a nativity pageant. The members of the choir wore their white and crimson robes. When my mother saw me dressed in choir robes, she became furious.

After the service, she told me: "I didn't raise my son to be a priest! You're never going back to that place."

By joining the church, I had acted out her rejection of Judaism yet she was furious when confronted by it. By stressing the outmoded character of Jewish ritual and her admiration of New England, she had initiated a process, the logic of which was to carry me into some form of Christianity. When confronted with her own creation, she recoiled in anger.

"You won't stop me!" I shouted back. This time things were different. I had given up the art lessons at her command, but now I was ready for revolt. The stakes were higher. I was not going to accept a Judaism she had taught me was meaningless, outdated, and superstitious or the impotence which seemed to accompany it.

From time to time I discussed my interest in the ministry with Minot Simons. One day he asked me if I had given any thought to the possibility of going to Stephen Wise's rabbinical school and becoming a Reform rabbi. He said: "You could do as much good serving your own people as in the Unitarian ministry. You know, Unitarians and liberal Jews have very similar beliefs."

Simons was in his sixties. He had behind him a lifetime of experience with the dreams and follies of his fellow men. He foresaw difficulties for the confused, anguished, young Jew who had joined his church. He was trying to guide my ambitions in somewhat more realistic directions.

"I want to be a minister, not a rabbi," I replied with a cool deliberateness that foreclosed further conversation. If my mother couldn't stop me, neither could he.

At the time, I was a senior in high school and had to give serious thought to college. My father could do very little to send me to college, save encourage me. I investigated the scholarships available at the New England colleges for candidates for the ministry. I also became active in citywide Unitarian youth activities and became acquainted with a number of ministers from other churches, several of whom tried to help me.

One day, one of my new friends wrote to me, suggesting that I change my name to one less obviously Jewish. He was in Oregon at the time and wrote that while Unitarians were theologically close to Reform Jews, they were socially distant. He also observed that there remained enough anti-Semitism among Unitarians that my name might create difficulties. He strongly urged me to choose an Anglo-Saxon name.

Elsewhere I have written that his suggestion fit in with my desire for flight, but that, at a deeper level, something in me rejected both the suggestion and the newly acquired Unitarian affiliation. By his frankness he helped me to see that there was a limit to the extent to which I could decently escape the absurd destiny of having been born a Jew in a home where Jewishness had so little positive meaning. In my flight I had elected an even greater impotence. I could only leave Judaism by a lifetime of self-falsification and self-rejection, always fearful that someone would discover my hidden stigma, my true identity. I feared impotence because it left me with absolutely no self. I could only become a minister by inventing a self that masked my origins, my history, and some elusive inner core of my being. That core may have been little more than the intersection of the hopes, fears, memories, and injuries of my progenitors. Slender, elusive, fictitious though it may have been, it was very real to me. It has been said that a man's person is his public mask. Nevertheless, I felt there had to be at least a minimal congruence between my inner world and my public mask.

In an adolescent crisis, I also learned the importance of my name. Nothing so identified me as did my name, yet I had no part in choosing it. Over and over again, teachers, clerks, and strangers had indifferently asked me:

"Who are you? What is your name?"

"Richard L. Rubenstein" I would reply, or sometimes "Richard Lowell Rubenstein," offering a name that identified me and reflected my mother's complicated relations with her parents, her halfway flight from Judaism, her unfulfilled literary and social aspirations, my father's patronymic inheritance and his passivity as head of the household. In the archaic sensibility of the race, few things are as important about a man as his name. In an adolescent crisis, I discovered that I could neither renounce nor falsify mine. I also discovered that there was a limit to the extent to which I could flee from identification with my father. I could not reject his family name nor could I deny the deposit of family inheritance contained within it. I had come into existence as a result of the loves and hatreds, the wars and defeats, the resentments and dreams of a hundred

47

generations of my ancestors. Far too many acts of parental love under the most harrowing of circumstances had nurtured those generations for me ever to deny my profound indebtedness by disguising my name. I had learned that self-contempt was a far greater burden to bear than the contempt of others.

I had begun my return to Jewish life. I did not return to Judaism because I was convinced that it was somehow "better" or "truer" than other religions. I returned because I came to understand that any other religious affirmation would have exacted an unacceptable measure of self-rejection and public deception from me. Whatever raging emotions confused my adolescent development, I wanted to feel clean about myself. I did not want my insides eaten away by the punishments I would inevitably have inflicted upon myself had I felt that the life I was leading was both a lie and a betrayal.

Nor did my desire to feel clean arise from any special virtue. I have never had any interest in acting out some abstract ideal of moral rectitude. I simply had the gut feeling that, were I unable to feel clean about what I did, I would make myself pay dearly.

I must sadly report that, although I have never since wavered in my unambiguous affirmation of my identity as a Jew, I ultimately found it difficult to remain actively involved in the established American Jewish community. The issue of truthfulness to myself brought me into the community. The same issue ultimately made it difficult for me to remain an active participant in its communal life. I have often urged my students to utilize one very simple measure in evaluating a theologian, the question: "Does this man mean what he is saying?"

It is a simple test but it tends to separate honest theology from dishonest, if not good from bad. When I found it impossible to affirm the traditional conception of the God who had chosen Israel in the light of the death camps, I made my position unambiguously clear. When I came to realize, to my horror, that one of the tragic causes of the twentieth century Jewish catastrophe in Europe was the perhaps unwitting betrayal of the community by some of its leaders, I made that position clear. Too many people had died to permit the luxury of ambiguity. I entered the Jewish community because of a need for a certain kind of existential truthfulness. I learned to my bitter disappointment that I could only serve that community as a rabbi by a kind of dissembling of which I was both somatically and psychologically incapable. In the long run, I was as little

48

able to misrepresent myself before Jews as I had been at sixteen before Gentiles.

It never occurred to me to choose business or law as a career. When I returned to Judaism, it was to become a rabbi. I could no longer abandon my quest for the priest's magic. Nevertheless, few young men were as ill-prepared to enter the rabbinate as I. I could neither read nor write Hebrew. I had almost no contact with the traditional way of life and my understanding of the Jewish situation had been distorted by my peculiar experiences. I did not even have the kind of street knowledge of Jewish life most boys pick up from living in a Jewish neighborhood.

I did receive help. Two Reform rabbis, the late Nathan Stern and Nathan A. Perilman, facilitated the transition. Stern became a kind of surrogate father. He was the rabbi of the West End Synagogue which was then located on West Eighty-first Street. When I met Stern in 1941, he was a bachelor in his sixties. He was a short, stocky man with white hair and a somewhat beaked nose. There was usually a twinkle in his eyes. He came from a prosperous German-Jewish family. He had received a superb education for his calling. He had earned the Ph.D. in Semitic Studies at Columbia and had studied at Cambridge University; around the turn of the century he received rabbinic ordination at the Hebrew Union College in Cincinnati. Stern came from a very different world than I, that of the affluent German Jews who had come to the United States in the aftermath of the unrest in Germany in 1848 and had quickly established a solid place for themselves in their new land. Had Stern turned to banking or commerce rather than religion, he might easily have developed into one of the "our crowd" types Stephen Birmingham has described in his book. He turned to the rabbinate at the moment when German Jews in America were most confident about their way of life and their adjustment to their new land. There were already hints of darkness on the horizon, but a characteristic Jewish myopia prevented all but the most prescient from taking note. Their confidence was reflected in the Reform Jewish ideology Stern had received as a child in New York in the eighteen-eighties and which he continued to affirm, albeit with adult sophistication, until his death in the mid-forties.

Stern's Judaism has been called "classical Reform." In reality, it was the social philosophy of a highly prosperous, optimistic, socially incestuous group of American Jews of German origin. Its cardinal affirmation was that Jews are in no sense a distinctive, national, or ethnic group. If

49

they differ from their fellow Americans (or Germans) at all, it is by creed alone. In Germany, for example, Reform Jews in the Bismarck era, long after the beginning of modern anti-Semitism, insisted that they differed from their "fellow-Germans" only in the small matter of religious creed. In all else they claimed that they were completely Teuton. Furthermore, both in Germany and the United States, they were determined to make religious belief truly a "small matter." Practically every religious practice that might distinguish Jew from non-Jew was abolished. The dietary laws, which had rigidly controlled what a Jew might eat and which served to reinforce Jewish social separation, were declared no longer binding. Bar mitzvah was discarded. In some synagogues religious services were held on Sunday rather than Saturday. The service itself was radically altered and shortened. It ceased to be an interminably long but emotionally compelling Hebrew service. It became a truncated, emotionally desiccated service in English or German.

The development of Reform Judaism is an example of what sociologists of religion have called the process of secularization, the process by which ever more areas of life are removed from the domain of religious control. In the United States secularization accorded with the aspirations of those German Jews who wanted to take advantage of the economic opportunities of post–Civil War America unimpeded by religious prohibitions. Reform Judaism became far more secularized in the United States than in Germany. The American experience was more congenial to radical breaks with the past. The German Jews who came over after 1848 did not come from urban centers but from the small towns and villages. In general, they were not accompanied by their better educated co-religionists. Their fundamental concern was to establish themselves commercially in their new communities. They succeeded more rapidly and more successfully than they had dared to hope. The United States was an expanding society. The peddler quickly became the shopkeeper; the shopkeeper often became the department store owner; the money changer became the banker. With prosperity came the ability to travel in style, to send one's children to good schools and universities, and to hold social positions of considerable substance. By 1900 the strategy seemed to pay off. The differences between them and non-Jews had been minimized. They were a distinctly privileged community. They thought of themselves as almost Protestant. They understood how to acquire and, more important, how to keep money. Confident in themselves, they saw their diluted Judaism as somehow a paradigm of religious rationality. At no point did it stand in their way, especially when the opportunity arose for the most affluent among them to escape the final stigma of Jewishness through marriage.

They were prepared for everything but the twentieth century. The twentieth century dawned for them in the eighteen-eighties when hundreds of thousands of Jews poured out of Russia, Poland, Lithuania, Rumania, and Hungary into an America that had yet to close its doors against the monumental transplantation of non–Anglo-Saxons from eastern and southern Europe. Today, that massive emigration of Eastern European Jews can be seen as the instinctive response of a whole people to the onset of a catastrophic deterioration of its situation. The death camps were, of course, the ultimate expression of the deteriorating situation.

Both my maternal and paternal grandparents were among the earliest Lithuanian Jews to intuit what was happening and to get out. My great-grandfather, Elijah Fine, also entertained the thought of leaving his native land. After his sons had settled in America he came over. He stayed only two weeks and then returned home. He was too traditional to adjust even to the Orthodox Jewish neighborhoods of New York City. My great-grandfather was atypical. My grandfather Jacob Fine was more typical. Although he was compelled to take liberties with religious practice, he had little respect for Reform Judaism. For the vast majority of Eastern European Jews in 1900, Reform Judaism was an inauthentic attempt to simulate German Protestantism. There was also deep and bitter resentment against the better established German Jews who were often regarded as at least as anti-Semitic as the average non-Jew but who dominated every significant American Jewish institution. The word "kike" was a German-Jewish invention. When I was a child, my paternal grandmother told me: "I have no use for German Jews. When I came as a young girl to Hamburg on the way to America they treated me with great contempt. All they were interested in was making sure I left Germany as quickly as possible."

My grandmother passed through Hamburg in the eighteen-eighties. Her first contact with German Jews taught her of the deep hostility that poisoned the relations of the two Jewish communities for generations. The Eastern European Jews saw the Germans as their better established coreligionists who offered them charity mingled with contempt and rigid social exclusion. The social exclusion was every bit as vicious as that practiced against all Jews by many Gentiles. Many Reform synagogues discouraged the membership applications of Eastern European Jews until the forties. In every major city German Jews set up country clubs from which persons of Eastern European background were excluded. German-Jewish young people were often warned by their parents that it was far better to marry non-Jews than Eastern European Jews.

From the German-Jewish point of view, the hordes of Eastern Jews were a fearful apparition whose very presence threatened their newly found status and security. A minuscule, assimilated German-Jewish community could comfortably be absorbed by Protestant America. When millions of foreign-looking, unassimilated, and seemingly unassimilable Jews suddenly appeared, it was inevitable that the German Jews would lose status by association with them. The first German Jew to be refused a reservation at an American vacation resort experienced that rejection at about the time the massive new immigration had commenced.

There was also a fundamental difference between America in 1848 and America in 1888 when the Eastern European Jews began to arrive in large numbers. In 1888 America was far more developed economically. Things were beginning to close in. Ambitious young Jews no longer saw unlimited opportunity in putting a peddler's pack on their back and moving off to the frontier. Their America was typified by the slum and the sweatshop.

America was different in 1888; so too was Europe. Thousands of intense, idealistic young Jews were stirred by the promises of revolution-ary socialism and even anarchism; even before Theodor Herzl wrote *Der Judenstaat*, other thousands saw the Jewish situation as permitting only a Zionist solution, a reconstituted Jewish nation in its own homeland.

Both the young revolutionaries and the Zionists terrified the circum-spect leaders of the German-Jewish communities. It was bad enough that the new Jews were foreign in appearance and culture. Unfortunately, too many of the newcomers seemed to be revolutionaries. By association, the revolutionary Jews might easily destroy the respectability the Germans had struggled so hard to win. The Germans often hated the Zionists even more than the radicals. The Zionists insisted that Jews would always be strangers to some extent everywhere save in their own homeland. This claim directly contradicted every effort the Germans had expended to find a secure place in America.

Nathan Stern was the first German Jew I got to know well. I admired his urbanity, his cosmopolitanism, and his wisdom. He had a fine scholarly library. He had traveled widely. He lived well and he had benefited from the experience that can come from a lifetime of service as a clergyman. He was a superb mentor for a turbulent adolescent. My relationship to him was predictably filial. It was somewhat clouded by the fact that my own revolt against my real father was at least partly responsible for turning to him as a surrogate father. As a bachelor, he welcomed the opportunity of guiding me into the rabbinate. For a period, he was apparently as much in need of a surrogate son as I of a surrogate father.

In one area our opinions definitely met. I was searching for a Judaism that was as close to liberal Protestantism as possible. Because of his background and training, he was violently opposed to Jewish nationalism in any form. He was a member of a small group of Reform rabbis who in the early forties founded the American Council for Judaism and issued an attack on the tendency of their colleagues to sympathize with Zionism. They insisted that Judaism was fundamentally a religious tradition devoid of all ethnic content. They expressed bitter disapproval of the growing sentiment among American Jews favoring a Jewish state in Palestine. About the time these rabbis were insisting that Jews differed from their fellow citizens in religion alone, the infamous Wannsee Conference was being held in Germany, at which the Nazi leadership decided that there could be only one "final solution" for Europe's Jews, the gas chambers.

Stern's anti-Zionism was seconded in those days by the other rabbi who guided me, Nathan Perilman. Perilman was an Associate Rabbi of New York's Temple Emanu-el. For years he held a senior position at the same congregation. Emanu-el was the 'cathedral' synagogue of America's wealthiest German Jews. In the early forties Herbert H. Lehman was governor of New York State and a leading member of the congregation. Its membership roster has carried the names of many of the most powerful Jewish (and formerly Jewish) families in the country. If any Jewish families had achieved a secure place in America, they were to be found among the leading families of Emanu-el. No rabbi could retain his tenure at Emanu-el in the early forties if he expressed the slightest sympathy with Zionism. Perilman was a convinced anti-Zionist in a congregation that stressed quiet elegance, dignity, and minimal distance from the ways of the White Anglo-Saxon Protestant élite.

I had fled Judaism because of my fear of Jewish impotence. The Judaism to which I returned had the appearance of power and confidence. The appearance was, of course, a façade. The plenitude of wealth and talent that had gathered at Emanu-el was incapable of acknowledging, much less of doing anything about, the greatest catastrophe in all of

Jewish history which was then unfolding in Europe. I cannot recall without a shudder the sermons I heard every week at Emanu-el. We were exhorted to have faith in the goodness of men and the ultimate triumph of democracy; we were instructed that the best and the highest in the Jewish spirit had given birth to the democratic ideals of our country. There were, of course, some moralistic denunciations of the Nazis, but no practical program was offered to give meaning to the self-pitying words. If the congregation was ever exhorted to do something realistic on behalf of the Jews of Europe who were marching by the millions to the crematories, it was not on any occasion when I was present. The rabbis were, of course, opposed to a Jewish state in Palestine. During the sermons my attention would sometimes stray. I often gazed at the costly stained glass windows and the monumental gilded ceiling. We seemed to be blissfully isolated from the agony of our times in that privileged sanctuary.

Nevertheless, as deluded as was the polite religiosity with pretensions to upper class respectability I found at Emanu-el, the congregation did make it possible to begin the task of coming to terms with my Jewish identity. Rabbi Perilman also made it possible for me to join the Junior Society of the congregation and I was able to get to know Jewish boys and girls of my own age for the first time since we left Long Beach.

Saturday evening December 6, 1941 the Junior Society of Temple Emanu-el held an enormously splashy formal dance in the large meeting hall of the congregation. I have often thought of what life was like for Europe's Jews the same evening. I wore Dr. Stern's hand-me-down white tie and tails. I couldn't afford the price of admission, but the Society's officers let me come anyhow. The dance lasted until about one in the morning. After it was over, a group of us went down to Armando's on Fifty-second Street, the "in" street for New York's café society, until after three in the morning.

"See you at the tea dance," one of my friends yelled at me as I left to stagger home.

Not content with a formal dance Saturday evening, we had planned a tea dance late the next afternoon. We were determined to start the holiday season early and have a smashing time.

We never got around to dancing that afternoon. At about three in the afternoon, one of my friends woke me up.

"Get up! The Japs have bombed Pearl Harbor! We're going to war!"

In that twilight zone between sleeping and waking, I didn't know whether my friend was really there or whether I was having a funny kind of a morning-after nightmare. My friend *was* really there. I *was* awake. Everything was real, even the nightmare.

We drifted down to the tea dance. Nobody was dancing. The joyous season had come to a startling halt before it began. In a few days I would be eighteen. Most of the boys in the Junior Society were between eighteen and twenty-one. Our lives had already changed in ways none of us could anticipate. With one of the girls I left Emanu-el and walked down to Times Square. It was jammed with a New Year's Eve–sized crowd, all looking up at the bad news that kept flashing on the Times's electric news sign. Finally, I took my friend home.

In the late fifties there was a period when people my age used to reminisce over where they were when the Japanese bombed Pearl Harbor. I was often fascinated by the stories people would exchange about December 7, 1941. My fascination turned to shame at a party once when a thin, fortyish man with a German accent quietly said: "For me it was a day like any other. I was in Buchenwald."

Shortly after, I received word that, because of the uncertainty created by the war, the Hebrew Union College was reopening an old program whereby it was possible to prepare for the rabbinate and finish college concurrently at the University of Cincinnati. Dr. Stern was then a trustee of the college. Both he and Rabbi Perilman urged me to prepare to enter the college. Rabbi Perilman also arranged for some scholarship aid from Emanu-el to ease the financial burden. I entered the Hebrew Union College in September 1942.

4

600,000 PAIRS OF SHOES

My years of study at the Hebrew Union College in Cincinnati, the seminary for the training of Reform rabbis, coincided almost exactly with the period during which Hitler's "final solution of the Jewish problem" was being carried out. Over one million Jews had been slaughtered by the time I entered the college in September 1942. When I left in June 1945, six million had perished. Hitler was dead, but he was victorious in the one war that really mattered to him.

Jean-Paul Sartre has observed that things happen in one way, we tell them in another. Happenings are transformed into stories with plot and meaning, a beginning and an end, by memory and hindsight. My memories of the college are highly selective. They tend to focus on my reactions to the great events that were taking place in the wider world rather than vignettes of student life. It is only in retrospect that the bizarre character of those years in Cincinnati have become apparent. Perhaps the most indecent aspect of our rabbinic studies in the years the death camps were operating at full capacity was the banal normality of our lives. We knew that mass slaughter was taking place. We had heard Hitler promise the extermination of the Jews, but somehow the catastrophe had little reality in our daily lives. The events had almost no impact on the way we lived or on our hopes for the future.

When I first arrived at the college, I was struck by the luxury of the place. Things changed somewhat as the war went on, but in 1942 the college was more like a country club than a school. We ate exceedingly well, far better in fact than most of us had eaten at home. Seconds were always available. The dining room was staffed by white-jacketed Negro waiters who also took care of our rooms. The college was situated in a pleasantly wooded area off Clifton Avenue, not far from the University of Cincinnati campus. We had an indoor swimming pool, a gymnasium, and excellent tennis courts. Images get mixed up retrospectively. I can still see the mounds of sweet butter, the lemon sole, the Friday evening roast chicken, and the steaks, but I cannot recall these images without envisioning our contemporaries, the starving Jews with burnt out, hollow eyes, caught in a limbo between life and death, dressed in the striped pajama uniforms of the concentration camps. We were truly innocent, not-knowing. We suppressed whatever knowledge we had of the European tragedy. We were primarily interested in living well, getting to know the local girls at a time when most of the local men were in military service, and studying only when we had to.

It did not take me long to understand why we were encouraged to live as well as we did. In the early forties Reform Judaism was largely an upper-middle-class, German-Jewish movement. Its strength was greatest among the more assimilated Jews of the South and Middle West. However, very few sons of prosperous German-Jewish businessmen had any interest in the rabbinate as a career. It was necessary to recruit young men from Eastern European, traditional backgrounds. Although the boys from the traditional backgrounds were far more knowledgeable about Judaism than those with Reform backgrounds, they were usually somewhat deficient in social skills. Their speech, table manners, and dress needed polishing. The normal course of study lasted six years after the B.A. degree, far longer than the average Ph.D. The length of time could not have been justified by any learning acquired. Even after ordination, few Reform rabbis could match the knowledge of Jewish sources possessed by their Conservative and Orthodox colleagues. The unduly long apprenticeship was in reality an acculturation process. The college had to transform its student raw material into socially acceptable functionaries who could serve the religious needs of the rich and the nearly rich. The surroundings were part of that process. So too was the

58

knowledge about proper dress the older students imparted to the novices. We speedily learned that J. Press and Brooks Brothers suits were more acceptable than the wide-brimmed, wide-lapelled styles then in fashion. The preferred manner of dress was imitation Ivy League. That was what the Reform congregations seemed to want, so much so that occasionally congregations would state their preference for blond graduates as candidates for their pulpits. The story may be apocryphal, but it is said that on at least one occasion, a request was made for an "Aryan-looking" rabbi.

I did not come to the college to become an imitation Protestant. I could have done that far better by remaining a Unitarian. I hardly knew what I wanted, save that my Jewish identity was a puzzle and a problem I was determined to unravel and I was intensely desirous of acquiring the priest's magic. Because of my limited knowledge of Judaism, there was much that was foreign to me when I first arrived. I was still woefully ignorant of both the Hebrew language and traditional religious practice. Because of the wartime emergency, I was one of a number of students who were admitted without proper preparation. The night before my first class in bible, I stayed up all night attempting to translate the first chapter of *Joshua* from Hebrew into English in order to give a decent account of myself in class. I also found the mealtime rituals strange. Meals were concluded with the *birkat ha-mazon,* a Hebrew blessing. I had never heard the blessing before and felt extremely uncomfortable when it was chanted. Eventually, I came to enjoy the chanting, but my first reaction was one of annoyance that both the blessings and the biblical texts studied in class were not in English. Initially, I found the college a very strange place and again saw myself very much as an outsider.

During my three years at the college, the dominant issues among the students were Zionism and the observance of traditional ritual. The faculty was largely anti-Zionist. Despite the European catastrophe the majority saw no reason to alter their deep opposition to the establishment of a Jewish state or their conviction that Jewish identity rested primarily upon religious belief. I shared that opposition until I sorrowfully concluded that the survivors of the holocaust dared not trust the postwar generosity or tolerance of any of the European host-nations for their survival.

Anti-Zionist convictions were espoused with especial force by the president of the college, Julian Morgenstern, a biblical scholar of considerable repute. Morgenstern came from a small midwestern town and currently lives in retirement in Macon, Georgia. He believed in "classical" Reform Judaism with its rejection of ceremonialism as well as of Jewish ethnicity. The year before I entered, he interviewed me at the Hotel Governor Clinton in New York. During the interview I told him that if being a rabbi meant being a Zionist, I could never be a rabbi.

Morgenstern smiled warmly as he replied, "That will be no obstacle."

Morgenstern had spent his entire life minimizing the difference between Reform Judaism and liberal Protestantism. His college had hired an elocution teacher to cleanse the students of the more obvious traces of Yiddish intonation in their accents. The Saturday morning chapel services were brief, uninspiring imitations of the services in the Protestant chapels of New England colleges and universities. Many years were to pass before the facts of ethnicity in American life were to be confronted with frankness by Reform Judaism. Zionism was fought because it implied that being Jewish was beyond both creed and free choice. Morgenstern's attitudes mirrored in the religious sphere the social aspirations of the German-Jewish group that dominated the college and the reform Union of American Hebrew Congregations at the time. Any attempt to suggest that there was an irreducible element of ethnicity in the Jewish experience was countered by the assertion that such thinking represented a capitulation to Nazi racial doctrines. The majority of the faculty believed that the war was being fought to realize the ideal of a truly democratic world and that, in the postwar period, Europe's Jews would have a share in that labor.

Most members of the faculty were apparently ignorant of the effect on European Jews of Europe's history and demography. They did not seem prepared to face the fact that Europe's Jews were everywhere regarded as a distinctive and unwanted national entity. They regarded anti-Semitism as an unhappy interlude which would diminish with the victory of the Allies and the resumption of mankind's march toward enlightenment and progress. They were convinced that the Jews of Europe had a responsibility to help to bring that fortunate time into being.

Perhaps no professor at the college was more out of touch with reality than the late Abraham Cronbach, who was professor of social studies. He taught bible to beginning students, but spent much of the class time expounding his extreme pacifism, anti-Zionism, and ethical relativism. Cronbach was firmly opposed to America's participation in World War II. In wartime, while his fellow Jews were being herded into the gas chambers, he insisted that Hitler was as right from his point of view as his opponents were from theirs. He argued that ethics were completely relative. Hence, there could be no such thing as a binding ethical standard. Nevertheless, his total rejection of ethical norms did not impel him to support his fellow Jews in their concrete efforts to create a life for themselves in Palestine. He denounced Zionism as "a species of partisan politics," insisting that his Jewish work was "in the domain of religion." In the midst of the worst onslaught ever experienced in Jewish history, this teacher of rabbis counseled a program of total pacifism and political uninvolvement.

During the entire period that I was at the college, I never heard a sober analysis of anti-Semitism as a *modern* phenomenon or as an expression of the concrete social, economic, and political disorders of the twentieth century. At the college, there was much mystifying talk about Israel's mission as a "light unto the nations." This was taken to mean that Reform Judaism was the most enlightened and rational of all religious movements. Both trinitarian Christianity and Orthodox Judaism were regarded as falling short because of the "irrational" and "superstitious" elements of their spiritual inheritance. In spite of the devastation of World War II, the fundamental goodness of mankind was constantly affirmed, as was the faith that proper education and social reconstruction would elicit that goodness from the majority of men. This "rational," "enlightened" faith was contrasted with the faith of those who believed in the doctrine of original sin and the depravity of Adam's progeny. At no time, for example, did I ever encounter a serious discussion at the college of the rise of nineteenth century racist thinking which divided the world into superior Nordics or Aryans and inferior Semites, Blacks, and Asiatics. Nor was there any consideration of the impact of technology on western Europe with its creation of a surplus of both men and capital. These twin surpluses led to the imperialist ventures in Africa and Asia which were a prelude to the Nazi policy of domination and mass extermination of Jews and other "enemies" of the Reich in the heart of Europe itself. Although I heard much about the enlightened character of liberal Judaism, I never heard a competent historical or sociological analysis of the social and economic forces that had led to the distinctive forms of marginal status experienced by European Jews and ultimately to the devastatingly successful assault upon them. We remained blissfully ignorant and utterly privileged in a world of death and dying. Only in the United States did Jewish institutions possess the security and the resources to attempt to comprehend scientifically what was taking place and to project realistic possibilities for the future. Such analyses were being initiated—and by Jews—but not at the college. There was a good deal of talk about the Hebrew Union College's role as a center of Jewish study in *preserving* knowledge of the *past*. There was pathetically little effort to understand the present. No attempt was made to utilize the intellectual tools of twentieth century social research to understand the desperate situation of our people.

The other major issue at the college was religious observance. Reform Judaism had arisen in large measure as a protest against the all-encompassing demands traditional ceremonial practice had made upon the individual Jew in every area of his private, public, and especially his commercial existence. Inevitably, a reaction against the more extreme forms of Reform anti-ceremonialism set in. The Nazi assault upon the Jews had caused a turning inward and a re-evaluation of Reform's attitude toward tradition; the influence of Franz Rosenzweig and Martin Buber was beginning to be felt, in part because of the influx of refugee rabbinical students from Germany.

The arrival of Professor Abraham Joshua Heschel in 1942 added impetus to the turn to tradition. Heschel came from a long and distinguished family of Hasidic rabbis. He was a product of the best traditions of Eastern European Jewish mysticism. He also had a Ph.D. from the University of Berlin. He was able to interpret to his students both the traditions of the Hasidic world and the insights of European existentialism and phenomenology. He had a powerful personality and was living proof of the vitality of the very traditions Reform Judaism claimed it had superseded. He was personally observant. By virtue of his knowledge, his strong personality, and the fact that he was far above the other faculty members as a thinker, writer, and creative spirit, he soon acquired a small but devoted following. Heschel satisfied the needs of a group of students for a leader who would be both a teacher and a spiritual guide.

When Heschel arrived, he was an impecunious bachelor. The college offered him a small stipend, far less than it offered other men who did not possess his gifts. He lived in the dormitory and took his meals with the students. People reacted very strongly to him. His disciples gathered together informally for prayer and study, and a group began to offer daily prayers every morning using the Orthodox prayer book. Some even took the seemingly radical step of praying with the traditional *tallith* and *tefillin*, the prayer shawl and phylacteries normally worn by religious Jews at morning services.

The appearance of a group under Heschel's influence devoted to traditional worship aroused great antagonism among some of the students. Heschel's disciples were referred to derisively as the "piety boys." Their newly found religiosity was regarded as somehow subversive of Reform Judaism. Undoubtedly, part of the antagonism toward the "piety boys" was the hostility toward Heschel. People were seldom neutral about him. They were either devoted or took a strong dislike to him. Over the years, my own feelings toward Heschel ran the gamut from respect to extreme antipathy. I was profoundly affected when I learned of his passing in January 1973. He had been my teacher at both the Hebrew Union College and the Jewish Theological Seminary. He had been influential in the shaping of my theological career at a number of crucial junctures. In spite of the estrangement that developed between us in the years before his death, I felt his passing as a deep loss. Perhaps the root of distance between us lay in the fact that one could enter Heschel's circle only as a *disciple*. At no time during the thirty years I knew him was I prepared for that role. I had sought the priest's role because of my own power needs. No matter how wise Heschel might have been, no matter how much I might have gained from accepting the disciple's role, I was unprepared permanently to assume the role of disciple. Other men derived much spiritual and intellectual profit from so doing. It was impossible for me. And Heschel knew it.

Another element in the turn toward tradition among the students was the impact of Reinhold Niebuhr and the rise of Protestant Neo-orthodoxy. After its wartime publication, quite a number of students read Niebuhr's *The Nature and Destiny of Man* with great appreciation. Niebuhr's stress upon the tragic and ironic elements in the human condition seemed to be a far more realistic appraisal of what we were experiencing than the more optimistic religious liberalism against which Niebuhr had reacted. The shift in Protestantism from liberalism to Neo-orthodoxy contributed to the reassessment of traditional Jewish modes of religious expression among an important group of students at the college. Neo-orthodoxy's protest against liberal religion's optimistic view of human nature and faith in historical progress was especially important. Few Protestant liberals were as naively optimistic on these issues as Reform Jewish spokesmen in spite of the fact that Jews had far less justification for optimism than did their Protestant counterparts.

As a mood of pessimism about human potentialities set in, many of the students were disinclined to trust their own instincts in the area of personal and religious behavior. They sought guidance in the historically authenticated insights of the great rabbinic teachers of the past. They became more willing to let their lives be guided by the discipline of religious tradition rather than to assert the authority of their own moral insights. In view of the way in which totalitarian leaders were asserting the primacy of their own will, with such disastrous consequences for the Jewish community, it is not at all surprising that the freedom to decide for oneself was no longer regarded as the boon it once was. The disciplines of traditional Judaism were a welcome alternative to the moral chaos that was regnant on the European continent. Very few students were untouched by the change in atmosphere. Most saw no conflict between their newly discovered attachment to tradition and remaining liberal Jews. A few saw a conflict so intense that it impelled them to leave the college.

One of the problems faced by liberal rabbis is that it is difficult for them to point to an authoritative body of tradition to guide them when their congregants seek direction in moral and religious questions. The lack of an authoritative tradition places a burden of personal responsibility upon the rabbi that some men may welcome but others find exceedingly threatening. Those with strong power needs may welcome the fact that their religious authority exceeds that of any other member of their community. Such authority may in fact be empty. As we have noted, real power in the community is in the hands of affluent laymen who are seldom inclined to follow rabbinic guidance when it contradicts their own interests. Rabbinic authority is often illusory. Nevertheless, for some men, even the illusion of power is better than none at all.

For others, authority can be a burden, especially in times of extreme social distress. Many of those who led or were about to lead communities during World War II were aware of their own limitations. They did not want to do "what was right in their own eyes," nor did they feel they could entirely trust themselves to give appropriate guidance to others. They welcomed the renewal of traditionalism which was being felt in Reform Judaism. Perhaps the best way to describe the situation is that a not unjustifiable failure of nerve was taking place.

I shared that failure of nerve but at that time I was too far removed from the world of traditional Judaism to accept its way of life. When I first arrived at the Hebrew Union College, I accepted uncritically Reform's faith in progress and enlightenment. Reform Judaism did not inhibit personal behavior through ritual. It seemed almost entirely devoid of myth. It was not until reports of the capture of the Nazi death camp at Madjdanek, Poland in the fall of 1944 that I began to wonder whether Reform's confident belief in progress was not as mythological, in the worst sense of the word, as the myths Reform believed it had overcome.

In the fall of 1944 I was permitted to accept a preaching assignment for Rosh Hashanah and Yom Kippur in Tupelo, Mississippi, although I had completed only two years of the eight year course. Normally, a student with so little knowledge or experience with Jewish tradition could not have led a small congregation even for the Holy Days, but the wartime emergency had resulted in a shortage of rabbis in the Reform movement. The older students were serving communities whose rabbis had volunteered for the military chaplaincy. Younger students were given a chance to lead smaller congregations to meet the emergency.

Tupelo was a provincial southern trading center. In my memory I confuse it with the bleak Texas town in which the movie *The Last Picture Show* was filmed. Because it was a trading center, a few lonely Jews gravitated to it and established themselves as merchants. Once a year, they brought in a student rabbi from Cincinnati. It was his task to give them the feeling that they had met a major obligation of their faith by observing its most important holy days and to give them a sense of connection with the wider Jewish world. The student rabbi was expected to offer assurance that all was well at the great turning point of the year, the season at which the enthronement of the gods and their victory over chaos had been celebrated in the ancient Near East from time immemorial. That year I found it impossible to give the congregation such assurance. During the Holy Day season, when the advancing Russian armies had captured the Polish town of Madjdanek and had discovered a vast Nazi death camp nearby, our worst fears concerning the fate of Europe's Jews had proven mistaken. We had erred on the optimistic side even in our most paranoid fantasies. Somehow mere numbers turn the reality of mass suffering and death into an abstraction. The image that made it impossible for me to regard the slaughter as an abstraction was the discovery of six hundred thousand pairs of ownerless shoes at the camp. The absence of the owners was a haunting presence I could not obliterate from my mind. In a small Mississippi town thousands of miles from the camps, I could no longer offer the gathering congregation the age-old assurance that all was well, nor could I celebrate the triumph of order over disorder, rule over misrule, nomos over chaos.

I had dutifully prepared a sermon urging the Jews of Tupelo, Mississippi to take advantage of the season to renew their faith in God, in the righteousness of his ways, and in the triumph of his kingdom. The six hundred thousand pairs of shoes made it impossible for me to deliver that sermon. Although Jews traditionally refrain from writing on Rosh Hashanah, I stayed up all night feverishly preparing another sermon. I was no longer capable of affirming the optimistic faith in progress and human perfectibility of Reform Judaism. Nor was I able to regard the doctrine that there was a God who had chosen Israel as his peculiar people as having even a shred of credibility. Chosen for what?—for Madjdanek and Auschwitz? I had attempted to accommodate myself to Reform's optimism against my own intuitive convictions. Unable to accept the mythology of either traditional Judaism or Christianity, I had sought to affirm the far blinder mythology of liberal religion.

Six hundred thousand pairs of shoes awakened me from my mythic revery. In my innermost being I had never really been deceived. My liberal faith was bad faith. I had only deceived myself. There was no all-powerful judge. No power in the universe had the slightest concern for the hopes, yearnings, or aspirations of human beings. The Jews of Europe were paying the ultimate price of their impotence. They were a primal exemplification of the fate of the powerless in a world, where, despite all contrary mythologies, power and interest alone are the final determinants of what is permissible and impermissible. No moral claim could force the Nazis to desist. They could continue to send people up in smoke as long as they dominated Europe, and it suited their interest to exterminate people as if they were insects. Years later, I read Arthur D. Morse's book *While 6 Million Died*, in which the author details the extent to which Franklin Delano Roosevelt and Cordell Hull, his secretary of state, were aware of the slaughter and describes their stony indifference to it. As I rewrote my sermon that Rosh Hashanah night, I understood that no power in heaven or on earth was sufficiently concerned with the fate of these people to do anything that might have diminished the horror. As a rabbinical student, I had heard sin defined as a want of conformity with the will of God. I had also heard much talk about Israel as the chosen people. The camps taught me that there was no such thing as sin and that powerlessness alone is the ultimate failing. Much will be forgiven the powerful. The powerless can call nothing their own. Even their memories belong to others. Popes and potentates render homage to the powerful, no matter what their moral status; the powerless are simply without status before the onslaught of their oppressors. Nor would things ever change. It was possible to dream of a time when power would be replaced by some other determinant of human affairs. One could dream, but only because the future was not yet. I did not realize it, but that Rosh Hashanah, I had caught a glimpse of the nothingness which I believe to be at the heart of all creation. My vision was utterly without consolation. This lesson the camps had taught me; but I already knew it in my innermost being. I was badly shaken when I returned to the college after the discovery of the camps.

Nineteen forty-four and forty-five was to be my last year at the college. The previous spring I had been placed on probation. The faculty had an institution known as "roll call." Twice a year they reviewed the work of each student and decided who would be permitted to remain. My record as a student had been poor. My turning first to Unitarianism and then to Reform Judaism was a surface manifestation of an inner turmoil which made it difficult for me to establish easy-going relations with fellow-students or professors. I was moved by a peculiar combination of unwarranted pride and an inordinate need for approval. Because of my limited Hebrew background, it was difficult for me to perform well in my studies. Students from traditional Jewish backgrounds invariably did far better in their studies than I. This intensified my wounded sense of self-esteem.

From a professional point of view, it seemed as if I were a very poor prospect indeed. It was expected that students at the college would develop the personality traits necessary to function well as Reform rabbis. This included the ability to get along smoothly with people, and I was anything but smooth. The immediate test of how well we developed was how well we managed with our professors. I failed that test rather dismally.

One obvious indication of my inability to make a proper adjustment was my preoccupation with cosmic issues. I was intensely concerned with the question of whether the biblical conception of God could be reconciled with what I was learning in my classes in philosophy at the University of Cincinnati. My favorite professor was not a member of the college faculty but the late Julius R. Weinberg, then a young assistant professor of philosophy at the university. Weinberg later went from Cincinnati, where a heavy dose of anti-Semitism in the Department of Philosophy made it impossible for him to advance beyond the rank of assistant professor, to a distinguished career as Vilas Professor of Philosophy at the Institute for Research in the Humanities of the

University of Wisconsin. He was both a logician and a historian of philosophy of the first rank. I understood almost immediately that, unlike most of the professors at the college, there was neither a hidden intellectual nor professional agenda in his relations with his students. He wanted to impart as honestly and as dispassionately as he could a disciplined knowledge of his subject. He was especially interested in the problem of the existence of God. He was not a believer and, because of the dispassionate character of his thinking and scholarship, he was most convincing. Both personally and intellectually I found him more open and direct than the professors at the college. I did as well in his classes as I did poorly in my Jewish studies.

I was not the only student who studied with Weinberg. Steven Schwarzschild, Arnold Wolf, Eugene Borowitz, and Samuel Dresner—all of them now prominent rabbis—were among those who were influenced by him. As far as the faculty of the college was concerned, there was nothing wrong with a student having theological doubts, provided such uncertainties did not interfere with becoming a well-functioning professional. Although I was not privy to the thoughts of the professors, I have on occasion wondered whether they had their own doubts which they held in check lest undue reflection interfere with their roles as rabbis and teachers. It is likely that they regarded an intense preoccupation with intellectual and philosophic uncertainties as a possible sign of personal immaturity. Since there were other signs of my inability to adjust, my teachers probably concluded that I would never become the kind of rabbi they were seeking to train. If such was in fact their judgment, they were undoubtedly correct. Although I developed the capacity to preach well and to be a good counselor, I was never able to feel at ease when I became a congregational rabbi.

The evening of the spring 1944 roll call we went down Clifton Avenue to get a hamburger. When we returned late in the evening, we noticed that roll call was still going on. There were only about a hundred students, but it took many hours to go down the list. I said, "I wonder who is being roasted tonight?"

I found out the next morning. I was summoned to the president's office where Dr. Morgenstern told me the faculty had come to the conclusion that I was not suitable as a candidate for the Reform rabbinate. He said that my relationship with the college would be terminated at the end of the semester.

I was caught by surprise. I knew that I had not been getting on well, but I had no idea of just how bad things really were. Above all, I was unprepared for what I regarded as the disgrace of dismissal. I knew that, were the dismissal to stick, it would be a hard thing for me ever to live down in my own eyes.

I was one of three students whom the faculty voted to dismiss. Fortunately, when the other students learned about the decision, they petitioned the faculty to give us another chance. After some deliberation, the faculty decided to put us on probation for a year. It is likely that the dismissals were really meant to shock us into shaping up. Whatever the faculty's real intentions, the incident served as a most effective warning.

Although I have since come to be grateful to the college faculty for expressing their doubts about my suitability as a candidate for the Reform rabbinate, I was bitter at the time. I felt that there were a few students who were using the college as a wartime hideout and who had no interest in anything more than finding a proper trade for themselves. They were left alone while I had almost been dismissed. I did not understand that no matter how cynical such men might be, they were far more likely to serve as well-functioning rabbinic professionals than I. They seemed to be a better investment of the college's resources.

Nevertheless, though my preoccupation with questions about God and my obvious emotional turbulence were, from one perspective, undeniably symptomatic of a disturbed personality, there was another side to the story. I had left Unitarianism because I could remain a Unitarian only by changing my name and living a lie. I had hoped that I would not have to lie as a rabbi. I wanted the priest's magic, but I did not want to deceive people from the pulpit. As I have indicated, there was nothing especially virtuous about my inability to deceive. I simply made a bad liar. It was easy for people to see through me when I lied. I could not look forward to a lifetime of lying from the pulpit. There was no way I could assure a congregation that I believed in a just and righteous creator, especially one who had chosen Israel, and who would ultimately weigh and judge the deeds of men. Nor was it possible to pretend that I was a believer when I was not. I know many men who have that capacity. They do much good in their communities. They present as true, beliefs that they feel their communities require, even though neither they nor many of their congregants believe a word of it. Such men have undeniably made a sacrifice of the intellect which is productive of much good for the people they serve. Perhaps a good deal of religion is a form of whistling in the dark, pretending to believe what in fact few people actually believe. But I

69

couldn't do it. I could not publicly affirm an image of God and of his relationship to Israel or mankind to which I could not privately assent. My preoccupation with philosophy and theology was in large measure an attempt at self-clarification so that I might function as a rabbi with some measure of intellectual integrity.

My situation was complicated by the fact that I regarded my inability to believe as a personal failing. Within both Judaism and Christianity unbelief has often been regarded as a moral as well as a theological failing. My unbelief intensified my generalized sense of guilt. Nobody was more painfully aware of my emotional turbulence than I. As a result, I tended to blame myself rather harshly whenever what I said or did met with general disapproval. It took a very long time before I reluctantly attempted to take a solitary stand against the dominant institutions and personalities of my religious community. And, I was very frightened when I did. In the decade of the sixties, it became a commonplace for sensitive young people to see through the alienating character of the institutional structures to which they had committed themselves. More was understood about alienation and alienating institutional structures in the sixties than in the forties. In my student years, I was initially inclined to feel that I was always in the wrong whenever my views conflicted with those of my teachers and peers. I felt that it was my responsibility to adjust rather than the community's task to reconsider its fundamental perspectives in the light of the drastically altered political and social realities of the time.

Nevertheless, I did not believe I was entirely mistaken. Outside of Palestine, the Jewish world was collapsing. Like most Jews, few of my professors or fellow students understood that the success of the Nazi onslaught was in part due to an unprecedented internal decay within the Jewish community. Certainly, the idea was never seriously discussed in either my classes or in student bull sessions that I attended. Although I was not capable of formulating with any degree of precision my reasons for believing that the external onslaught was conjoined with a vast inner decay, I intuitively perceived that such was the case.

Years later I came to understand that the Nazi onslaught was the final chapter in a bitter history which began with the emancipation of the Jews of Western Europe at the time of the French Revolution. Those Jews who prospered or hoped to prosper professionally or financially tended to regard their religious background as the last obstacle to full acceptance in the non-Jewish world. In every generation after 1789, many of the sons and daughters of the previous generation's leaders sought to escape from

70

the stigma of Jewishness through conversion to Christianity and/or intermarriage. The Western European Jewish community was thus almost entirely devoid of a viable lay élite. Men and women who were pariahs in their own eyes acted as if they were an élite. The more successful they became in the larger world, the more they saw themselves as pariahs because of their Jewish origins. In the Middle Ages the rabbinate provided an alternative élite. In the nineteenth and twentieth centuries, the rabbinate, especially in Western Europe, was reduced by the bourgeoisie to the status of subservient, emasculated, though well-paid functionaries.

The final chapter in the story of the inner decay of European Jewry came when the *Jüdenräte,* the Jewish Councils, composed principally of lay communal leaders, were organized by the Nazis to assist in the selection, transport, and extermination of Europe's Jews. The story of the *Jüdenräte* is one of the most heartbreaking of the war. Whatever may be history's judgment on those Jewish leaders who collaborated with the Nazis, it is impossible to regard the phenomenon as other than a hideous symptom of the internal deterioration of a two-thousand-year-old community. Furthermore, on the basis of more than twenty years of professional experience with the American counterparts of the European Jewish leaders, it is my sad conviction that far too many of them would behave as did the leaders of the *Jüdenräte* were they ever put to a comparable test. Throughout history, there have been many occasions when one of the greatest hazards endured by ordinary Jews has been their own leaders.

I grasped intuitively that the institution at which I was a student was part of that very same decay in spite of its surface prosperity and well-being. There was little doubt that I was dis-eased but the dis-ease within my soul was far more a reflection of a larger Jewish dis-ease than I had any way of knowing. My inner life was profoundly disturbed, but the institution which constituted my primary religious and social reality was itself too diseased to offer any promise of healing. The college offered me the promise of a relatively prosperous career. Beyond that it offered very little.

My last year at the Hebrew Union College coincided with the final apocalyptic year of World War II. As the Allies moved closer to the heart of Germany, ever more death camps were discovered with their mounds of unburied dead and their masses of living dead. I could not possibly harmonize the European horror with the smug, complacent atmosphere at the college. With each newly discovered death camp, it became less possible for me to find any credibility in Reform's liberal theology. The thought that I would spend my life ministering to an affluent American Jewish community seemed more like a life-sentence to immensely distasteful labor than the promise of a rewarding career.

The mood at both the college and in the congregations remained upbeat in spite of all that had happened. At the time, Rabbi Joshua Loth Liebman was one of the leading Reform rabbis. His *Peace of Mind* became a national best-seller shortly after I left the Hebrew Union College. Its pop-psychoanalysis and its faith in democracy, progress, and enlightenment were expressive of the dominant mood of Reform Judaism in the face of the worst disaster in over three thousand years of Jewish history. It was a mood I could not share.

During my last year at the college I continued to do well in philosophy at the University of Cincinnati and poorly at the college, although not as poorly as in previous years. I found my work at the university less conflict-ridden and more involving than my rabbinic studies. Julius Weinberg remained a far more acceptable model than any of the professors at the college. I became ever more appreciative of the fact that whenever he offered an opinion on any subject within his area of competence, *he meant exactly what he said.* The prospect of leaving the college and eventually pursuing graduate studies in philosophy became an increasingly attractive alternative during that final year.

Abraham Heschel was one of the few professors at the college whom I respected. During the short time he had been in America, he had written a number of articles which had attracted favorable comment and his name was well known within Jewish scholarly circles. As a Polish Jew who had watched from a distance as his family, relatives, and friends were systematically exterminated, the smugness and the optimism of Reform Judaism were far more offensive to him than they were to me. As the facts of the death camps became known, there was less opposition at the college to the establishment of a Jewish State than there had been at the beginning of the war, but in spite of all that had happened, opposition to a Jewish State remained strong among the faculty and some segments of Reform's lay leadership. Perhaps more than any man on the faculty, Heschel understood how urgent was the need for a homeland for the survivors. There was much about the college that offended Heschel deeply. With his strong sense of what was authentic in Jewish experience, he could not have had a high regard for the imitation Anglo-Saxon life

72

style, which was almost unconsciously fostered upon the students. In the spring of 1945 he accepted an invitation to join the faculty of the more traditional Jewish Theological Seminary of America located in New York City.

I was in great conflict about remaining at the college myself. Heschel urged me to quit and pursue work in philosophy. He knew that I had no desire to live a traditional Jewish life, but he was in sympathy with my rejection of the liberal optimism of the college. He warned me against remaining at the college simply because of the security it offered. I am permanently indebted to him for his counsel.

Things came to a head about the time the students tendered a farewell reception to Heschel. Although as I have mentioned, Heschel had many student admirers, there were some who resented him because he was going to a rival institution. Even those who disliked him, and there were many who did, resented his departure. Jay Kaufman, who became Executive Vice President of B'nai B'rith, before his premature death, was chosen as chairman of the reception. Kaufman had been a leader of the students who were not especially friendly to Heschel. His choice as chairman of the occasion was indicative of the conflicting emotions which Heschel's forthcoming departure elicited among the students.

Nor did Heschel make things easier when he was presented with a testimonial by Kaufman on behalf of the student body. I have never forgotten his response.

"Gentlemen, it is often said that only students graduate. That is not true," he said. "It is also possible for professors to graduate."

Heschel made it clear that he had little regard for the college and was leaving for what he considered to be the superior institution. I heartily agreed with him then. After I came to know some of the other institutions of learning supported by American Jews, I revised my judgment. The college is certainly no worse than any of the other major institutions. It performs an indispensable function by training scholars and rabbis. Furthermore, the college has become a far more sophisticated institution today than it was thirty years ago.

Heschel's reception came shortly after the final collapse of the Third Reich. It was an apocalyptic time. Nineteen forty-five was the year of the apocalypse for those of us for whom World War II was the *war* of our lifetime. Apart from the discovery of ever more death camps, 1945 witnessed the demise of Hitler, Mussolini, and Roosevelt, the collapse of Germany, the surrender of Japan, the exit of Churchill from England's wartime leadership. A million Jews moved from death camps to displaced persons' camps. Jewish life and culture on the European continent had come to an end, yet it was by no means certain that the Jews of Palestine could overcome the dual obstacles of British opposition and Arab enmity to create a viable, self-governing community. It was a time of the catastrophic end of the old order and the infinitely painful beginnings of the new.

I first became aware of the name of Adolf Hitler in 1932 when I heard that there was a man who wanted to become chancellor of Germany who was promising that he would get rid of Germany's Jews if he did. Although I was only eight years old, I avidly followed the events in Germany to the extent that they were reported in the *New York Daily News*. I can still see the *News*'s headline that von Hindenburg had defeated Hitler in the 1932 elections. I can remember my short-lived sigh of relief that a majority of Germany's voters had rejected Hitler. From the time I was eight until Hitler's death, I followed the events in Germany as if they were neighborhood happenings. I began to read the *New York Times* and the *Herald-Tribune* when I was ten. Hitler's assumption of the title of Führer, his breaking of the Versailles Treaty, his invasion of Poland which led to World War II were among the most crucial public events of my boyhood. The horizons of my world as a child and adolescent were very largely determined by what was happening in Europe. In April 1945 Hitler was dead. The struggle against him had finally carried the day at an awesome cost for mankind.

Franklin Delano Roosevelt became president of the United States the same year that Hitler became chancellor of the German Reich. I was nine years old at the time. He passed from the stage of history when I was twenty-one in the same month that witnessed the death of both Hitler and Mussolini. I first heard of Roosevelt a year or two before the 1932 presidential elections. The children at school said that Herbert Hoover was a bad man who was responsible for the breadlines, the men who sold apples for a nickel, and the depression. Someone said that the governor of New York was a good man and that he would change things. In the first grade, we saw Hoover as a bad guy and Roosevelt as an extremely good one. Like most middle- and working-class Americans, I trusted him perhaps more than his performance warranted. I was convinced that he understood Hitler's challenge and that his wisdom and leadership would carry us through to victory. When he died, it seemed as if he were the only president I had ever known.

If Hitler represented the polarity of satanic demonism on my horizon, Franklin Delano Roosevelt incarnated the mythic forces that were destined to triumph over evil, disorder, and misrule. The combat of the children of light against the children of darkness, of the forces of nomos against chaos, of Christ against anti-Christ have been some of the ways in which mankind's mythic imagination has perennially represented the decisive cosmic conflict, that between the forces of good and the forces of evil. I was under the illusion in my last year at the Hebrew Union College that I was a non-believing secular man in whom none of the archetypal images of the mythic imagination were operative. I did not realize that I had transformed the principal actors of contemporary world history into demigods who were engaged in acting out the primordial cosmic combat of good and evil, light and darkness. The events of contemporary history were real. They were making a profound difference in the lives of hundreds of millions of people; they spelled death for yet other millions. Yet, I had transformed them into mythic events during my childhood and youth. Perhaps it will always be necessary for historians of one generation to demystify the leading personalities of the previous generation. It may be that all good history must be to some degree revisionist because of the tendency to transform the dominant figures of one's own time into heroes and demons of cosmic dimensions. As I grew to manhood, the press, radio, and cinema had mythicized and iconicized these creatures of flesh and blood. Lacking a religious tradition I could appropriate as a source of meaning and value, I participated unwittingly in this process of mythicizing the dominant historical figures of the period.

In April 1945 both the wise and virtuous father and the satanic adversary of my psychic horizon had suddenly exited. So too did their field of combat. The wise and virtuous father had been victorious but, like Moses, he did not live to accompany his people into the Promised Land. He had fallen along with the satanic adversary. His place had been taken by a man of human scale, Harry S. Truman, the former haberdasher of Independence, Missouri. The triumph of virtue had been celebrated. We called it V-E Day, Victory in Europe Day. The defeat of the Nazis was a blessing to all mankind, even the Germans, but with the passing of Hitler, Mussolini, and Roosevelt, I lost something I was never to regain, a mythic cosmos with which to interpret the leading events of my time. I could not mythicize Harry Truman, Clement Attlee, or the war against Japan. Shortly thereafter, the cosmic combat was to reappear for millions of Americans in the form of the Cold War. Although I believed that it was necessary to limit the westward expansion of the Soviet Union, the Cold War never had the same mythic dimensions for me as the events culminating in World War II. The drama came to an end at the very moment I was contemplating resigning from the Hebrew Union College and Abraham Joshua Heschel was urging me to quit. In retrospect, it would seem that my decision to seek a new beginning was as much conditioned by the loss of my mythic horizons as it was by the very real conflicts I had about liberal religion and a lifetime career as a Reform rabbi. I was, however, completely unaware of my own myth-making proclivities or the extent to which they were influencing the course of my life. Living in a man-made world far more than in the world of nature, I was profoundly shaped by the implosive effect of the public events of my time as they were mythicized and filtered into my brain by the communications media. In April 1945 I decided to leave the Hebrew Union College.

5

A RABBI'S CURSE

When I entered the Hebrew Union College I was very much involved with two girls I knew in New York. However, Cincinnati was much farther away from New York than it is today. Phone calls were expensive. The Pennsylvania Railroad's Cincinnati Limited took about fifteen hours. When I could afford it I took the train. More often, I would get out on U.S. 22 and try to hitchhike to Columbus, Pittsburgh, the Pennsylvania Turnpike, Harrisburg, and New York.

Hitchhiking was difficult, especially in winter. I often waited for hours in subzero weather and snowstorms for my next ride. One ride through the Pennsylvania mountains was particularly harrowing. I rode with a truck driver who was despondent over his wife's infidelities. He kept on saying: "If it's written on your ticket that you've got to go, you've got to go. I don't care what happens to me any more." It was a wet, icy night. He was carrying a full truckload of nitroglycerine. Fortunately, we made it through the night.

Inevitably, I began to turn my attention to the girls in Cincinnati. Eventually I met Ellen van der Veen.

I was attracted to Ellen partly because of her family background. The van der Veens were assimilated Jews and cultivated Europeans. Although my mother was violently to oppose my decision to marry Ellen, ironically I found the van der Veens attractive because of my mother's values. Given my upbringing, I could not feel at home with a woman who came from a traditional background.

At first, Ellen had a touch of adolescent awkwardness about her, but it was obvious that the awkwardness was soon to pass. She was a tall, beautiful, slender, exceedingly well-proportioned woman. She had dark brown hair, brown eyes and a long, oval face. Her nose was rather long. This bothered her although it was harmonious with her face. She was very athletic and played an excellent game of tennis, a game I have never mastered.

Had Ellen come to marital age in peacetime in Holland, she would have been a much sought-after young woman. In America things were different. She was thrown on her own a great deal. She had problems with her English in school. She spoke English with no trace of accent, but for several years her vocabulary was extremely limited because she never received formal language instruction. This made it difficult for her to express herself. Her teachers often responded to her as if she were of low intelligence. In Holland she had been a good enough student to get admitted to the élite classical gymnasium. At Cincinnati's Walnut Hills High School, her performance was at best mediocre.

There was also a social transition. In Holland her family was well-connected. After the war one of Max van der Veen's cousins became foreign minister of the Netherlands. Other friends and relatives prospered as bankers, stockbrokers, and merchants. In Cincinnati, Ellen was a refugee who fitted in best with the German-Jewish immigrants but who was regarded as an outsider without money by the boys and girls from established Jewish families. While in high school, she tried to join *Habonim,* a Zionist youth organization, but she did not mix easily with the more traditional Jewish young people who naturally gravitated to Zionist activities. The van der Veens were the only Dutch Jewish family in Cincinnati.

Ellen was an outsider who never really found herself in Cincinnati. She was more of an outsider than any girl I had ever met. I was largely attracted to her because she was a very beautiful woman who matched my fantasy of what my intended bride was supposed to look like. I had no idea that the reason Ellen fit the image was because of her vague resemblance to my mother. The resemblance alone could not have elicited a strong response in me. Undoubtedly, an important element in my response was the fact that we were both outsiders who were aware of what was happening to the Jewish people but who could feel at home almost nowhere with our own people.

Our sexual involvement was complicated. There was a great deal of passion between us, yet, from the outset, something was withheld. I know that some hidden corner of my being never fully consented to the relationship nor permitted me to give of myself completely to Ellen. I believe that a portion of Ellen's feelings were always withheld from me. We were lonely young people with the passions of our time of life. We could neither give up the relationship nor could we ever wholeheartedly consent to it.

In all likelihood, Ellen's resemblance to my mother both drew me to her and prevented me from giving of myself completely. Because we were such outsiders, the conflict-ridden nuances of our relationship ultimately proved decisive. Things would have been different had we grown up in a traditional culture in which both of us did what was expected of us during courtship and marriage without much worry about emotional complications. Unfortunately, we had no larger structure into which we might insert ourselves. We were two people alone who were attempting with only partial success to find some warmth and companionship.

Nor could I escape a sense of guilt for our sexual involvement. The van der Veens were careful to leave us alone when we were together at their home, whether we were in the living room after a date or in Ellen's room. In spite of the fact that I did not get along with their friends— whose friends did I get along with?—and they found it very strange that their daughter might become a rabbi's wife, they did not interfere. During the first year of our courtship, I was still a student at the Hebrew Union College. We often made love in my room at the college dormitory. It was against the rules but that rule was broken by most of the students. Nevertheless, I felt that there was something wrong with our intimacies, as if I were taking advantage of her or doing something dirty. I could not get over the idea that there was something cruel and sadistic about masculine sexual activity.

Had Ellen and I been more at ease in our relationship, we might have been able to see each other less. The very uncertainty drove us to intensify our bond. We were almost afraid to be away from each other lest we lose each other. After I left the college and was turned down by the armed forces in the spring of 1945, Ellen and I got jobs as counselors at a summer camp in New Hampshire. We were able to spend the summer together in the country. We had less time together than we expected. She had to live in a girls' bunk and I in a boys' bunk. The activities of the camp consisted largely in a series of ever-intensifying team competitions which reached an almost orgastic climax the last week of the season. The camp was no vacation for the little boys and girls. It was a vital part of their education. They were properly instructed in the facts of upper-middle-class life. Nothing was more important than to be on the winning team. The children were daily exhorted to beat the other teams and made to feel worthless when they lost. We were unable to get into the spirit of the place, but at least we were together.

In August of 1945 while we were in New Hampshire, America beat the other team by dropping the bomb on Hiroshima. Ellen and I read the *New York Times* report with a sense of horror while we were by ourselves in the fields. We knew that our world had suddenly become even more precarious than it had been during the war, that sooner or later America's enemies would have the capacity to produce and deliver similar weapons. Ellen could never forget how close her own escape from the death camps had been. She had nightmares about being pursued by the S.S. for years. As we read the story of the dropping of the first atomic bomb, we knew that the threat of mass death had been universalized. The Nazis had been vanquished, but it was now technologically feasible instantaneously to transform whole cities into death camps.

I returned to the University of Cincinnati in September 1945 but not to the Hebrew Union College. Because I had enrolled in a joint program at the college and the university, I did not yet have my B.A. I resolved to concentrate in philosophy in the hope of entering a graduate program the following year. My father's financial situation had improved somewhat during the war and he gave me what help he could. I was also given assistance by my mother's cousin, Louis Fine, an attorney in Norfolk, Virginia.

My life at the university was very different from what it had been when I was a student at the college. I lived in a miserable, dirty, lice-ridden rooming house near the campus, the only quarters I could afford. I had to work to support myself in spite of the help I was receiving. For a while I worked as a timekeeper in a plant in Covington, Kentucky, across the Ohio River from Cincinnati from 6:00 P.M. to 2:30 A.M. every day. I never got home before three in the morning and had to pull myself up for an eight o'clock chemistry class every morning. I ate poorly. I bathed irregularly. To save money on laundry—there were as yet no laundromats—I wore a wool plaid shirt for days on end. The insects which were endemic to the rooming house literally got under my skin. For a while I hardly knew what I was doing. Naturally, I had only minimal contact with the students at the Hebrew Union College. I no longer had either the security or the status I had had when I was one of them.

My schedule of work and study was impossible. Something had to break. It was I. About the middle of the year I got sick and realized that I had to find a less demanding job. In order to get admitted to a good graduate school, I needed grades of distinction level. This was impossible with my work load. I was also troubled by my relationship with Ellen. I was afraid of sliding into a permanent commitment for which I was unprepared. Today, many students live together without getting married. Some relationships last; others eventually break. In 1945 it would have been unthinkable for Ellen and me to live together without marriage. I decided that we ought to break up and told Ellen so. She was not happy about breaking up, but had no choice. However, we continued to see each other at the university because we were in many of the same classes.

Several weeks after we broke up I arrived early for a philosophy seminar. I felt sick, discouraged, and thoroughly exhausted. Nobody else was in the room. I buried my head in my arms. In my misery I wanted to shut the world out. As I rested, I felt someone's fingers running through my hair. It was Ellen. Her touch lightened my sadness and my isolation. We started all over, but we now knew that sooner or later we were going to get married.

As my choice of bride became more certain, my choice of career became less so. Philosophy looked like a more attractive vocation when I was a student at the Hebrew Union College than after I had left it. During my last year at the University of Cincinnati, a career in philosophy seemed increasingly to be a life devoted to *theoria,* to beholding and contemplating the world, rather than to *praxis,* practical activity in the real world. The courses offered in the Department of Philosophy at Cincinnati emphasized the contemplative aspects of philosophy. Weinberg was interested in logic and the history of philosophy. We received a good grounding in the Greeks, especially Aristotle. He also introduced us to the world of medieval philosophy and to such thinkers as Descartes, Spinoza, Malebranche, Leibniz, Locke, Berkeley, Hume, and Kant. However, we received no training in Hegel, Marx, Feuerbach, Kierkegaard, or Nietzsche. The men who trained us were under the influence of the University

81

of Chicago—St. John's College "great books" approach to intellectual history. They were reacting against the pragmatism and relativism of their own college days. They were disinterested in nineteenth and twentieth century continental philosophy. Although Karl Marx's crucially important early writings had been discovered in 1932 they still had had no impact on our department in 1946. Kierkegaard was beginning to be translated into English but his writings were neither understood nor appreciated. There was so much work to be done coming to understand Thomas Aquinas, Duns Scotus, Nicholas of Cusa, and Immanuel Kant that the study of the puzzling Dane who wrote about anxiety and faith, who composed a *Diary of a Seducer* under a pseudonym, and who offered apparently subjective impressions on Christ and Socrates seemed to be a diversion from the main business of philosophy. Nietzsche was regarded as a proto-Nazi. Hegel was disposed of with a few references. We had, of course, heard of the French existentialists—from an article with photographs in *Vogue*—but we regarded these people as denizens of a café world, frivolous and unworthy of our study.

In a word, we were largely ignorant of the truly formative thinkers of the contemporary world. This was partly due to the fact that our department, like most such departments, was influenced more by Anglo-Saxon philosophy than by French and German thinkers. We had just emerged from a war in which the most prominent expression of German culture was the death camp. There was a fetid stench about German culture which made it almost impossible to appreciate anything that came out of that country. The stench was not lightened by our knowledge of the extent to which so many German professors, including Germany's greatest philosopher, Martin Heidegger, had prostituted their vocations for the sake of Nazi ideology. In the fifties and sixties, men like Herbert Marcuse, Walter Kaufmann, Karl Löwith, and Paul Johannes Tillich were to offer Americans a more balanced assessment of German philosophy. In 1946 it was too soon after the war to permit such a reassessment. Ironically, in America contemporary philosophic movements such as existentialism, phenomenology, Marxism, and Hegelian studies were often given the recognition they deserve in theological seminaries before they were studied seriously in most academic departments of philosophies.

At a time when the six million exterminated Jews had hardly found their rest and the survivors of the camps were being herded into refugee camps, a life devoted to the study of Aristotle, Aquinas, and Kant seemed too severely abstracted from the currents of contemporary history to offer much fulfillment. I believe I would have found philosophy far more relevant to the world of 1946 had I been exposed to thinkers like Hegel, Marx, Nietzsche, Brentano, Sartre, and Merleau-Ponty, but I was exposed to none of them. I found myself discontented with the uninvolved and apparently scholastic nature of my studies. I was not prepared to spend my life playing the Glass Bead Game. In spite of the social and intellectual myopia prevalent at Hebrew Union College, students there were at least given minimal training with which they could serve their own community. I seemed to be engaged in a very private enterprise at a time of unprecedented communal distress.

I could not admit my discontent. I had broken with the college. I had lost the security I had had as a rabbinical student. The loss enhanced my sense of personal virtue, but it enhanced little else in my hungry, lice-ridden existence. Ironically, had life at the college been less secure, it might have been easier to return there. The very hardships I was enduring obscured my judgment. I came to equate personal hardship with virtue and ease almost with vice.

My doubts about pursuing a career in philosophy were settled by the universities to which I applied for graduate study. Both Columbia and New York University turned me down. My academic record was at best spotty. I had had to take freshman chemistry twice before I received a passing grade. I earned only a D in calculus and physics. My record was covered with C's. Only in philosophy did I have grades of distinction level until my last term when I was required to take the senior seminar led by Howard Roelofs, the chairman of the department. Roelofs was a Harvard Ph.D. and an intellectually committed Episcopalian whose distaste for Jews was unredeemed by even surface politeness. There was a streak of meanness in the man that served as an unpleasant horizon for his passionate intellectual defense of his religious faith. At the beginning of the senior seminar, Roelofs announced that there would be neither a final paper nor a final exam. I did not realize it but this meant that Roelofs was free to grade his students as subjectively as he pleased. With full knowledge of my interest in a career in philosophy, he gave me a C, thereby ruining whatever chance I might have had of entering a graduate program at one of the better universities, especially at a time when returning veterans were taxing existing facilities.

Shortly after graduation, the van der Veens invited me to spend a weekend with the family at Brown County State Park near Nashville, Indiana. During the weekend I asked Ellen to marry me. She consented.

83

I was twenty-two. I had a B.A. degree in philosophy and only the most confused of career intentions. I decided to return to New York in the hope of working for a year and building a reserve with which I might get married and continue my schooling. Ellen decided that the one school in the country where she could get the training she wanted was New York's New School for Social Research. Her parents agreed to send her there. In reality, we both understood that our tenuous engagement would have fallen apart if I were in New York and she remained in Cincinnati.

Getting a job in New York was not difficult; getting a suitable job was another matter. I worked for a while selling pots and pans in Macy's basement. I quit and took a job selling cameras at B. Altman's. In 1946 there was a pent-up demand for quality cameras. As a result, at Altman's as elsewhere, they were pushing an American-made half-frame 35 mm. camera called the Univex Mercury. Photography had been my hobby since high school days. I was convinced that the Mercury's body and lens were of poor quality and that the camera was overpriced. As soon as the better quality German cameras reached America, the Mercury disappeared from the market.

I wasn't a good salesman. I could never encourage a customer to buy something I didn't believe in, whether it was the Univex Mercury or, at a later time, some highly dubious theological propositions about God. When I expressed skepticism about belief in the biblical God of history as a rabbi, I was not unaware of the consequences. When I voiced skepticism about the shoddy Univex Mercury, I didn't realize that some of the customers were in fact Altman's staff buyers. After two weeks on the job, I was summarily fired.

I then secured work with the American Jewish Committee doing research on Jewish education. The work was interesting, pleasant, and far more in keeping with my interests and temperament. The job with the Committee made me realize that, in spite of my theological conflicts, I was profoundly involved in what was happening to my own people. The job led in turn to a research position with the Jewish Education Committee of New York and a part-time teaching position at Temple Israel, one of the Reform congregations on New York's Upper West Side. I also returned to Jewish study, taking evening courses for laymen at the Jewish Theological Seminary. I was impressed with the depth of insight expressed in much of rabbinic and medieval Jewish literature. I was also impressed by the fact that most of the people best qualified to understand that literature had been murdered by the Nazis. There seemed to be an almost sacramental quality to my renewed studies. I was studying not only for myself but also for the dead. For me, there could be no such thing as a purely contemplative study of Jewish literature after Auschwitz.

My horror at the world that made Auschwitz possible continued to grow. Part of that feeling was undoubtedly due to my perception that the violence and destructiveness in the larger world seemed to mirror a potential for anger, violence, and destructiveness within my own soul. Above all, I dreaded any kind of emotional spontaneity. I was fearful that were I to let go I might fall apart. Although Ellen and I were now engaged to be married, we actually became less physically intimate than we had been in Cincinnati. Horrified at what had happened to Europe's Jews, impressed with the integrity and authenticity of traditional Judaism, the very Judaism that Hitler had assaulted most successfully, both Ellen and I were increasingly attracted to a disciplined life of obedience to Jewish religious law. For my part, it seemed to be the best way to control my potentialities for explosive violence. It was also our response to the Nazis. We were in effect saying, "You tried to destroy this tradition. We won't let you. As long as people like us keep this way of life going, you have not been victorious." Furthermore, a traditional way of life accorded with my revulsion against the optimism of liberal religion in the age of Auschwitz. Implicit in the tradition's insistence that men required a body of law and custom with which to govern their lives was the perception that without such guidance men are capable of unspeakable viciousness. Although I have never believed in the literal truth of the doctrine of the Fall of Man, I have always believed in its psychological truth. The Fall had certainly been empirically validated by the events of our times. For me it was further validated by the raging chaos of my own soul. Thrown as I had been on my own resources and lacking any objective norms which might offer moral guidance, I came to regard my own situation as demanding a choice between the anarchy of moral and religious normlessness and the order and discipline which belief in the God of the covenant of Abraham, Isaac, and Jacob might give my life. I never really believed in the God of the covenant; nevertheless, I was so horrified by the depths to which men without God had descended that I felt impelled to submit to the uttermost letter of the law of that God. Sooner or later, I was convinced, Auschwitz would invite repetition. I accepted Ivan Karamazov's observation that if there is no God, everything is permitted. When Dostoevski shaped the character of Ivan, the hell of Auschwitz could only be anticipated by an act of poetic imagination. In 1947 imagination had been outstripped by reality. *I believed at the time that if there is no God, Auschwitz may indeed be permitted. I could not live in such a world. It seemed far better to commit the ultimate act of bad faith, of submitting to a nonexistent God than to add even a particle of reality to the possibility of a future Auschwitz.*

I had hoped to return to school after a year at work. I could no longer plan to work for a Ph.D. in philosophy. Increasingly, I thought about getting married and returning to the Hebrew Union College to complete my rabbinic studies. I sought out Julian Morgenstern on one of his visits to New York to determine whether it would be possible to return. He indicated that the college would permit me to return and I began to plan accordingly.

I got married sooner than I had expected. During my year of work I lived once again in my old room in my parents' apartment. My mother strongly disapproved of the engagement. She felt that I had no business getting engaged before I had settled the issue of a career. She also disapproved of the van der Veens, insisting that they were "bourgeois," which they were, and "too interested in money," which they weren't. She warned me that they would "corrupt" me with their values. She strongly disliked Ellen and perhaps perceived, as I could not, that our relationship was more complicated and problematic than I could admit. In the meantime, as I became more committed to traditional Judaism, Ellen supported me all the way. It would have been perhaps better for our relationship had she been more critical of what I was doing. It is my belief that she compensated for her own ambivalence by accepting uncritically any and all decisions I arrived at.

One day in a fit of anger my mother said some particularly unpleasant things about Ellen. This infuriated me. I took my belongings and went to a hotel. Ellen and I decided that it was ridiculous for me to live in one place and she in another when we were going to get married sooner or later. It was close to the Passover season. We called up the van der Veens and told them we wanted to come to Cincinnati and get married immediately. Ellen's parents made the arrangements. On short notice, a reception was arranged which was to be held at their home after the wedding. My old friends and professors from the college were invited; so too were Julius and Ilsa Weinberg and all of the van der Veens's friends. My parents were invited but they refused to come. Their refusal cast a shadow over the occasion for me in spite of my determination to act on my own.

The sudden decision to get married precipitated a further crisis. Although Julian Morgenstern had indicated the college's willingness to readmit me, my friends in New York urged me to seek admission to the rabbinical department of the Jewish Theological Seminary instead. Two people were especially insistent in encouraging me to become a Conservative rabbi: Dr. Leo Rosenzweig, a Lithuanian talmudist with a Ph.D. in philosophy from a German university, and Samuel Dresner who had been my classmate at the college and who was now a freshman at the seminary. Rosenzweig was my teacher in the courses I took at the seminary. I respected both his Jewish learning and his philosophical training. He was a neo-Kantian, as were many of the Lithuanian Jews who studied philosophy in pre-Hitler Germany. Dresner, Heschel's disciple, had become extremely traditional and urged me to come to the seminary.

"You can't really go back to that place," he said. "Stay here and really learn something."

It did not take much to persuade me. I wanted to find a career in Jewish service. I didn't really want to serve as a congregational rabbi. I liked to preach, but I disliked calling on people I didn't know when they were sick or in mourning. Above all, I did not want my life controlled by men and women who sought power over the rabbi to compensate for their lack of it outside the synagogue. Perhaps, I also intuited that I had a tendency to challenge some of the more complacent assumptions of the community on religious and social issues and that this was bound to upset people. In the back of my mind I had not abandoned the idea of an academic career. I understood that the seminary would give me a far better training in rabbinic literature than the Hebrew Union College. The traditionalism of the seminary fitted in with my psychological needs. Ellen and I had decided to observe the dietary laws and keep a traditional Jewish home. We thought that the life we were planning was more in harmony with my becoming a Conservative rabbi. Socially, we felt far more at home among nonobservant Jews. Nevertheless, the direction of our lives was toward Conservative Judaism.

There was also a sociological factor operative which only became apparent in retrospect. The postwar period witnessed an enormous growth in the number of churches and synagogues, especially in the newer suburbs. Because of the Great Depression, the thirties had been a period of retrenchment for religious institutions. The first half of the decade of the forties was a period of marking time. After the war, there was a reservoir of pent-up demand for new housing, new communities, new schools, and new universities, as well as new churches and synagogues. This demand exploded at about the same time the first generation of

87

American-born Jews of Eastern European background were becoming homemakers in the suburban developments that were springing up in every metropolitan area. These new developments led to the building of hundreds of synagogues. A comparable development on a larger scale took place among the Christian denominations. By background most of the young Jews who were beginning to establish families in West Newton, Massachusetts, Shaker Heights, Ohio, Highland Park, Illinois, and the San Fernando Valley were more traditional than the Reform Jews who had founded the older, better established communities. It was apparent that Conservative Judaism was going to be a formidable rival to Reform. In the late forties and throughout the fifties the mood of Conservative Judaism was that of the American economy, one of confident expansion in spite of periodic, minor setbacks. The movement was led by Louis Finkelstein, an exceedingly complex personality who was given to excessive hyperbole in describing his institution's place in the world. Finkelstein had become chancellor of the seminary in the early forties. In 1947 he was at the peak of his energies as a leader. He was assured that the road ahead would bring great success to him and his movement. He was apparently convinced that his seminary had a central role to play in the religious life not only of the Jewish but also of the Christian communities of America. It is my conviction that in his enthusiasm, Finkelstein confused an accident of demography and economic development with authentic religious vitality. Nevertheless, some of the organizational optimism of Conservative Judaism must have impressed me at the time. I decided that it would be impossible for me to return to the college.

It was by no means certain that the seminary would take me. Even after three years at the college, I had none of the elementary knowledge of the Talmud, which the seminary requires of entering students. I thought it prudent to discuss my interest in the seminary with Abraham Heschel. He encouraged me to apply. Without his willingness to support my application, it would have been impossible for me to make the move. He knew the story of my career at the college. If there was to be any question of my record in Cincinnati, his judgment would be crucial. And a serious problem did develop after I was married. When the college faculty learned that I had once again changed my mind they were understandably angry. Somebody on the faculty proceeded to write a letter to the seminary faculty warning them that I was a poor student as well as emotionally unstable. Without Heschel, I would not have been admitted to the seminary.

When Ellen and I arrived in Cincinnati for the wedding, it was thought that I intended to return to the college. The day before the ceremony, we were invited to tea by the professor of bible, Sheldon Blank. We had not gotten on well when I was a student and the invitation was his way of indicating that I could start off with a new slate when I returned. It was a generous gesture.

"So, you'll be back with us in the fall, Dick?" Blank asked.

"No sir, I've decided to enter the seminary."

Blank went blank. He froze. We stayed with him and his wife for a while, but it was only out of politeness. I had not gauged how deeply the departure of Heschel and Dresner had been resented. It was one thing for me to leave the college for a nonrabbinic career; it was quite another to enter the rival institution.

Ellen and I were married in a simple, private ceremony by Rabbi Louis Feinberg, the local Conservative rabbi. Ellen looked as lovely as I have ever seen her. Standing under the bridal canopy, I gave her the ring and recited the ancient formula: "Behold, thou art betrothed unto me with this ring in accordance with the Law of Moses and Israel."

A number of my friends from the college were present. My best man was Nathan P. Levinson who is today the *Landesrabbiner* in the West German Province of Baden. He serves the university town of Heidelberg.

Word of my decision to enter the seminary had spread through the college. The students who came to the wedding reception wished us well, but there was an undertone of tension at what should have been a joyous occasion. The tension finally exploded. Dr. Samuel Atlas, who taught Talmud at the college and who had been one of my favorite teachers, became livid with anger. He was a short, round, fat man with beady, piercing eyes. He wore thick-lensed, horned-rimmed glasses that exaggerated the piercing effect of his eyes. Like Leo Rosenzweig, he came from Lithuania, had a German Ph.D. in philosophy and was a neo-Kantian. He had known the world of traditional Judaism from earliest childhood. He was a stranger in midwestern Cincinnati. He seemed envious of Abraham Heschel who had been able to find a position at the seminary. Atlas had attempted several times to interest the seminary faculty in inviting him to teach there, but to no avail.

"You are doing an insane thing," Atlas said to me. He began to raise his voice. His face turned red. People gathered around us. "You will never be able to live that kind of life. In six months you'll be eating ham sandwiches on the sly. You are taking your bride into a life of horror. She

89

doesn't belong in that life; neither do you. You will be ridiculous as a Conservative rabbi, if indeed you ever become one. You've burned your bridges now. You'll never be able to come back to the college and you'll never make it through the seminary!"

Atlas had Orthodox rabbinic ordination. He knew how deeply he was violating the spirit of the occasion. In his fury it didn't matter. Ellen and I were badly shaken by what was in reality a rabbi's malediction on our wedding day. My parents had withheld their blessing. My teacher was prophesying that our plans were destined to turn out disastrously. Unfortunately, there was a kernel of truth in what Atlas was saying. Although Ellen and I reassured ourselves afterwards that his curse was without substance, we really knew better. It didn't matter that his own motives were mixed. Out of my horror of the Auschwitz-world which I believed to be regnant in contemporary history and which I feared might explode in the depths of my own soul, I had chosen the path of bad faith. I had sought a morally intact cosmos at any cost. I had chosen the path of obedience and servitude to a heavenly master whom I was convinced did not really exist. Atlas's dire prophecy did not come true in six months. I did become a Conservative rabbi. I did not eat ham sandwiches in public or on the sly, but neither Ellen nor I were ever able to be at home in the life we entered as man and wife.

6

THE END OF
THE LAW

Ellen and I began married life in 1947 in a furnished room near Columbia University. Housing was scarce. Our resources were exceedingly sparse. We shared the kitchen and bathroom with a number of other people, most of whom were students at one of the institutions in the Columbia–Morningside Heights neighborhood. Our room was on the ground floor facing the street. It had been the living room of an apartment which had seen better days before it was subdivided into rooms for students. We did our best to brighten our room with posters, art reproductions, and an occasional piece of our own furniture. We had little privacy and hardly enough space, but it didn't matter. We were beginning our marital adventure and we were together. It also helped that most of the other tenants were our age and in a comparable situation.

We both worked. I taught at Temple Israel at first and continued my part-time research job with the Jewish Education Committee. Sam Dresner introduced me to Wolfe Kelman, a student at the seminary. Wolfe has served almost all of his rabbinic career as executive vice president of the Rabbinical Assembly of America. Shortly after we met, Wolfe helped Ellen to get a job with the Youth Division of the United

Jewish Appeal. It was the period immediately before the birth of the State of Israel. Ellen became deeply involved in helping to raise money for the young nation which was about to face its test of birth and war. We wanted to do all we could to help the beleaguered Jews of Israel to become masters of their own destiny.

Wolfe became a very important influence upon me from our first meeting. He was my age but he had far greater experience with the Jewish world. Like Abraham Heschel, he came from a long line of Hasidic rabbis. He was part of a Hasidic aristocracy of which neither Ellen nor I had had any prior knowledge. His father had been a rabbi in Toronto. After his premature death, Wolfe's mother brought her family to the Borough Park section of Brooklyn, then as now a citadel of Orthodox Judaism.

Before meeting Wolfe, I had known a number of men who were at home in traditional Judaism but none my own age who were also at home in the secular world. Wolfe introduced Ellen and me to his family. We were frequently invited to share the Sabbath with them. Mrs. Kelman was an attractive woman, deeply committed to her inherited Hasidic traditions. She was raising her family as committed Orthodox Jews under difficult circumstances with great dignity. From earliest childhood Wolfe and his brothers had been at home in the world of Talmudic literature. Knowledge of the complexities of Jewish religious practice was second nature to every member of the Kelman household. No matter what the sacrifice, Mrs. Kelman insisted that all of her children receive as excellent a Jewish education as was available in North America. She also insisted that they complete their secular educations as well.

When Ellen and I decided to commit ourselves to a more traditional life, there was something abstract about our resolve. We had little contact with the living tradition. Things changed when we met the Kelmans. Mrs. Kelman encouraged Ellen in her efforts to overcome the feeling that there was something unnatural about what we were trying to do. She also served as a model, perhaps even a surrogate mother. It was impossible to be a guest in her house without being deeply impressed by its spiritual and cultural integrity. We were brought into contact with a religious world that had remained intact in spite of all the assaults visited upon it. We were always mindful of the fact that thousands of households of comparable dignity and devotion had been contemptuously slaughtered by the Nazis. Both Ellen and I had been brought up to look down on Orthodox Jews as backward, unenlightened, and perhaps superstitious. We had good reason to revise our judgment after we met the Kelman family.

92

The extraordinary dignity of the household intensified our revulsion against the compromises of middle-class Judaism. Learning and piety were the measures of personal worth in the Kelman home. We were immensely impressed by the fact that we had come upon people who could neither be bought nor corrupted by the bourgeois world. The experience was revelatory. With Mrs. Kelman's encouragement, Ellen became increasingly conversant with the requirements of a traditional household. Soon Ellen and I began to feel somewhat more at home in our new life. However, Orthodox Judaism never ceased to have an element of strangeness for us that precluded our ever making a wholesome adjustment to it.

Given my poor Talmudic background, it was impossible for me to enter the Rabbinical School of the seminary without further preparation. The Talmud is an enormously complex work that consists primarily of the record of discussions of Jewish religious law, lore, and legend carried on by rabbis in Palestine and Babylonia from about the first to the fifth centuries of the Christian era. The language of the discussions is primarily Aramaic. It is complicated by the ambiguities of its unvocalized and unpunctuated text. A word can often have more than one meaning and one is often uncertain whether a question is being asked or an answer being given. Immersion into the study of the Talmud has been likened to immersion into the sea itself because of the immensity of the work and the difficulties which impede mastery of its contents. Without a skilled teacher, it is impossible to acquire even a rudimentary knowledge.

Unable to enter the Rabbinical School, I entered the *mechinah*, the preparatory department of the seminary. I quickly realized that the *mechinah* would prepare me to pass the entrance exam but little else. The level of instruction was such that I would never have gained any real grasp of rabbinic literature had I rested content with the *mechinah*'s offerings. I sought supplementary, individual instruction from a young postdoctoral student at the seminary, Ezra Band* of Basel, Switzerland. Although he was not much older than I, Band had received Orthodox rabbinical ordination in Europe and a Ph.D. for his studies in religious thought at Basel, where he had studied with Karl Barth. I was as impressed with Band as I had been with Kelman. He seemed to be a living link to the chain of Jewish tradition that had been almost totally obliterated by the Nazis. He was also a link with a European intellectual life I had learned to

* Band is a pseudonym.

93

respect as a result of my contacts with the refugee professors at the Hebrew Union College. It was especially important to me that he had been Barth's pupil.

There was, however, something indefinably disturbing, one might almost say demonic, about the man. He was thin and short with a sallow complexion. There always seemed to be a film of the city's exhaust products on his face which was seldom entirely clear of pimples. He had a pallid indoors look. Although his movements were quick and energetic, he did not seem very robust. On the contrary, his coloring suggested that his natural habitat was the sidewalk café, the dingy hotel, and the library carrel, that he was a stranger to the world of nature. He was fascinating to a certain class of overly cultivated women who were perhaps more interested in exploring the hidden, the unusual, and the mysterious than in openly celebrating the uncomplicated joys of physical love. Perhaps a certain boredom with the ordinary had to set in before a woman might take up with Band. When we first met, some of the seminary students called him the crown prince, because he seemed to be courting Emunah Finkelstein, the chancellor's daughter. He always wore the longest and the most ostentatious prayer shawl when he came, as he did frequently, to those services at the seminary synagogue that were presided over by Dr. Finkelstein. In spite of his display of piety, he talked a great deal about blasphemy, the holiness of sin, and mystical antinomianism. At one of our earliest meetings, he made the accurate prediction that I would soon find more meaning in the pagan gods of Canaan than in the Lord God of Israel. When his friendship with Miss Finkelstein suddenly cooled, he came less frequently to services at the seminary synagogue.

According to the Talmud, a man's rabbinic teacher is more important to him than his own father. One's father brings one into this world; one's teacher brings one into the life of the world to come. Ezra Band was my first teacher of Talmud. I can no longer remember what tractate he chose for instruction, but I have a vivid memory of his long digressions on Sören Kierkegaard, Paul of Tarsus, and Sabbatai Zevi. Band's theological strategy was to demonstrate the impossibility of all commitments devoid of religious faith. He sought to generate faith out of horror of the secular alternatives. He was, however, perhaps more skillful than any secular humanist I had ever met in arguing for the very world without God he called upon me to reject.

I had no problem with Band's dialectical approach to belief in the existence of God. My own turning to traditional Judaism was largely based upon a similar dialectic. I was convinced that I was confronted with the necessity to make a spiritual decision: I had either to choose a Godless world, whose quintessential expression was Auschwitz, or obedience to the commandments of the Lord God of Israel. Out of fright and despair I chose the Lord God of Israel.

Nevertheless, there was always danger of backsliding because a life of obedience to the commandments was fundamentally out of keeping with my normal life style. It was therefore necessary for me constantly to be mindful of the perils of such a retreat. As a result, I became fascinated with the more prominent forms of mystical antinomianism as they had surfaced in Jewish history. I saw Paul of Tarsus's proclamation that Christ is the "end of the Law" as the classical expression of mystical Jewish antinomianism. I mistakenly regarded Paul's proclamation of the "end of the Law" as opening the floodgates of moral and ethical subjectivism within Christendom. One of my spiritual alternatives appeared to be the choice of either the antinomianism of Paul or the *halakhah*, the body of Jewish law and tradition to which Ellen and I were committing our life. Paul's way seemed to lead to a thoroughgoing moral anarchy in which all things including Auschwitz would be permitted. The way of *halakhah* alone seemed to offer a life of moral security.

Between Talmudic discussions of an ox which gored a cow, Ezra and I discussed Paul's "antinomianism." On the surface Paul's proclamation of the "end of the Law" was an expression of the spiritual wasteland we had rejected. At another level, we were both fascinated with the rabbi who became Christendom's greatest and most perennially influential theologian. We were also intrigued by Sabbatai Zevi, the heretical seventeenth century messianic pretender. We were strongly influenced by Gershom Scholem's great work, *Major Trends in Jewish Mysticism*, which had been published in 1946. Scholem's work has been perhaps the most influential single work of Jewish scholarship published in the twentieth century. When it first appeared, his chapter on Sabbatai Zevi had an almost revelatory character for me. Sabbatai Zevi's strange career can be reckoned to have begun in 1648 when Bogdan Chmielnicki, a Ukrainian rebel, led his people in revolt against their rapacious Polish overlords. At the time the Jews of Poland and Ukrainia were caught between the Polish landowners and their Ukrainian peasant tenants. Denied access to more normal ways of earning a living, many Jews were compelled to become tax collectors for the Poles, and, as such, despised by the Ukrainians. In their revolt, the Ukrainians slaughtered over one hundred thousand Jews. This was the greatest catastrophe endured by the Jews until the time of the Nazis.

The condition of the community plummeted to a level of desperation hitherto unknown even during the worst anti-Jewish outbursts of the Crusades. The question of when and how redemption would come assumed an unprecedented urgency. When Sabbatai Zevi, a man of manic-depressive tendencies, was proclaimed the messiah of Israel in Palestine in 1665, a very large proportion of Europe's Jews permitted their yearning for redemption to convince them that redemption was actually at hand. Many were so convinced that Israel's redeemer had come that they sold their possessions to make ready for the miraculous return to the Holy Land.

Shortly after Sabbatai Zevi was proclaimed messiah he was brought to Adrianople where Turkish authorities gave him the choice of conversion to Islam or execution. The "redeemer" of the Jews chose to become an apostate! Confronted with the apparently disconfirming evidence of the messianic pretender, the Jewish world was forced to choose between a totally unanticipated kind of *credo quia absurdum*, the affirmation that its hopes were in the process of being realized by its apostate messiah, or the dreary recognition that the community had been tragically deluded by its own hopes. Hundreds of thousands of Sabbatai Zevi's followers were so dependent upon the joyful promise of redemption that they could not cease believing in him even after his defection.

Sabbatian theologians offered a mystical interpretation of his conversion. They contended that it was part of God's plan that the messiah became an apostate. The evil that impeded redemption was too great to be overcome by mere goodness. The messiah had chosen a more effective way to overcome evil, the redemptive holiness of sin. He had chosen to descend to the depths of iniquity and impurity to overcome those cosmic forces opposed to God's plan. Sabbatai Zevi's followers were divided on the question of whether they were to act out the messiah's strategy to foster redemption in their own lives or whether the messiah's immersion in evil sufficed. The radical Sabbatians proclaimed the sacramental character of acts that negated the surface meaning of God's law. They also asserted that it was necessary for the believer to imitate the messiah's redemptive negation of the Torah. This was especially true in the sexual area. Formerly pious Jews practiced all kinds of sexual excesses as an expression of the distinctively Sabbatian version of the messianic "end of the Law."

From the perspective of traditional Judaism, it was clear that, in their cosmic impatience, the Sabbatians were sinful in attempting to bring about the end before the time of redemption had been fulfilled. I saw Sabbatianism as an object lesson of the dangers of religious enthusiasm and the failure to maintain observance of the *halakhah* in all strictness. When I studied the Talmud under Band's tutelage I saw myself as literally upholding by my life and learning the forces of cosmic discipline, order, and morality against the antinomian moral excess which the Sabbatians and their spiritual heirs had bequeathed to mankind. I was especially impressed with Gershom Scholem's assertion that Sabbatian antinomianism was one of the underground sources of the Reform Judaism I had so recently rejected. I saw every Orthodox rabbi as a heroic guardian of civilization, morality, and decency against the anarchic outrages of moral chaos. I wanted to be one of the guardians.

On one level, my apollonian quest for discipline was satisfied by studying the Talmud and by the interludes of conversation during which my brilliant teacher and I would ponder in horror what life would be like without the law. On another level, the Sabbatians attracted me at least as much as they horrified me. In my daydreams I beheld naked Orthodox Jews, not yet bereft of their beards, gathering in Sabbatian synagogues to enjoy orgiastic sexual coupling with beautiful maidens who lay spread out upon unrolled Torah scrolls waiting to receive the redemptive sacrament of promiscuous love. I imagined unclothed, lustful, dark-haired beauties offering themselves in every imaginable act of love as their mystical identification with Israel's holy messiah, Sabbatai Zevi. And, of course, I saw myself as one of the wild Sabbatian lovers.

My imagination made me a participant in Sabbatian orgies; my behavior was that of a repressed, overly intellectual rabbinic student who kept the *halakhah* with ever greater stringency and insisted that his wife wear a covering over her hair whenever she was in public. I also refused to shake hands with women lest mere touch lead to unpardonable adulteries. There was, in all likelihood, a direct relationship between my sternly monogamous ways and the wildness of my Sabbatian fantasies. The daydreams of excess reinforced my zeal to obey God's law. Undoubtedly, my zeal was a never-ending goad to ever-wilder fantasies. By refusing to touch a woman's hand, I had eroticized even the slightest contact with the opposite sex.

Could I have been a crypto-Sabbatian? I hovered between love of God and dreams of sinful liberty. Ezra's personality heightened those tendencies. Ellen and I were simultaneously attracted and repelled by him. One day Ellen was preparing for a bible lesson in an empty room in the seminary dormitory. I entered the room while she was engrossed in study. She did not notice me. I came up behind her, put my right hand on her breast and fondled it. She relaxed and became limp. We continued for a few minutes until I broke the erotic atmosphere by speaking.

"My God," she said, "I thought you were Band. I felt hypnotized and couldn't resist." Band had a seductive, disturbing effect on both of us.

Band had only a limited amount of time. I required a kind of immersion in the study of the Talmud that was simply not available at the seminary. Wolfe's brother-in-law, Rabbi Melech Silber, suggested that I discuss my needs with Rav Isaac Hutner, the Rosh Yeshivah or principal of the Mesivta Chaim Berlin. Chaim Berlin was far more strictly committed to Orthodoxy than the better known and more prosperous Yeshivah University. It was also less in direct competition with the seminary. It was therefore possible to attend Chaim Berlin without compromising my relations with the seminary.

Chaim Berlin was located on Stone Avenue in the Brownsville section of Brooklyn. In those days Brownsville was a decaying lower-middle-class neighborhood that still retained traces of its former glory when illustrious characters like "Lepke" and "Gurrah," the leaders of Murder Inc., a Jewish appendage to the Mafia, made their headquarters there. The school was located in a converted bank building. The faded elegance of the structure was still visible in the marble floors and bronze gates of the first floor where the bank's public business had once been transacted. The marble floor was usually dirty. The walls were covered with dust and cobwebs, adding a touch of decay to yesteryear's elegance. Nothing had been done to spruce up the building. This was partly due to the perennial financial crises which made it seem as if the yeshivah was always on the brink of being permanently closed. There was also a deeper reason for the ugliness: Orthodox Judaism has always been deeply distrustful of sensuous spontaneity. A tradition that prohibits men from shaking hands with women cannot be expected to encourage the growth of a rich aesthetic sensibility. This world is a stage upon which God's law is to be obeyed; undue attention to beauty would be a waste of time better spent in the study of that law. God was to be adored as the cobwebs multiplied.

The most important room in the yeshivah was located on one of the upper floors. It too lacked adornment save for a small ark containing the scrolls of the Torah. This room, the *beth ha-midrash*, served as both synagogue and study hall. Over a hundred students could usually be found sitting around tables in small groups. There were also some older men, the rebbes, interspersed among them. The room was very noisy. At every table students were engaged in reciting aloud the text of a Talmudic tractate or discussing its meaning.

In spite of the din and the drabness, the age-old tradition of Talmudic study was preserved intact. The rebbes at Chaim Berlin were largely ignorant of contemporary historical scholarship which is capable of critically examining the Talmudic literature and arriving at an increasingly accurate picture of the men and the societies that produced the successive layers of that literature. Nevertheless, the Talmud was a living document for them. Chaim Berlin may have offended my aesthetic sensibility; it moved me morally and religiously. There was an authenticity manifest in the lives of its best teachers which seemed to be radically different from anything I had seen elsewhere in American Judaism. The very traditionalism of the institution added stature to the men who taught there. They transcended the lower-middle-class drabness of their surroundings by living according to a code that was the distillation of the wisdom and experience of a hundred generations of their people. They were proud of the fact that it was their vocation to hand that tradition down to yet another generation. There was also the factor of Auschwitz although it was seldom mentioned. Chaim Berlin was one of the very few yeshivoth that had survived the holocaust. The great yeshivoth of Europe were no more. Israel was about to face its life-and-death struggle for independence. In 1947 there was the distinct possibility that the survival of traditional Judaism rested with a handful of impoverished institutions, neglected by the prosperous American Jewish mainstreams, institutions such as Chaim Berlin and Mesivta Torah Va-Daath in the Williamsburg section of Brooklyn.

Rav Isaac Hutner was a somewhat rotund, hearty man with dark hair and a beard. He had an immensely powerful personality, which was evident in the physical power of his handshake, as well as in a certain electric air about his presence. It would be unfair to say that his personality dominated those around him. That would convey an image that would not be entirely accurate. Yet, he did dominate as an exceptionally sensitive medieval father confessor might have influenced those who habitually turned to him for counsel and absolution. As were so many Talmudists of distinction, Rav Hutner was a Lithuanian Jew. He had studied at the Slobadka Yeshivah, one of Europe's greatest centers of rabbinic learning. Unlike Samuel Atlas of the Hebrew Union College and Louis Ginzberg of the Jewish Theological Seminary, Hutner had sought no western-style Ph.D. He was not interested in being a modern Orthodox Jew. His religious cosmos had never suffered the cultural and theological lesions the men who had gone to German universities had had to endure. Nevertheless, Hutner was no obscurantist. He was an immensely perceptive intuitive psychologist who maintained his moral authority over his disciples long after they left the yeshivah to work in Orthodox Jewish day schools and to serve as Orthodox rabbis in the larger and more compromised American Jewish community.

Rav Hutner's school had as one of its functions the training of rabbis. Yet, the man did whatever he could to *dissuade* those he ordained from accepting even the most Orthodox pulpits.

"It is a *mitzvah*, a service of God, to keep the laws of the Torah," he would say, "it is no *mitzvah* to become a rabbi of a synagogue."

On other occasions he would say, "Judaism needs good *baalay batim*, religiously committed laymen (literally, "masters of households"); it doesn't need more rabbis."

He understood that it would be impossible even for his disciples not to make compromises once they made a profession out of their learning. Such compromises were unpardonable breaches of God's law. He had no desire to see the initial stages of corruption set in the moment a man was hired by a synagogue. He thought of schools that train pulpit rabbis as trade schools. In his eyes, they were necessary evils, but they were also a waste of time for men of spiritual integrity.

At times, he expressed a kind of admiration for honest unbelievers which he withheld from those who maintained a compromise position. He told of one great rabbi who was asked, "Rabbi, why is it that the 'lefties' seem to prosper so much more than the 'righties'?"

"Because *emet* [truth] is on their side."

"How can that be, rabbi? How can truth be on the side of those who keep none of the commandments?"

"Because it is *emet* that they are 'lefties' and it is not *emet* that we are 'righties.' If it were, we would prosper, not they."

Although I had been at the Jewish Theological Seminary for only a short time, I had come to see that that institution was as compromised as had been the Hebrew Union College. It is difficult for me to describe the impact Rav Hutner had upon me. Apparently, I needed a father-surrogate whom I could respect. Such men were rare at both the college and the seminary. Hutner was a strong, perceptive person in his own right. He also carried with him the moral authority of thousands of years of tradition. He was certainly the most authoritative yet humane interpreter of what I regarded as God's law I had ever met. Twenty-five years later, a part of me still regrets that I could not permanently remain his disciple. I know that he cannot be happy with the direction my career has taken. Nevertheless, of all my religious teachers, I retain the greatest respect for him.

When I first met Hutner, I told him about my nonreligious upbringing, my encounters with both Unitarianism and Reform and my decision to enter the Jewish Theological Seminary and become a Conservative rabbi. He offered no objection to the plan. He told me that he would think about what I needed to "learn Torah." He asked me to return in a week.

When I returned, he said that Rav Asher Zimmerman, one of the teachers at the yeshivah was willing to give me an hour's private instruction five days a week. I would spend every weekday morning in the *beth ha-midrash* sitting at the Rav Asher's study table. At some point during the morning he would instruct me in a section of the Talmud. I would then review the section until I knew it well. If I had questions, I could ask Rav Asher. My teacher would only charge me a token seven dollars a week. He had chosen Rav Asher partly because of his great learning and piety and partly because his native language was English. Instruction in Talmud was normally given in Yiddish in both Eastern Europe and in American Orthodox rabbinical schools. I knew no Yiddish. It was important that my teacher be able to express himself with precision in English. Most of the rebbes could speak English but they had no experience in teaching or interpreting the Talmud in English.

Rav Asher was a thin man of medium height in his middle thirties, with a mustache and balding brown hair. He was American-born, but his parents had sent him to pre-war Poland to the Mirer Yeshivah for his rabbinical training. He had never had any secular schooling. He was regarded with great reverence by the students. He lived in the most Orthodox section of Williamsburg with his wife and their small children. He was an extremely patient teacher who was determined not only to introduce me to the study of the Talmud but to win me over to "a life of Torah."

Rav Asher had never seen a movie. He believed movies were a waste of time that could be best spent on Torah. He never looked at picture magazines. He regarded the relatively modest pin-ups carried by *Life* and *Look* as unduly unclothed. Study of the Torah and observance of its

101

commandments were alone worthy enterprises for him. He had no time for games or physical exercise. There was for him only one way to spend one's days. If he possessed any religious doubts, they were so deeply hidden that he was entirely unaware of them.

One day shortly after the Israeli War of Independence he told me that he had heard from a friend in Israel the real reason for Israel's victory over Egypt near Beer Sheba, Abraham the patriarch's place of settlement in ancient Palestine.

"It was dark," Rav Asher said. "The patrol had lost its way. The men were in danger of getting lost in the desert. When things seemed at their worst, an old man with a white beard suddenly appeared out of nowhere and showed the patrol an unknown path. The Israelis were able to ambush a much larger Egyptian force. When the battle was over they looked for the old man, but he had disappeared. Somehow, they all knew who he was. He was Abraham *avinu*, Father Abraham, come to rescue his children."

Rav Asher admitted that the old man's appearance could have been imaginary, but he indicated that he didn't really think so. He believed in the miracle as he believed with full faith in all of the miracles told in the Bible.

Once we got to know each other, Rav Asher would often invite Ellen and me to spend the Sabbath in Williamsburg with his family. We were moved by the experience. Rav Asher excelled in one of the most demanding of scholarly disciplines, Talmudic studies. At the same time, there was an unselfconscious ease about his life as an Orthodox Jew which both Ellen and I respected and to which we aspired.

I regarded Rav Asher as the polar opposite of Ezra Band. In spite of his Orthodox ordination, Band seemed to be part of the Auschwitz-world I was attempting to escape. Band's instruction had the effect of intensifying my own Sabbatian temptations. Rav Asher calmed me. He gave me the assurance that the life of moral and religious certitude to which I aspired was within my grasp.

When I began lessons with Rav Asher, I kept the dietary laws and faithfully offered prayer three times a day, as is customary among traditional Jews. Our new way of life was infused with confidence and enthusiasm. Ellen and I saw ourselves as having miraculously escaped from both the secular world and corrupt middle-class Judaism. Our new life gave us a commitment that solidified the problematic bond between us. We were partners in this spiritual venture. Traditional Judaism reserves the term, *baal t'shuvah,* for one who repents his old life and begins to live in accordance with God's law. We were assured that there was greater rejoicing on high for a *baal t'shuvah* than for one who had never tasted the temptations of a life without Torah. We enjoyed the attentions we received from our new friends so much that we were often tempted to overemphasize the miseries of our old life and how wonderful it was that we had found the better way.

As the months passed, my respect for Orthodoxy and my questions about Conservative Judaism grew. Conservative Judaism began to seem even more objectionable than Reform. Reform Judaism made no pretense that it had kept the tradition intact. Only those who had already broken with tradition would be attracted by it. Perhaps Reform might help them to preserve their ethnic if not their religious identity. Conservative Judaism seemed like *ersatz* Orthodoxy. It often gave the appearance of retaining the ethos and the authentic liturgy of the Orthodox synagogue. In reality, there were vast areas of belief and practice in which it had compromised itself.

Not surprisingly, I was most disturbed by Conservative Judaism's compromises with Orthodoxy's insistence that any suggestion of an erotic element in worship be repressed. In traditional synagogues not only are men and women seated separately, but women are also required to sit behind a *mehitzah,* a partition. Women may not officiate in any capacity at services and a woman's voice, especially in song, is regarded as a seductive incitement. In 1947 many new synagogues were beginning to spring up that permitted mixed seating. The founders of these synagogues were convinced that there was little difference between Conservative and Orthodox Judaism, save for the fact that "families could sit together." They argued that the mixed seating would lead to a more meaningful religious life for the entire family, because all could worship as a unit. I was convinced that Orthodoxy's insistence on the separation of the sexes and its repression of the erotic was based upon a profound religious and psychological intuition. I felt very much like those Roman Catholic conservatives who opposed the reforms of Vatican II. It was their conviction that, were even one crack to appear in the sacred fortress which held back the onslaughts of secularity and relativism, the whole structure would collapse. Mankind would then be condemned to an existence in which neither moral nor spiritual authority retained even the slightest hold. I was fearful that wherever Conservative Judaism abandoned Orthodoxy's insistence on strict sexual definition and discipline, the worst excesses of Sabbatianism would eventually reassert themselves. This fear was, of course, reinforced by the knowledge of how potent my own Sabbatian fantasies continued to be. It was almost as if I were crying out, "Give me a straitjacket, O Lord, lest I outdo Sabbatai Zevi. . . ."

Neither Reform nor Conservative Judaism could serve as my spiritual straitjacket. Orthodoxy seemed to be the only possible defense against a life of moral, spiritual, and, perhaps, psychological chaos.

Once again, I was faced with a crisis. I was admitted to the Rabbinical School of the Jewish Theological Seminary in September 1948. Classes were to begin after the fall sequence of holidays, Rosh Hashanah, Yom Kippur, and the eight days of Sukkoth. I no longer wanted to enter the seminary. I wanted to become an Orthodox rabbi. I saw myself as defending order against chaos by saving assimilated Jews like myself from the spiritual perils of the contemporary world. It was useless, I thought, to fight the world's Nazis unless one were purified of all taint of that which led to Nazism in one's own soul. Only perfect fidelity to God's revelation could lead to such a purification. To become a Conservative rabbi now seemed tantamount to rebellion against God. At the core of my being I still did not believe in such a God. Nevertheless, my fright compelled me to hearken with ever greater scrupulosity to his revelation. It seemed as if I had only one remaining alternative, to become an Orthodox rabbi.

There were, however, difficulties. I was aware of the fact that those who knew me tended to regard my changes in religious commitment as evidence of acute instability. On the surface I refused to let this get to me. But, at a deeper level I was profoundly disturbed by the recognition that there was much justice in that opinion. Another consideration was that Ellen was pregnant. There was a limit to the financial and emotional insecurity I could inflict upon her. It was doubtful whether I could complete the studies at Chaim Berlin in an endurable period. It would be difficult enough to become a Conservative rabbi. I had the intellectual ability to become an Orthodox rabbi, but the cost in time and emotion would be even greater.

Neither Rav Hutner nor Rav Asher Zimmerman encouraged me. They indicated that I would be welcome at Chaim Berlin, but Rav Hutner suggested that the wiser course would be for me to find a nonreligious profession while continuing to live as an Orthodox Jew. In retrospect, this would have been the most practical solution had I been primarily interested in obeying God's commandments. I did not perceive that my hankering for the priest's magic remained greater than my desire to obey

God. From the time I wanted to be a Unitarian minister my interest in an omnipotent profession never faltered. Even my flirtation with the academic study of philosophy was no exception. If I could not serve as a priest, I could at least possess the saving knowledge of the mystery of existence. Rav Hutner's suggestion that I serve God as a mere layman was clearly unacceptable.

Ezra Band was the only one who encouraged me to leave the seminary. He reinforced my conviction that the seminary represented the kind of compromises that would ultimately lead to a contemporary form of Sabbatianism. He presented me with the hope that I might be a defender of civilization itself were I to make the proper decision. He warned me that, were I to remain at the seminary I would be worse than the most contemptible bourgeois because I understood what was spiritually at stake in choosing the compromises of Conservative Judaism. Most people simply did what they had to in order to survive in a corrupt world. If I went to the seminary, I might cover myself with the title of rabbi, but, in reality, I would be a cheating, despicable merchant. My rabbinic office would at best be a pretense, at worst a contemptible fraud. If that was what I wanted, he argued, why waste four or five years at the seminary? It would be far cleaner to go into business and make my way in the secular world.

Band almost convinced me. One evening while Ellen was in Cincinnati with her parents, Band and I decided to go over to the seminary dormitory and tell Wolfe and Sam the "good news" of my latest decision.

Band was almost manic in his enthusiasm. He rolled his eyes and gesticulated energetically as he said, "Isn't it wonderful, he's going to leave this terrible place and go to Chaim Berlin!"

"If it's so bad," Wolfe asked him, "why do you stay?"

"I'll leave as soon as I can. I have to make my plans carefully," Band answered. "But think of the drama. A man with Rubenstein's background leaving all this corruption and compromise to go to the *Mesivta!*"

"Whose drama," Wolfe calmly asked, "yours or his? You goad him into leaving while you stay. He's got a pregnant wife. He's made enough changes. Do you want to wreck him?"

As Wolfe spoke, I began to see Ezra as a peculiar kind of Mephistopheles. Faust was enticed with the lure of Gretchen, *Walpurgisnacht*, and Helen of Troy. Band was seducing me with the promise of an impossible ideological purity, made all the more questionable by his own refusal to take the same path. An animal instinct warned me that life was superior to ideology, that sooner or later I would be compelled to join the human race and make some compromises in order to keep myself and my family intact. With his fundamentally sympathetic knowledge of Orthodoxy, Wolfe was protecting me from myself.

When Ezra saw that the drama was not going to take place, he cooled toward me immediately. He became extremely contemptuous. He said very little to me thereafter but at each of our subsequent meetings it was as if he were saying: "You may fool the rest of the people around here, but you can't fool me. I know you for the contemptible, pretentious bourgeois you are. I prefer an honest cheat to someone like you."

Ezra's contempt was the counterpart of my own self-contempt. His disdain for bourgeois Judaism was reminiscent of my mother's. His disapproval was reinforced by echoes of an infinitely more potent and archaic source of authority and values. During the time I was a student at the Jewish Theological Seminary, I never ceased to despise myself for having permitted practical considerations from interfering with the purity of my resolve. I was convinced that my decision to become a Conservative rabbi was an offense against God. I did not feel less guilty because I did not really believe in the God I was offending! After ordination I had again to face Ezra at Harvard. He spent several years there as a postdoctoral fellow. Whenever we met, he would reinforce my negative feelings about myself for having become a Conservative rabbi and for having contaminated myself by daily association with ordinary middle-class Jews.

Partly in order to ward off both his accusations and my own, I resolved to be as strictly traditional as I possibly could. Life may have forced me to become a Conservative rabbi, I reasoned, but nothing prevented me from living a thoroughly Orthodox personal life. From the moment I entered the seminary until I was helped by psychoanalysis to regard myself with a less anguished vision, I experienced a pervasive and never-ending sense of uncleanliness and moral pollution about the kind of rabbinic vocation I had chosen.

The crisis about my decision to enter the seminary was only one side of my encounter with Orthodox Judaism. Other aspects of the encounter had an even more profound effect on Ellen and me. Almost immediately after I began to study with Rav Asher and long before my crisis about entering the seminary, Rav Asher raised the question of whether Ellen and I would observe the laws of *taharat ha-mishpahah*, the laws of family purity. Orthodox Jews follow the biblical injunction that, seven days after

106

the menstrual period, a woman must be purified by full immersion in a fount of "living waters" before she can again become sexually available to her husband. Reform Judaism has long regarded such taboos as primitive superstitions of no relevance to enlightened Jews in the twentieth century. Conservative Jews have been embarrassed by the subject. In spite of the claim that their movement was essentially faithful to the observance of Jewish law, they have been as indifferent as Reform Jews to the laws of family purity.

When Rav Asher raised the issue, I was unenthusiastic about the prospect of Ellen going to the *mikveh*, the ritual bath, every month. I responded politely but dismissed the suggestion. Nevertheless, a seed had been planted. I felt there was a certain logic to Orthodox Judaism's insistence that God really cared about the conditions under which I made love to my wife. The Orthodox insistence that marital sex had to be minutely regulated seemed in some respects *less* repressive than liberal Judaism's attitude, which was to leave the individual entirely on his own resources in dealing with the complex emotions which attend both menstruation and sexual intercourse. Fear of menstrual blood is one of the most widely attested masculine responses to the mystery of femininity in practically every culture. No relationship is as fraught with emotion, both pleasurable and anxious, as the sexual relationship. It soon became apparent to me that part of Orthodox Judaism's fundamental integrity was its ability to give these complex realities an ordered place within the spiritual life of its adherents.

I resisted Rav Asher's suggestion for a time, but my passion for ideological consistency impelled me to ever greater compliance with *every* aspect of God's law. If God had given the commandments, who was I to decide which to obey and which to reject? There could be no lacunae in my religious practice. I reasoned that selective obedience was sinful. It also placed me in the very predicament I had sought to escape. If the final decision were mine, what, I asked myself, could prevent me from fulfilling the laws concerning prayer while at the same time indulging in adulterous excess? Sabbatai Zevi's image never left me. The law could only give me the moral certitude I sought, were I to commit myself to it all the way.

I came to understand that there was in fact only one sin in biblical religion although it took many forms. That sin was disobedience. *Every* biblically ordained commandment became a test of my willingness to disobey myself, in order the better to obey God. It was not for me to

107

question why God had commanded me to observe the laws of family purity. My task was to try to understand *what* God required of me, not *why* he had done so.

Ellen and I initially experienced our new commitment as an enormous spiritual gain. Just as we were partners in forsaking our former life in the matter of prayer, study, and diet, we were now partners in forsaking our old sexual ways. Whatever ambivalence existed between us in this area was seemingly diminished. We now felt that we were delighting in the joys of the bridegroom and the bride in a way that was pleasing in the sight of the Lord. There were moments when it almost seemed as if he were present as a third party at our celebrations of love. Our actual love-making achieved a kind of chastity. For the first time, I was free of all sense of guilt in my sexual relations.

Observance of *taharat ha-mishpahah* further intensified our disdain for bourgeois Judaism and our own pride that we were no longer a part of it. This was, of course, before I faced the crisis of whether I would become a Conservative or an Orthodox rabbi. I came to regard most of the leaders of Conservative Judaism as insincere men who pretended to a piety they did not possess. At the seminary, I heard a great deal about Conservative Judaism's fidelity to Jewish law, but whenever I asked about *taharat ha-mishpahah,* I was met by silence and embarrassment. Understandably, some people at the seminary began to regard me as an eccentric given to extreme positions. In retrospect, it would seem that whatever I gained by fidelity to the law was offset by a heightened sense of pride and a kind of spiritual arrogance that I was somehow less compromised and less evasive in my religious commitments than most of those I knew. There was little modesty in my position. My "vocation for the summit" had not been altered by my "conversion." I now sought to feel that I was better than others by virtue of the greater logic and consistency of my spiritual position.

After I had begun to observe the laws of *taharat ha-mishpahah,* there remained a glaring example of my unwillingness fully to obey God's commandments. The first positive commandment given by God to Adam and his progeny was to be fruitful and multiply, yet when Ellen and I made love, she used a birth control device. Both of us felt that it would be impossible for us to have children for years to come. Whether I entered the seminary or Chaim Berlin the following fall, it would be years before I could be ordained and get a full-time job. If Ellen and I were to have any degree of economic security, it was imperative that we both work.

Having children as I embarked once again on a career as a full-time student was utterly impractical. Yet, I could not ignore the commandment to be fruitful and multiply. I was again faced with the same problem: Who was I to decide which commandments to obey? I again asked myself whether I had any right to permit economic considerations to compromise my religious commitments.

Beyond the practical considerations, there was the simple but largely unrecognized fact that neither Ellen nor I were emotionally ready to become parents. We required a greater measure of psychological, if not economic, stability. The turbulence of our lives was simply too great to permit us fully to assume the parental role. Yet in spite of the practical problems, the decision to have children was inevitable. I was earning two thousand dollars a year as a Hebrew teacher. My income was insufficient for a family life of even the most disciplined frugality, and Ellen and I were given to impulse spending. Nevertheless, I told Rav Hutner that Ellen and I would cease to violate the commandment to be fruitful and multiply.

I was very frightened as I contemplated the prospect of becoming a father. Ellen went to the *mikveh* for ritual purification after her menstrual period. When she returned home, there was an inner glow about her. She seemed more beautiful than ever. We made love without reserve and with a warmth and a wholeness we had never before experienced even on our wedding night. In spite of our fears, we wanted a child that night.

I have always felt that my oldest son was conceived that evening. Within a short time we learned that Ellen was pregnant. It was the best time of our marriage. We were apprehensive about money; we were peculiarly unfinished emotionally, but for a short time we felt that there was a profound rightness about what we were doing. In the midst of a world of war, death, and unbelief, we had given ourselves wholly over to a greater power; we had given ourselves to the power of life. In spite of the harsh difficulties I was to face as a father, I have never ceased to be grateful to Rav Hutner for encouraging me when he did.

Unfortunately, there was little certainty that life would indeed triumph. In her fifth month Ellen began to stain badly. It looked very much as if she might miscarry. Her obstetrician told her that it was imperative that she remain off her feet and have nursing care at all times if the child was to be born at all. We were totally unprepared for this catastrophic turn of events. We had saved up enough money to pay for the doctor and a normal hospital stay, but no more. Fortunately, by this time

109

I had entered the seminary's Rabbinical School and we were able to receive help from emergency funds made available to us by the seminary. On April 19, 1949, she gave birth to a very healthy son.

Thousands of years ago, scripture records that God spoke unto Abraham:

> As for you, you shall keep My covenant, you and your offspring to come, throughout the ages. Such shall be the covenant, which you shall keep, between Me and you and your offspring to follow: every male among you shall be circumcised. You shall circumcise the flesh of your foreskin . . . . At the age of eight days, every male among you throughout the generations shall be circumcised. . . .

As it had been for over a hundred generations, so it was with Aaron. According to Jewish tradition, it is the duty of the father to circumcise his own son. Since few fathers have either the skill or the calm to carry out so delicate an operation, it is customarily performed by a *mohel,* one skilled in the techniques of the operation and possessed of a reputation for religious rectitude. Aaron received the sign of the covenant at a ceremony conducted in accordance with strict Orthodox tradition. His body and his psyche were altered by an archaic rite which linked father and son in an unbreakable bond to Israel's primal antiquity. Ellen and I had been carried along by the supra-personal force of life itself when Aaron was conceived. At his circumcision, Aaron and I were swept along by an ancestral culture which enveloped the entire family. Aaron was thousands of years old the day he was born.

There was a palpable air of tension and anxiety at the ancient rite as the *mohel* took out his surgical instruments and prepared to remove the child's foreskin.

What if the instrument slips? I thought.

Will it hurt my baby? I wondered. Did I perhaps want it to hurt my baby? I rejoiced in the birth of a son, but Ellen's attentions would now be divided. Where there had been two, there would now be three. Was there some corner of my being in which I wanted the knife to slip? Could I possibly be one of the castrating fathers psychoanalysts have written about? After all, those psychoanalysts were themselves mostly Jewish. Perhaps they knew something I didn't know. There was something indelibly primitive about the ceremony, yet the participants were highly educated men, rabbis, professors from a rabbinical school, and rabbinical students. In what century was the ceremony really taking place? Was I with Father Abraham in the Negev or in America?

I was assured by the *mohel* that the ceremony was performed before the child developed any localized sense of pain.

"It's nothing," he said, "don't worry. It'll all be over in a few moments."

But it wasn't "nothing" and it wouldn't be over as long as Aaron lived. Something uncanny had taken place. The circumcision was the first act in which I had asserted my unchallenged authority as a father over my first born son. For seven days the child had been lovingly tended by his mother. On the eighth day, he had been abruptly taken away from the woman's world and forcibly introduced into the world of men and the service of a masculine deity. His diffused ego was given a masculine focus far earlier than would have been the case had nature been permitted to take its course. Culture had triumphed over nature; the city over the countryside in that eight-day-old infant.

His body had been fundamentally altered by circumcision; so too had his psyche. Can one be changed without the other? Whenever he thought of that archaic injury in later life, he would always wonder whether there was worse to come. In addition, I had put my mark on his masculine organ. I had no doubt that he was my child. Nevertheless, I had claimed him as my own as Father Abraham had once claimed Isaac, in spite of Sara's questionable night visits with Pharaoh and Abimelech, king of the Philistines.

On the eighth day . . . Aaron hadn't been asked. There would come a time, perhaps when he was seven or eight, when he would do the asking. I did when my brother was circumcised. Perhaps his thoughts would be similar to the ones I had. I remember thinking to myself: Is this what Daddy did to me when I was little? What would have happened if the knife had slipped? Suppose I'm really bad, what would Daddy do to me?

There are those who claim that circumcision reduces masculine sensitivity and so dampens passion that a circumcised man can never let himself go as completely as an uncircumcised man. I have no scientific way of evaluating that suggestion but it ought not to be rejected too hastily. The acculturation process within Judaism has the effect of limiting the physical and emotional hold a woman can have over a man. That process begins on the eighth day.

The book of Exodus contains traces of an even more archaic rite practiced by fathers upon their sons on the eighth day in the almost forgotten reaches of Israel's pagan antiquity. God is depicted as demanding:

> Sanctify unto me all the first-born, whatever opens the womb among the Israelites, both of men and of beast; it is mine.

Most scholars agree that the earliest sanctification of the first born of *both* men and animals involved the setting aside of the first born as sacrificial offerings. This is stated almost explicitly in Exodus 22:28,29:

> The first born of your sons you shall give to me. You shall do likewise with your oxen and your sheep; seven days it shall be with its dam; on the eighth day you shall give it to me.

Every year on Rosh Hashanah, the lesson from scripture retells the story of Father Abraham's ascent to Mount Moriah to offer his first born son by Sara as a "burnt offering" unto the Lord. As Abraham raised his knife to slaughter the child, the dire necessity was miraculously averted. A ram was provided by God in place of the child. Orthodox Judaism has never permitted the memory of the archaic sacrificial slaughter of the first born entirely to disappear. Every Jewish father is required to "redeem" his first born son on the "thirty first day of his birth" in a ceremony known as the *pidyon ha-ben* or Redemption of the First-born Son.

On Aaron's thirty-first day, my family joined with a small group of rabbinical students and teachers at our apartment in New York to take part in Aaron's *pidyon ha-ben*. On the surface, the occasion was a joyous family celebration of the happy addition to its circle. Customary Jewish delicacies were served. Beneath the surface something at odds with all pretense to rationality and modernity took place. Aaron was brought into the room on a cradle of pillows placed upon a silver tray. I then handed him over to a *cohen*, a hereditary priest, a man who could by family tradition trace his lineage back to the Israelite priesthood of biblical times. As I presented Aaron to the *cohen*, I repeated an ancient formula:

> This, my first born son, is the first-born of his mother, and the Holy One, blessed be He, has commanded that he be redeemed as it is said: "And those that are to be redeemed of them from a month old shalt thou redeem, according to thine estimation, for the money of five shekels after the shekel of the Sanctuary. . . ." and it is said:

112

"Sanctify unto me all the first-born, of man and of beast: It is mine."

I took out five silver dollars, the symbolic equivalent of the biblical shekels and placed the money in front of the *cohen*. The *cohen* asked me in accordance with the prescribed ritual:

> Would you rather give your first born son, the first born of his mother, or would you rather redeem him for the five *selaim* [shekels] which you are bound to give according to the Torah?

I had rehearsed my part. I knew what I was required to respond:

> I would rather redeem him. Here, you have the value of his redemption which I am bound to give according to the Torah.

However, as I recited the formula I asked myself: What am I really redeeming him from? What would the *cohen* do if I told him I would rather keep the money? The fleeting thought was immediately suppressed. At the time, I had no conscious awareness that I might have been tempted to alter the customary ritual. Years later I found myself fascinated by this strange and awesome ritual. On one occasion, as I permitted my imagination to flow freely, the following scenario was enacted in my fantasy:

Richard: *I want my money. God can have the boy.*

Cohen: *You've no right to keep the money. The Torah has commanded you to give up the money and redeem your son.*

Richard: *Redeem him from what?*

Cohen: *I don't know . . . just redeem him.*

Richard: *That's nonsense. You know as well as I do what I'm supposed to redeem him from.*

Cohen: *Maybe so, but that's all the more reason for you to give me the money. I'm not a bloodthirsty man.*

Richard: *You don't have a choice. The Torah also commands me to give my first born son to God. You're God's holy priest; take him for God.*

Cohen: *I can't. My wife and I have our own children. I don't need yours.*

Richard: *I'm not giving him to you. I'm giving him to God through you. You know what God really wants. Stop playing games. Do your duty as a priest.*

Cohen: *I know what God doesn't want. Nobody in three thousand years has*

113

behaved the way you have at one of these ceremonies. This thing was settled by Father Abraham. Haven't you ever gone to the synagogue on Rosh Hashanah? Haven't you ever heard a rabbi tell you God didn't want the life of the child. He wanted the ram instead. Your money is just like Isaac's ram. God is permitting you to give your money and keep your child.

Richard: *I don't need him. He'll only get in the way. It's hard enough taking care of Ellen. Besides, she'll give him more attention than me. I'm not ready to be a father yet. I want to be a great scholar, not an ordinary rabbi. How can I be a great scholar and support a family? You take him and give him to God. What is between you and God is none of my business. Just take him. I'll keep the money.*

None of this outrageous fantasy consciously entered my mind during the ritual. Nevertheless, there is a dark side to my nature which I can more easily acknowledge and manage today than I could then. There is one detail which suggests that more may have been going on beneath the surface than I was prepared to face: Aaron was not my first born son's first name. It was his middle name. Neither he nor I have ever liked his real first name. Aaron's suppressed first name is Isaac.

In the actual ceremony, after my declaration that I preferred retaining my son rather than my money, the *cohen* took the money and handed my Aaron back to me, saying,

This [the money] instead of that [the child]; this in exchange for that; this in remission of that. May this child enter into life, into [obedience of] the Torah and into the fear of Heaven. . . ."

The child was now mine rather than God's.

The fundamental purpose of the ceremony was both to acknowledge and to deflect whatever latent infanticidal tendencies I had toward my son. As Abraham had been commanded to circumcise his son, I had circumcised mine; as Abraham had offered up a surrogate for the life of his Isaac, I had done so for mine. For the moment Jewish tradition enabled me to believe that I had exorcised my infanticidal tendencies. Within a short time, my own wife was to call me the murderer of my second son.

Shortly after Aaron's *pidyon ha-ben*, Ellen and I were again faced with the religious issue which led to her first pregnancy: Could we disobey God's first commandment? The question was more urgent this time because of my sense of guilt for having entered the Jewish Theological

114

Seminary. The use of a birth control device would have been further proof that Ezra Band was right after all, that I was really a spiritual fraud. Nevertheless, if the pressure to have another child had intensified, so too had the practical obstacles. Ellen's health had seriously deteriorated during pregnancy. She badly needed a respite before having a second child. Unfortunately, we were too dependent upon the need for ideological purity to be realistic. Ellen became pregnant again almost immediately. The pregnancy itself was without incident, but she was neither physically nor psychologically prepared for the ordeal that was to follow.

Nathaniel Ephraim Rubenstein was born in June 1950 in New York City. When Ellen returned from the hospital, we had no resources with which to secure help for her. Our apartment was on the top floor of a building on Claremont Avenue in the Morningside Heights area of New York. It was a small but pleasant apartment during most of the year. In the summer, it was infernally hot as the sun beat down upon the poorly insulated roof. Ellen had to care for the two infants alone under extremely difficult conditions. I felt that it was her job to take care of the babies and mine to study the Talmud. Regrettably, my attitude was by no means unique among traditional Jews. My help was less than adequate. Within a month she was close to emotional and physical collapse.

As her situation became desperate, Ellen's parents intervened. She needed rest badly. They proposed that Ellen and the babies go to a mountain resort where she would not have to take care of the house and prepare meals. At the end of the summer it was arranged that she would visit Cincinnati, remaining there until after the Jewish holidays. I had been engaged to preach at the services of a congregation in Baltimore during Rosh Hashanah and Yom Kippur. We would have had to have been separated for the Holy Days in any event.

Both Ellen and I were grateful for the van der Veen's generous offer, but our newly found Orthodoxy created further difficulties. It was important that the resort be Orthodox in every detail. The food had to be kosher; the Sabbath strictly observed. We found an apparently suitable place through our Brooklyn friends. Unfortunately, everything about the place was strange and ugly to Ellen. The atmosphere, the people, the cuisine, the aesthetics were different from anything she was used to. It was one thing for us to attempt to live an Orthodox life together; it was very different for Ellen, worn out and discouraged as she was, to enter into so foreign a framework by herself.

I did not accompany Ellen to the country. Her father drove her and the children there. I gather from Ellen's description that the rest turned out to be a horror story. She was worse off among strangers than she would have been at home doing her own chores. The Sabbaths were not the joyous occasions they were supposed to be. They were a form of torture she had to endure. According to Orthodox custom it is forbidden to turn lights on or off on the Sabbath. This was no problem in our apartment. We simply left a light burning in the living room. We opened the bedroom door when we needed light. We shut it when we wanted to sleep. At the resort Ellen and the children were confined to one dreary, ugly room which was illuminated by a naked light bulb that hung on a chain from the ceiling. It was a prison cell for her. There was no way to turn off the light without desecrating the Sabbath. Nathaniel's feeding schedule compelled Ellen to get up several times during the night. Aaron would also cry occasionally. Ellen had little opportunity for the sleep she so desperately needed. When the boys ceased crying, the naked bulb became an instrument of torture compelling Ellen to remain awake. She kept faith with God's commandments but her situation was becoming unendurable.

Things seemed to improve when she arrived in Cincinnati. The van der Veens provided her with day help. Lucy van der Veen took over many of the burdens Ellen had been carrying. Ellen seemed to get some of the rest she needed, although Nathaniel still required night feeding. Apparently, Nathaniel was especially disturbed the night before Yom Kippur. He cried a lot. Ellen got up several times to calm him down. The next morning Ellen found him lying on his stomach dead.

At the time Nathaniel was found I was preparing to conduct Yom Kippur services in Baltimore. It was the second year that the huge Baltimore congregation had invited me for the Holy Days. Dr. Rosenblatt, the rabbi, had sounded me out as to whether I might be interested in becoming assistant rabbi of the congregation after graduation. I had acquired a taste for preaching and the sense of power it gave me, especially on Israel's most sacred days. If ever anything I did as an adult was in fulfillment of an infantile wish, it was my preaching. As I rode the Pennsylvania Railroad from New York to Baltimore, I was confident of my power to weave a spell over my listeners. I would control the way they saw me. I would control what they heard. I might not be God's mouthpiece but I was the next best thing: I had the authority to stand before the community and interpret his word. I did not know that as I

116

looked forward to the fulfillment of my childhood will to power, my own child lay dead in Cincinnati.

Officially, it was described as a crib death. We never really found out what happened. We might have learned the cause of death if there had been an autopsy. Both Rav Hutner and Professor Saul Lieberman, the professor of Talmud at the seminary, counseled against an autopsy as contrary to Jewish law. The uncertainty was worse for Ellen than it was for me. Although she never said so to me, I have always had the feeling that she, like so many other mothers in the same situation, could never get over the feeling that she was somehow responsible for Nathaniel's death. Our marriage began to deteriorate immediately. I could feel a chilling sense of distance as we met in Cincinnati before the funeral. It was impossible for me to offer her any consolation. We were condemned to live with each other, but an icy wall now stood between us.

In the years that followed, our mutual anger would occasionally boil over. We would then say things we later wished we hadn't. Whenever she became really angry with me she would scream: "You murderer, you killed your own son!" My wife's hideous accusation hit the mark. I felt like a murderer. I had not given her the help she needed when she was strained beyond endurance. I had permitted her to go to a miserable Orthodox country place which only intensified her distress. I had left her alone with two infants at a time when her need for me was greatest. I was convinced that I had no time for anything but work, study, and prayer. The burden of the household rested with her. When that burden crashed down on the family with Nathaniel's death, I felt there was justice in Ellen's accusation. In my own eyes, I was an infanticide. I also found myself more deeply bound to Ellen by guilt than I had been by love. Divorce would have been unthinkable, but whatever warmth had formerly been present between us was fast dissolving. I felt I owed her an unnameable something. I had to make "it" up to her, yet I was incapable of spelling "it" out. I felt no need to atone for my son's death before God; I felt every need to atone before Ellen. This need bound me to her long after we should have gone our separate ways.

In spite of our ordeal, I find no fault with Orthodox Judaism for what had occurred. Orthodox Judaism was never meant to be the private religious affirmation of two pathetically isolated young people, divorced from the customs and life style of their parents and siblings. Mrs. Kelman could maintain a viable Orthodox household, as could Rav Hutner and

117

Rav Asher Zimmerman, because their web of primary relationships had provided them with support systems for that kind of life from earliest childhood. Orthodox Judaism had always been a communal and a familial rather than an individual way of life. There is no place in Orthodox Judaism for the single one, magnificent in isolation, casting aside all familiar relationships the better to enjoy solitary intimacy and fellowship with God. Ellen and I had attempted to live an Orthodox life apart from our families and against the grain of the acculturation process which had given us our fundamental personalities.

After the funeral and the mourning period, as I have written elsewhere, there was only one man I wanted to see, Rav Hutner. He knew that something was very deeply wrong and tried to comfort me as he could. "I want you always to remember that *Ribbono-shel-Olam*, the Master of the Universe, never writes guarantees in this life," he said. "I hope this doesn't cause you to lose your *emunah*, your faith."

I protested that nothing had changed. For over two years it seemed as if my fidelity to tradition had not been affected by the family catastrophe. Nevertheless, Rav Hutner's original intuition was accurate. The change took its own time to surface. As the excruciating wound began to develop its overlay of scar tissue, I began to emerge from my numbness. I slowly became aware of the fact that my compulsive quest for consistency had led to the death of my son and had left my family life disrupted beyond almost all hope of repair.

118

7

SURFACE AND
DEPTH

Nathaniel was dead. Divorce was unthinkable but inevitable. Ellen and I tried to piece together our lives. Rav Hutner had expressed concern about my *emunah*, but I was determined once again to be fruitful and multiply. Ellen became pregnant a third time within weeks of the child's passing.

Hannah Rachel Rubenstein was born July 1, 1951. The Sabbath after her birth I attended services at the Avondale Synagogue in Cincinnati where Ellen and I had been married. I was called up to recite the blessings for the reading of the Torah and to name my daughter. After the naming ceremony the rabbi invoked God's blessing on mother and daughter. Surface and depth were in conflict in that ceremony. On the surface, there was rejoicing that Aaron had a healthy baby sister. Beneath the surface, there was regret that a girl rather than a boy had entered the family circle. The day she was born Hannah was heir to her parents' compelling need to atone for the death of a brother she was never to know. Today, after years of struggle, Hannah is a warm, sensitive, highly intelligent young woman of great personal strength. Nevertheless, many of the problems she had to cope with took shape long before she ever saw the light of day. In addition to the normal burden of wounded Jewish memories, Hannah inherited the special burden of memories her parents had hoped would be alleviated by the birth of a second Nathaniel. A boy might have lessened their sense of guilt. The birth of a baby girl seemed to intensify it.

During my sophomore and junior years at the seminary, I supported my family by working as a Hebrew teacher in the Conservative synagogue in South Orange, New Jersey. South Orange was Philip Roth country. Most of the members were second-generation Eastern European Jews who came from Newark's heavily Jewish Third Ward. The men had taken the normal Jewish routes from immigrant poverty to second-generation prosperity. Some had gone to law or medical school. Others had seen their small businesses grow into larger enterprises. There were few professors or intellectuals. The Patamkin family in the movie version of Philip Roth's *Goodbye Columbus* would have felt very much at home in the congregation. There was, however, an edge of insecurity to the highly visible prosperity of the congregants. The Third Ward was never far away geographically or psychologically. The middle class status of the majority of the members was too recent to be regarded as a secure acquisition.

When I first came to Congregation Beth El of the Oranges and Maplewood, Leo Geiger was the rabbi. Geiger had been born in Palestine and came from a learned rabbinic family. He had a lined, rugged, clean shaven face. He was personally attractive in a masculine way, without being handsome. There was nothing new about his status. For generations his forebears had been learned and pious leaders of his people. He had ceased to be Orthodox as a young man, but Judaism's ancestral culture was second nature to him.

It was inevitable that there would be trouble between Geiger and his board. It was nobody's fault. There was little about them that was not brand new. I had heard the term *nouveau riche* used to express contempt since I was a child, but the newly rich are merely those who have succeeded within the recent past in escaping from the lot of the permanently poor. Every old-rich family in America was new rich at one time. Max Weber has observed that the aristocratic claim that old money is better than new is simply a device for keeping élite status in short supply. Nevertheless, harsh psychic scars are often acquired in an overly rapid ascent. Such scars were visible among Beth El's board members. It was impossible for Geiger, whose status derived from a distinguished lineage and an almost instinctive knowledge of things Jewish, to feel at ease with the go-getter leaders of his congregation.

Geiger was very kind to me. He was supportive of my work as a teacher. He also sought to moderate my rigid Orthodoxy. He did not argue. He encouraged me in my studies. Without a trace of condescension, he suggested that I would eventually "calm down" and assume a more moderate religious position.

I also came to know some of the leaders because Geiger invited me to give lectures on contemporary Jewish thought as part of the adult education program. It was my first experience as a teacher of adults. The course was called "The Twentieth Century Jew in Search of God." I covered the established "greats" such as Hermann Cohen, Mordecai M. Kaplan, Franz Rosenzweig, and Martin Buber. While offering the course, I conceived the idea of writing a book called by the same title. I never wrote it. I did not write my first book until I had painfully and reluctantly arrived at vastly different convictions than those maintained by the great Jewish thinkers of the first half of the century.

It was soon apparent that I was happier and better suited to teaching adults than children. In spite of my overly rationalized, Orthodox point of view, my students apparently found the experience rewarding. I enjoyed lecturing. For several years thereafter my classes were a part of Beth El's adult program.

As I got to know the adults, I realized the depth of their hostility toward their rabbi. The congregation complained that the rabbi was "arrogant" and that he acted like a "know-it-all." I saw him as a kindly and understanding leader of great sensitivity, but it was clear the leaders were determined to get rid of him. Geiger believed the congregation was dominated by a small clique led by a rich attorney whom Geiger saw as possessing an insatiable need for power and status. Because he was Jewish and newly rich, there was a limit to the status the attorney could attain outside the Jewish community. It was therefore especially important that his leadership be unchallenged within the congregation.

Geiger had come to the small, newly founded congregation after serving in the chaplaincy during World War II. He had led the congregation through the excitement and pain of the building fund drive and the erection of the synagogue. By 1950 the congregation was large, prosperous, and well-established—and determined to get a new rabbi.

My sympathies were with the rabbi, partly because he had been genuinely kind to me and partly because I was soon to become a rabbi myself. However, it was obvious that Geiger was expendable. Rabbis come and go. They are itinerant professionals. Congregations outlast them. It was also apparent that the affair was unfortunate for all concerned. Neither the rabbi nor the leaders could subordinate themselves to the other side and both sides demanded some subordination. Geiger believed that the moral authority of his office deserved more respect than it received. The leaders were self-made men who regarded the synagogue as their home base and the rabbi as their employee. Their energies and their money had built the congregation. They were ambivalent about their "employee." They wanted a rabbi who merited respect and high status, but they wanted his status to enhance *them*. They wanted a man they could look up to—and Geiger was such a man—but at the same time they wanted a man who would give them what they had paid for—a kind of servile recognition they could get nowhere else. It was an impossible arrangement. The very qualities that made them want Geiger rather than a lesser man made it impossible for him to give them what they really wanted.

At first, the mutual disappointment expressed itself in little slights and contests which seemed to end inconclusively. In reality, the outcome was inevitable. Those who paid would have the final say. Geiger finally realized he had to resign. He did so about the time Nathaniel was born. He then accepted a pulpit in Albany, New York.

A year or two after moving to Albany, Geiger invited me to lecture at his new congregation. I was glad to see him again. He assured me that there was a world of difference between Albany and South Orange. He told me that the new congregation respected him and trusted his leadership. The people were less pushy and *nouveau riche*. He was happy he had left South Orange. It was a hard thing to do, but it had proved to be a blessing in disguise.

Shortly thereafter, I learned that Leo Geiger, who was apparently a healthy man in his mid-forties, had suddenly dropped dead of a heart attack. My first reaction was shock. After reflection, I came to the sad conclusion that his heart attack was as inevitable as had been his resignation from South Orange. Geiger thought he had found the *right* congregation. There was no right congregation for Geiger, not because he was a bad rabbi but because he was a good one. Had he been less qualified or a grayer, more obsequious personality, his chances of survival would have been greater. I do not know what Geiger's feelings were before the heart attack, but it is my guess that he finally realized that he had boxed himself into a corner. It was too late to start over again. Albany was not really very different from South Orange, or Great Neck, or Glencoe, or

Scarsdale. The same kind of people ran most congregations. There was only one way out, and he took it.

Geiger was the first of a series of rabbis I came to know who dropped dead of heart attacks in mid-career. As I became more conversant with the strange forces that moved men to become clergymen, especially the forces that had moved me, I became convinced that most of the heart attacks were silent suicides. I also came to the conclusion that the days of human sacrifice were by no means over. In ancient times, it was the role of the king-priest to reign for a fixed term and then to be offered up as a sacrificial victim. It was the law of the sanctuary that the king must die. As I saw the rabbis die, I realized that that law was still in force in many places. The ancient priest-king-victims apparently consented to their *moira*, their allotted destiny, more readily than do modern men. Nevertheless, I began to wonder about my *moira* and what I might consent to in my time.

I have never been able to forget the opening section of Sir James George Frazer's *The Golden Bough*:

No one who has seen the calm water of the Lake of Nemi lapped in a green hollow of the Alban hills, can ever forget it. Diana herself might still be lingering by this lonely shore, haunting these woodlands wild. In antiquity this sylvan landscape was the scene of a strange and recurring tragedy. On the northern shore of the lake stood the sacred grove of Diana Nemorensis, that is, Diana of the Woodland Glade. The lake and the grove were sometimes known as the lake and the grove of Aricia. In that grove grew a certain tree round which, at any hour of the day and probably far into the night, a grim figure might be seen to prowl. In his hand was a drawn sword, and he kept peering warily about him as if at every instant he expected to be set upon. He was at once a priest and a murderer; and the man for whom he was watching was sooner or later to murder him and hold the priesthood in his stead. For such was the rule of the sanctuary; a candidate for the priesthood could succeed to the office only by slaying the incumbent priest in single combat, and could himself retain office only until he was in turn slain by a stronger or a craftier. Moreover— and this is especially significant—he could fling his challenge only if he had first succeeded in plucking a golden bough from the tree which the priest was guarding.

What drove a man to become a priest-murderer in the certain knowledge that the priest-murderer was fated to become priest-victim? Dimly, very dimly, I began to ask myself whether the summit to which my vocation impelled me might be like that of the priests of Diana Nemorensis—and Leo Geiger. Geiger's death gave me the first hint of how truly strange the priestly vocation might yet prove to be. Perhaps I had unwittingly started on a path that would end by my becoming the human sacrifice some community was unwittingly seeking.

Christianity had settled the issue of human sacrifice, not by denying that a sacred victim was required, but by proclaiming that God had graciously permitted himself to be the victim *par excellence once and for all*. There is irony in the Christian solution of the sacrificial problem for one afflicted with a "vocation for the summit." The ultimate expression of such a vocation is the desire to become God. However, so exalted a status is not without its vulnerabilities. Christianity affirms that the God-man is the perfect sacrificial victim. Tentatively, I began to wonder what I might find at the end of my climb to the priestly summit. My motives for the climb were mixed, but they included the quest for God-like omnipotence which expressed itself as power over my peers. Leo Geiger's sudden death offered a most disquieting hint of the ironies of such power when finally attained.

As I began to suspect that Geiger might have silently elected his own death, some very strange ideas entered my head: *Did Geiger, like the ancient priest-kings, give his people what they really wanted? Jews have no Jesus to die for them. Nor do they have any sacrament of the Mass in which they periodically consume the body and the blood of the savior-victim, making the once-and-for-all sacrifice a perpetually present, sensuous event. Since the fall of the Holy Temple, Jewish worship has been a bloodless affair, excluding what could not be confined to the abstractions of the written word. Throughout the Middle Ages, paranoid Christians were unable to believe that Judaism could really be bloodless. From time to time, they accused the Jews of killing innocent Christian children and drinking their blood at the Passover season. The accusation was nonsense, but madmen are not without their instinct for truth. Jews did not lust after Christian blood, but they may have lusted after the blood of their own interpreters of God's holy law. Every time I see a crucifix with Jesus's bloody body nailed to it, I ask myself, is this what it's all about? After all, they did call him rabbi.*

At the time, my dark suspicions were only surmises that I immediately suppressed. No Jew in his right mind would ever lift his hand against his rabbi. But, he might unconsciously wish him dead and the wishes might get through. Wishing might make it so.

No Jew in his right mind would ever lift his hand against his rabbi. But were all Jews in their right mind? In the summer of 1950, a leading Conservative rabbi returned to the Jewish Theological Seminary to spend the summer there as a visiting professor. He took an apartment opposite ours on Claremont Avenue. When ill-starred Nathaniel was born, the rabbi agreed to be the godfather at the circumcision ceremony. We were honored that so famous a rabbi was willing to take part in our family celebration. His name was Rabbi Morris Adler of Detroit, Michigan. On February 12, 1966 while Rabbi Adler was conducting Sabbath services, Richard Wishnetsky, a brilliant but demented young man, took out a revolver and murdered the rabbi in full view of the worshipping congregation. No Jew in his right mind would lift his hand against his rabbi. Perhaps someone not in his right mind might act out temptations normal men keep locked up within themselves. Occasionally, when Jews gather together, someone will say in jest that being a rabbi is no job for a Jewish boy. Perhaps the jesters know more than they can admit even to themselves. Leo Geiger was the first of many rabbis I knew who by dying may have given their flocks what they really wanted.

After Nathaniel's death, I found it difficult to teach effectively in Beth El's Hebrew school. My class consisted of twelve-year-old boys and girls who were preparing for their bar and bat mitzvah celebrations. Most of them regarded Hebrew school as a necessary evil, to be tolerated only until the ceremony took place. They were energetic young people who resented the additional classroom confinement after regular school hours. It might have been possible to work with such a class had it not been for my depressed state of mind. Under the circumstances, I was unable to control the class. At the end of the year, the congregation did not renew my contract. They did, however, ask me to continue my adult classes. Our parting was amicable. My heart was not in Hebrew teaching.

I had hoped to remain at South Orange until ordination. I did not want to serve as a student rabbi in a small congregation in which men and women sat together, contrary to Orthodox practice. However, there were no other congregations available. Wolfe Kelman had become director of placement for the Rabbinical Assembly of America and had made it possible for me to succeed him in his old part time job of director of student placement. He urged me to moderate my stringent position on mixed seating in the synagogue. I did not want to, but I had no alternative. I could not afford to comply with the biblical injunction to be fruitful and multiply unless I led a congregation with mixed seating. Rav Hutner had anticipated my dilemma. He had urged me to prepare for a secular career so that I would not be compelled to compromise on matters of religious practice. After leaving South Orange, compromise was inevitable. I dared not place Ellen in further jeopardy. When a small Conservative congregation in Ridgefield Park, New Jersey, across the river from Manhattan, invited me to serve as their rabbi, I accepted.

Although there was much stress in my personal life during my years at the seminary, my academic career was certainly not marked by the kind of intellectual conflict that had characterized the years I spent at the Hebrew Union College. There was, however, one impression that predominated from start to finish. When Chancellor Louis Finkelstein met our class for the first time in October 1948, he told us: "You have not come here to become great scholars. If that is what you want, you would be better off studying in the library of the British Museum. You have come here for only one reason—to sit at the feet of great men." It was by no means certain that our professors were great men. They were, however, among the greatest *scholars* in their respective branches of Jewish studies. At a certain level, neither Finkelstein nor his scholarly colleagues could conceive of any preeminence that would equal scholarly greatness in Jewish studies. This was a reflection of the fact that for two thousand years Jews had been without military or political power of any consequence. It was impossible for a Jew to become a Michelangelo, a Napoleon, or a Cosimo de' Medici. They could become learned rabbis. When the Romans needed scholars, they often used Greek slaves. In contrast, the Jewish people saw its love of learning as its emblem of superlative merit rather than the best adaptation to circumstances available to a defeated group of wanderers.

Nor were all forms of scholarship equally esteemed. There was a definite hierarchy at the apex of which stood Talmudic scholarship. Because of his unrivaled authority as a Talmudic scholar, the most powerful man on the seminary faculty was Aaron Kleinman.* Every professor was expected to have regular office hours for the students. Kleinman's office hours were from eleven-thirty to midnight every other Wednesday. His message to his students was undisguised.

During my senior year, I sought an interview with Kleinman during

* Kleinman is a pseudonym.

his office hours. I told him that I wanted to continue my studies after graduation in the hope of eventually becoming a scholar. In ancient times, the Hebrew word for one ignorant of rabbinic literature was an *am ha-aretz*. When I told Kleinman of my hopes and my willingness for further sacrifice to achieve a solid foundation in Jewish learning, he responded: "Rubenstein, if you study for fifteen years maybe you'll reach the level of an ancient *am ha-aretz*."

The term *am ha-aretz* is one of contempt and opprobrium in rabbinic Judaism. I had a very good idea of the vastness of the subject matter. I also had a realistic idea of my own limitations. I was not a poor student by seminary standards; in spite of my personal difficulties and the deficient background with which I began, I completed the seminary's course in the minimum time and was graduated *cum laude*. This made no difference to Kleinman. Like most of his students, I was an unworthy *am ha-aretz* in his eyes.

When I realized how great was his disdain, I asked him how he could affix his name to his students' rabbinical diplomas. The seminary's formula of ordination differs from the traditional formula, which certifies that the bearer is empowered to render decisions in matters of religious law. The status of seminary graduates is diminished by *adding* to the title they receive at ordination. They are not ordained as "Rabbi" but as "Rabbi, Teacher and Preacher in Israel." The seminary formula for ordination is: *Rav yithkaré w'haham yithkaré.* ("He shall be called rabbi and he shall be called wise.")

When I asked Kleinman about his signature, he replied, "He shall be *called* rabbi and he shall be *called* wise," emphasizing the word called. "What's the harm in that? Somebody has to do the dirty work."

Having recently lost my child, I hardly regarded a funeral or a wedding as dirty work. I was appalled. As I left the man's office, I thought of Rav Hutner who had a very similar background. Rav Hutner did not have a high regard for Conservative rabbis, but he had not accepted a post at the seminary.

Perhaps the most famous member of the seminary faculty in recent years was the late Abraham Joshua Heschel. His position at the seminary was not very exalted during my student years. He was a mystic, a Hasid, and a Polish Jew. Kleinman was a Lithuanian Talmudist. Lithuanians tend to respect the products of the great Lithuanian Talmudic academies far more than they do other Jews—no matter what their accomplishment. I caught some of this disdain as a little boy when my Lithuanian

127

grandmother, Anna Fine referred to a Polish Jew from Galicia as a *"Galitzianer hazir,"* a Galician pig. In later years Heschel's worldwide status eventually enhanced his status within the seminary, but from 1948 to 1952 rabbinical students were required to take only one single hour a week for one year with him.

While I was at the seminary, a group of us asked Heschel to lead a seminar on contemporary theology. I wrote a paper on Sören Kierkegaard for the seminar. After I read the paper in the seminar, Heschel called me into his office.

"Dicky, you must never become a pulpit rabbi." Heschel always called me Dicky.

"Why?"

"The paper had depth. There was something in it which was different from the others. You'll waste your time if you become a rabbi. You must teach somewhere."

After Nathaniel's death, I had no interest in further financial sacrifice. In spite of my reluctance to compromise on ritual matters, I looked forward at the time to becoming a congregational rabbi and earning a living wage. I tried to convince myself that I could prosper as a rabbi and at the same time continue my studies. "Professor," I asked, "can't I study in the rabbinate?"

"You can," Heschel answered, "but the demands will be too much for you. You'll have to prepare a sermon every week, maybe two. You'll have to go to meetings, more meetings than you'll be able to stand. You'll start out convinced that you can achieve something, but you'll give up sooner or later. You'll hate yourself when you do. Don't do it. You've got something you don't want to lose. Dicky, don't become a rabbi!" He then turned very sad. "When I think of what our people have accumulated over the centuries that nobody will ever know about, it seems like a second holocaust. Hitler destroyed our people. Now we let their spirit die. We train rabbis for sisterhoods and men's clubs, but nobody knows our people's literature. You have a lifetime of work ahead of you. You have the mind and the depth to do it. You mustn't become a rabbi. You'll only waste your time."

Heschel had never spoken to me like that before. There was an urgency bordering on desperation in his voice. Kleinman had exhibited his contempt. Heschel had no contempt. Nevertheless, both men had said that the rabbinate was a second-rate profession, that first-rate men would become scholars. Their attitude was shared by almost every member of the faculty. Most of our teachers were convinced of their special superiority because they were *not* congregational rabbis. In a thousand ways they conveyed their message to us. "You are second rate. You aren't much better than clerks. There is only one summit for a Jew, to become a scholar. You'll never make it. If you insist on trying for a doctorate, we'll give you our own D.H.L. (Doctor of Hebrew Letters), but everyone knows that's only a correspondence course degree. Be content to do the dirty work. Somebody has to conduct services, officiate at marriages, and bury the dead. Be happy you can at least do that. It's not a bad living, but always know your place and *never challenge our authority*." The message was never explicit but it did get through to us. Our rabbinic superegos were shaped by the conviction that we would never be as wise or as learned as our teachers. We were never to trust our own judgment in matters of religious belief or practice. When in doubt, we were expected to turn for guidance to the fountainhead of Jewish wisdom, the faculty of the Jewish Theological Seminary. In ancient times the rabbis had said: "If they [the former generation of rabbis] were like angels, we are like ordinary men. If they were like ordinary men, we are like donkeys." The sons could never attain to the wisdom of the fathers.

We could preach to ignorant laymen. If we were in love with our own voices, we had plenty of opportunity to hear ourselves. On matters of consequence we were supposed to turn to our betters. At the apex of this hierarchy stood Aaron Kleinman. It was not possible to graduate from the Jewish Theological Seminary as a rabbi until one was thoroughly convinced of one's spiritual and scholarly inferiority.

I was ordained a rabbi in June 1952. I was twenty-eight years old. Almost ten years had passed since my freshman year at the Hebrew Union College. I now made plans to work for a Ph.D. I applied for admission to Harvard's program in the History and Philosophy of Religion. Twelve years had passed since I had entered college, but I was convinced that I needed further schooling. I have written about some of my motives for remaining a student in *My Brother Paul*. One of the strongest was fear of death. As long as I remained a student, I could indulge in the fantasy that I was the son, and that my teachers were the fathers. I could delude myself that time was not really passing and that I did not really have to fear death. Nathaniel's death altered my perceptions, but it took time for the full impact of his passing to work its change in me.

There were related motives, all arising out of my curious vocation for the summit, which in turn arose out of the sense of guilt, shame, worthlessness, ugliness, and impotence which I had experienced since earliest childhood and which I have attempted to describe in this work. Once I became a rabbi, it was not enough to be an ordinary rabbi. I wanted to be a Jewish theologian, if possible a Jewish Reinhold Niebuhr or Paul Tillich. Nor would an ordinary Ph.D. have sufficed. When I was a senior at Townsend Harris High School my mother had encouraged me to apply to Harvard, but I had to abandon the idea when I realized how unrealistic it was in view of the family finances. Apparently, I had never really given up that project. Nor was my archaic desire to control the way people saw me without influence in my decision. It was not enough to be Rabbi Richard L. Rubenstein; I wanted to be Dr. Richard L. Rubenstein, and the doctorate had to come from Harvard.

Nevertheless, although it was illness that drove me on, it was illness in search of healing. Whatever measure of wholeness I was eventually able to achieve came about as a result of the path I was compelled by illness to choose. Had I been born to a primitive Siberian tribe, I might have been recognized as a Shaman. My illness, my vocation, and whatever healing I've attained have all been the expression of a unified striving.

After receiving word from Harvard that I had been accepted, I was invited to become rabbi of Congregation Beth Emunah of Brockton, Massachusetts. The congregation had just split away from the local Orthodox synagogue with harsh feelings on both sides. Beth Emunah did not have a building and the normal growing pains of a young congregation lay ahead. I accepted the position because Brockton was less than twenty-five miles from Cambridge and the officers indicated that they would not object to my studies, provided they did not interfere with my duties as rabbi.

Ellen was unhappy about moving to Brockton. We had been in Ridgefield Park less than a year. The congregation wanted me to stay and promised a decent raise. Ellen urged me to remain in Ridgefield Park and study at Columbia. The congregation was small but relatively stable. It had not split away from an older congregation nor did it face the problem of building a new sanctuary. The people in Ridgefield Park were accustomed to young rabbis who spent most of their time studying. There was wisdom in remaining, but I was determined to move. I did not want to pass up the opportunity to study at Harvard.

When we arrived in Brockton, Ellen and I had to adopt a very different kind of life than we knew in New York. Brockton was a small, grim, shoe manufacturing town. In 1952 it had produced one figure of more than local fame, Rocky Marciano, the World Heavyweight Boxing Champion. Ridgefield Park was in reality a neighborhood of the Greater New York metropolis. Jews in a small town like Brockton are far more involved with their synagogue and their rabbi than Jews in a metropolitan neighborhood. In spite of the unresolved marital problems Ellen and I were attempting to cope with, it was our responsibility to be professional models of middle class Jewish rectitude and piety. We were able to manage this initially by continuing to appear almost completely Ortho- dox. Although both of us had begun to change, we remained publicly very traditional. Since most people were not interested in what lay beneath the surface, what mattered was that we appeared to be living a harmonious, well-ordered, religiously observant life. I was known as an intellectually inclined young rabbi who was extremely strict in religious practice. My congregants had few hints of how deeply troubled we were beneath the surface.

On the surface, my career began to show promise. I did well at Harvard and was awarded a graduate fellowship. I took a course on the Epistles of Paul with Henry J. Cadbury. He liked my research paper and encouraged me to revise it for scholarly publication. I also took a course with Sydney Ahlstrom, who was then a young instructor, on "Paul and the Western Christian Tradition." He also liked my work on Paul. Their encouragement eventually led to the writing of *My Brother Paul* almost twenty years later. The Boston Bureau of Jewish Education invited me to give adult education lectures at Zionist House on Commonwealth Avenue one afternoon and one evening a week. My adult lectures became popular, repeating my South Orange experience. The Zionist House lectures led to invitations to lecture in a number of Boston synagogues, churches, and other institutions.

Things also went relatively well at Beth Emunah during the first year. I liked preaching. The Unitarian and the Universalist churches in Brockton merged. They offered Beth Emunah the building of the Universalist Church for twenty-five thousand dollars. Beth Emunah accepted. Had the congregation built its own structure, it would have cost at least one hundred thousand dollars at the time. We were spared the worst agonies of a building fund drive. By May 1953 Beth Emunah had remodeled the church building. With much celebration the congregation moved into its own very adequate quarters.

I was the rabbi of a growing congregation. I was acquiring a good reputation in the Boston area. My doctoral studies were progressing. Two paths seemed to open before me: With a good rabbinic record and a doctorate from Harvard, I might reasonably hope to be called to a large synagogue as the senior rabbi; the other path was to seek an academic appointment upon completion of my graduate work. If one did not know much about me, one might have concluded that a promising, predictable, normal career lay ahead.

Nevertheless it was impossible to conceal everything that was going on underneath the surface. The bitter mutual estrangement that poisoned our marriage was worsened immeasurably by the fact that we felt compelled to maintain the appearance of being a happy, contented couple whose lives were being fulfilled by our commitment to a life of obedience to God's law. Some changes became apparent. People noticed that I was no longer as Orthodox in thought or practice as I had been the first year in Brockton. I continued to observe the dietary laws, but I became somewhat lax about daily prayer. My theological opinions became less rigid. My sermons reflected the shift; I began to refer a good deal to Kierkegaard and Freud. Ellen told me that people would be more at ease with me when they realized that I had become less Orthodox. It didn't turn out that way. My shifts were slight, but they made people uncomfortable. Life was uncertain enough for most members of the congregation without a theologically wavering rabbi whom they instinctively understood to be deeply troubled.

There were other changes. Ellen and I realized that we needed help badly. In spite of my adolescent interest in Freud, I became openly hostile to psychoanalysis after I turned to Orthodox Judaism. My hostility increased as my marriage deteriorated. On one occasion, I had lunch at a restaurant with Rabbi Maurice Zigmond, the director of the Harvard Hillel Foundation, and one of his friends. When I learned that the man was a psychoanalyst, I became gratuitously unpleasant. The analyst later told Zigmond that he had seldom seen a man who was more in need of analysis than I. My antagonism toward psychoanalysis was a reflection of my resistance to seeking help. Nor was my resistance wholly irrational. I dimly perceived that my unhappy relations with Ellen were symptomatic of a deeper disorder that would eventually require therapeutic intervention. Nevertheless, after so many stormy changes of affiliation and commitment, even the certainty of present misery seemed preferable to further change, with its unpredictable effect upon the web of relationships I was building for myself. I was miserable with Ellen, but I liked Boston,

Harvard, and my studies. I did not want to lose the very real satisfaction I had gained. I knew that analysis would change me in ways that no one could anticipate. My antagonism was born out of fear of the future.

In the fall of 1953, I had no choice but to risk further change. I turned to a Boston analyst (I'll call him Dr. A.) who agreed to take me on for psychoanalytic therapy. Dr. A. was highly recommended. I was impressed by the fact that he had four Harvard degrees, including a Ph.D. and an M.D. While I was seeing Dr. A. for the first time, Ellen had her first interview with another analyst. When she came home, she said: "I don't like the man I saw today. You probably have the better analyst because you're the rabbi. I want to meet him before I make up my mind." I had no reason for thinking that I had the better analyst. We had both received our recommendations from a training analyst of excellent reputation. Nevertheless, Dr. A. agreed to meet with Ellen.

When next he saw me, Dr. A. told me that an analyst normally doesn't see both husband and wife; but he believed there were good reasons for breaking that rule in this instance. I was desperately in need of help. I felt that I had no choice but to accept his judgment. I later came to regret the decision. It was impossible for me ever to relate to Dr. A. without being mindful of the fact that he was also hearing Ellen's most intimate secrets, many of which I would never know. Instead of exploring the unconscious roots of my marital disorder, I drew Dr. A. into my war with Ellen. I attempted to influence Ellen through him, thus creating a very different and less effective kind of transference than would have developed had Ellen and I consulted different analysts. It was only after Ellen and I had parted in 1963 and I consulted another analyst, this time in Pittsburgh, that I was able effectively to explore what my relations with women meant to me.

During the years I was Dr. A.'s client, I learned very little about what had been going on between Ellen and me. However, I did learn a great deal about my complicated subterranean motives for becoming a rabbi. I also gained some insight into the less visible aspects of my relationship with those I served. On the surface, I normally received both respect and courtesy. Beneath the surface, some very strange things were taking place. Through analysis I came to understand fully something that I had perceived only dimly before: that I had voluntarily elected the role of sacrificial offering and that, were I to remain in the active rabbinate, the time would assuredly come when I would be compelled to enact the terminal atavism of archaic religion. I would become my congregation's human sacrifice. No bloody knife would ever be lifted against my throat or heart, yet my body would silently consent to its *moira*. Before my natural time, my heart would give out. Some congregation would be blessed with an opportunity mournfully to celebrate funereal rites for its fallen priest-victim. In a thousand devious ways, my flock would goad me on, altogether unconscious of what they were really doing. And I too, as unconscious as they, would have played my part in the ancient drama. They would have wanted to honor, respect, obey—and kill me. I would have wanted to be honored, respected, obeyed, and slain. Each of us would have given the other what we wanted as we played out our parts in the foreordained drama. Like Leo Geiger and a host of other prematurely dead rabbis I have known, the time would have come when I realized that I had no further escape save the grave.

I had become a rabbi largely because of my pathetically distorted will to power. Even in my first years as a rabbi, I perceived how the gods do seduce their priests. They lure us on with our yearning to be like them, but they cast over us a spell of forgetfulness. Ancient men knew that the gods, especially the male gods, must suffer and die. To be a god means to suffer as they suffer, to die as they die. My vision was too narrow. I envied the gods their power. I ignored their passion.

I read and reread Freud's *Totem and Taboo*. I could seldom forget his image of the sons killing the primal father. Every time some overly enthusiastic lady came up to me after a lecture or a sermon and said, as many of them did, "Oh rabbi, you were so good, I could just eat you," I wanted to reply, "Madame, I know exactly what you mean."

Nor was Jesus far from my thoughts. After all, he had had his flock and he knew what they wanted. On his last night, he gathered together his disciples and, breaking bread and distributing wine, he said to them: "This is my body. This is my blood." He knew what they wanted. He gave it to them. Jesus brought the game out into the open. He understood what it meant to be a god.

Analysis was one major change in our lives; another was Ellen's decision to return to school and complete her undergraduate studies at Boston University. In the course of time, she built a life of her own that was independent of her role as a rabbi's wife. When I left Brockton to accept the position of rabbi of Temple Israel in suburban Natick in September 1954, it was easier for both of us to get into Boston. Ellen completed her B.A. and then enrolled in a master's program in psychology. She also got a part time job with the Veterans Administration as a psychologist in training. In addition to her job and studies, she became interested in modern dancing.

As Ellen developed her own life, there were times when we had very little to do with each other. At other times, we became involved in violent, recriminatory arguments. When we tried to come together, the wounds we had inflicted upon each other were too severe to permit any real reconciliation. When the pain seemed unendurable, I would tell Dr. A. that I intended to call a lawyer and file for divorce. However, I was not really prepared to take the final step. I expected Dr. A. to dissuade me and he always did.

One of the attractions of the new position in Natick was a rent-free home. However, there was a price to be paid for what ostensibly came free. Had I separated from Ellen, our personal problems would have become a matter of public notice immediately. Things were bad enough without involving the housing committee of the congregation in our marital problems. I had urgent reasons for remaining in Boston. I wanted to complete my studies; I did not want to terminate the analysis. I was fearful that were I to lose my new job, I would be unable to find another in Boston. I felt trapped and impotent.

There were even more compelling motives for remaining in the situation. I simply could not leave my children. Ellen and I did not separate until I became convinced that I could be an effective father in no other way. Nor had I yet come to understand my complicated involvement with Ellen. I could not leave her until that issue had been resolved. I was tied to her not only by guilt but by the conviction that our unhappiness was the result of the chronic instability with which the marriage began. As my analysis progressed, I became aware of the extent to which my pain was part of a drama I had co-authored. In spite of my recurring outbursts of self-pity, I was beginning to understand that we were locked in an emotional *Totentanz*. We required each other as the beloved enemy we could freely wound. The cycle of blow, resentment, counter-blow and revenge never stopped. At the same time, we continued to appear as models of happy, contented, pious, yet thoroughly modern Jewish parents.

Nevertheless, it became increasingly difficult to hide our difficulties. In retrospect, I would guess that a number of people in the Boston area knew that we were having problems. In spite of my fears, people who knew were generally discreet. My problems were not used to hurt or embarrass me.

I had wanted the limelight all my life. I wanted to matter to people. Having become a public figure, I began to hate what I had so long sought to attain. I especially hated the rent-free house. It was a small, pleasant, suburban ranch house on a large corner lot on Natick's Beacon Street, not far from Wellesley College and the Wellesley shopping center. When I first came to Natick, I thought the house would add to my security. My salary was the same as it had been in Brockton, but the rent-free house actually represented a substantial increase in real income. Unfortunately, I had not reckoned on the congregation's housing committee. The chairman of the committee dropped in with some regularity to inquire whether anything needed repair. He was always cheerful. He honestly wanted to be helpful, yet we always felt that he was a potentially dangerous intruder. I was afraid of being "found out." When we invited members of our congregation to our "home," we had the feeling that we were the guests and they the hosts, especially if they were officers. The house diminished our sense of privacy at a time when we required it to mend our splintered lives. It was in many ways more prison than home.

During the period of my worst marital difficulties, I reexamined my commitment to religious practice. My decision to become religiously compliant arose largely out of fear of chaos, both the chaos within my own soul and the more distant chaos of the secular world. It was not the fault of traditional Judaism that my attempt to comply with its norms produced an even greater chaos than that which I sought to avoid by religious conversion. As I came to understand that I would have to find an alternative route to personal wholeness, the dietary laws, and even daily prayer no longer seemed relevant to the problems Ellen and I were trying to resolve. My task could no longer be that of finding an obedient relationship to my creator nor of becoming some kind of "light unto the nations." In view of what I was going through, every time I heard a rabbi talk about the covenant between God and Israel or of our need to be a "light unto the nations," I felt like throwing up—quite literally. My fundamental need was to discover the forces in my own personality that had carried me, against all conscious intent, to elect so destructive a familial relationship. I was no "light unto the nations." If it were possible to achieve insight into the roots of my perplexing behavior, a second task awaited me, that of becoming a loving, trustworthy husband and father. I had sought magically to "save" the world. I had proven almost incapable of the elemental task of preserving myself or my family. I had been critical of my father's exaggerated promises as a child, but he had never projected

136

for himself so vaunting a life-plan. Ever since childhood, my aspirations had been grandiose, my emotional horizons cosmic. The time had come for a narrowing of horizons to more modest, realistic, and realizable limits.

One minor incident stands out as a turning point in my attitude toward religious practice. In my second year in Brockton I was summoned to a special meeting of the congregation's Ritual Committee. The chairman appeared very distressed. When the committee was assembled, he declared with great solemnity, "Rabbi, a serious complaint has been lodged against you. I'm afraid you have some explaining to do."

Oh my God, I thought, *they've found out about us. What's going to happen now? Perhaps I can stall. I've got a contract. They can't just fire me. They'll have to give me some notice . . . Maybe not . . . Maybe they can fire me! Perhaps I'd better leave quietly and avoid scandal. Maybe I can get a Hebrew teacher's job and not have to leave Boston.*

I was in a panic but I managed to hide my fright.

"What's the complaint, Nathan?"

"Rabbi," he said with the utmost gravity, "you were seen entering the kosher butcher shop without a hat. You're supposed to set an example. I hope this never happens again."

You petty bastard, I thought. *Is that what you think I should worry about? If you only knew what was on my mind!*

Of course, I kept my thoughts to myself. I couldn't decide what he really wanted. Could he be using the incident to put me on the defensive or was he genuinely concerned that I might cease to be a worthy exemplar for the congregation? In any event, I was in no mood to challenge him. He went on to question whether I was too liberal in my interpretation of the Bible in my sermons, but that wasn't really what was bothering him.

"Nathan," I said meekly, "I went into the butcher shop without thinking. If it disturbs the congregation, I won't do it again."

About the time the Ritual Committee made their complaint, I read once again Freud's *Totem and Taboo.* I was especially struck by a passage in which Freud described the ways in which kings are made to pay dearly by their respectful yet resentful subjects for their extraordinary status:

The attitude of primitive peoples to their chiefs, kings and priests is governed by two basic principles which seem to be complementary rather than contradictory. A ruler "must not only be guarded, he must also be guarded against" [Frazer] . . . . It is not to be wondered at that a need was felt for isolating such dangerous persons as chiefs and

137

priests from the rest of the community—to build a barrier round them which would make them inaccessible. It may begin to dawn on us that this barrier, originally erected for the observance of taboo, exists to this day in the form of court ceremonial.

The parallel was there. I was the one man in the congregation who had to be careful about what he ate and when he wore a hat. In theory, I was supposed to set an example. That was clearly nonsense. Not a single adult in the congregation would have changed his life style because of my example. The hidden cost of the status for which I had so long striven was becoming clear. The community wanted to be on the safe side. They required a representative figure who would observe the law for them, in the remote possibility that the law might really turn out to be God's law. The rabbi was their representative. Yet, they resented his out-of-the-ordinary status. Their lives were spent in drab anonymity. Nobody gathered together weekly to hear them talk. Thus, their insistence that the rabbi obey the law as their representative figure was also an expression of their resentment against him for having assumed the very role they could not dispense with.

Nathan had his victory, the congregation its revenge. Today, I am convinced that the committee and its chairman knew as little about what was driving them as I did about what was driving me. We were all sleepwalkers in matters religious. God was on their side against their rabbi. I was furious, but could do nothing with my anger save contain it. I couldn't win this battle but I never forgot it. What a rabbi wore on his head in a kosher butcher shop may have been important to them; it no longer was to me. The Ritual Committee seemed unable to tell the difference between surface and depth. God himself had drawn up the contract, one of whose clauses pertained to the wearing of hats in a butcher shop. All that was required was that they find somebody to keep their side of the bargain. I had been hired as that person. I was expected to place the moral and religious authority of my ancient office in the service of their narrowly restricted field of attention.

Nevertheless, there is something to be said on their behalf. Communities are held together by appearances that often appear trivial. Perhaps Nathan and his committee intuited that their rabbi was changing in ways that disturbed them, but which they could not identify. If so, they might have seized upon a trivial issue in order to indicate their concern. Perhaps they felt compelled to elevate trivia to cosmic status to avoid facing problems about which they could do nothing. Much of life is beyond choice. At least one can choose whether one goes hatless in a butcher shop. Moreover, I am no longer certain that any of those men were ignorant of the depth dimension of existence. It is possible that they kept their gaze firmly placed upon the surface of things because that was about all they could manage and still retain their equilibrium. That may have been their wisdom. I know their marriages were by no means as imperiled as mine, but their day-by-day lives tended to be drab, colorless, repetitive, and with few genuine gratifications. Beneath the placid surface of middle class contentment during the Eisenhower years, many of these men had their hidden moments of desperation. They too had to keep things going. The surface had to be kept in order in their lives as well as mine.

I could, however, no longer believe that surface and depth could be brought into harmony in my life through fidelity to what was alleged to be God's commandments or by "living a Jewish life." For the time being, it was important that I maintain the appearance of commitment to a traditional way of life for the sake of the congregation. As long as I remained their rabbi, they required a certain image of me. It was not their fault that there was a goodly measure of illness in my motives for becoming a rabbi or that my values were changing. Nevertheless, as soon as I decently could, it was my intention to seek a situation in which those I served would have a more limited investment in my public image.

8

HOLY MAN
IN ISRAEL

Another turning point occurred with the death of one of the members of my congregation. I had known him only for a short time. Today I have forgotten his name. When I came to Brockton, he was alive, healthy, and well. A month later, I was told that he had died and that his family needed me immediately. It was my first funeral.

I can still see the ashen faces, cleansed only by a superabundance of tears, the black dresses of the women, the puzzled, almost little-boy despairing looks of the men in their best, ill-fitting dark suits, and the slightly obscene professionalism of the overly solicitous funeral director. The body lay in an open coffin at the front of the funeral home auditorium. The family tearfully awaited my arrival. They took their last look before the coffin was sealed. Each was required to perform the rite of *keriah,* the biblical act of rending one's garments, in America reduced to the cutting of an attached black ribbon, as they recited the blessing of submission to the justice of God: *Baruch . . . dayan ha-emet* ("Blessed be the true Judge.").

I never felt comfortable with eulogies. It seemed insulting to the dead to exaggerate who they were or what they accomplished, yet the temptation was always there. The real problem was never that of praising the dead but of consoling the living before an omnipotent necessity to which all must submit. What does one say to eulogize those whose lives were anonymous and without worldly attainment? The highest praise I could offer was the simple fact that they had kept things going for themselves and their families. Before coming to Brockton, I might have looked down on such people. After Nathaniel's death and the terrible estrangement that drove Ellen and me from each other, I was no longer contemptuous of people who simply kept things going as best they could. *Would that I could do as well,* I often thought to myself.

I learned very quickly not to probe too deeply when asked to conduct a funeral. I always asked those closest to tell me about the deceased. The stories were, of course, too good to be true. I cannot recall a single instance when anybody spoke ill of the dead. On the basis of what I was told, I would have to conclude that the deceased had the most perfect of marriages, that there was seldom anything but overflowing love between parents and children. If ever there was family strife, it was between siblings, usually those siblings who chose to absent themselves from the funeral . . . *de mortuis nihil nisi bonum.*

The most sorrowful moment came when the coffin was lowered into the ground as I recited the age-old formula: *Al m'komo ya'vo b'shalom* ("May he come to his place in peace."). Once again earth had taken her own back unto herself. Every time I conducted a funeral, I saw the grave as an open mouth, the mouth of the Great Mother. In the beginning, as babes we ate of the mother's substance; in the end we are all destined to be eaten by her. Hers alone is the final victory.

The Jewish funeral service is magnificent in its truthfulness, dignity, and elegant simplicity. There is one moment in that service that I have always found especially moving. Upon departure from the cemetery precinct after the interment, one washes one's hands and recites in Hebrew:

He will swallow up death forever, and the Lord God will wipe away tears from all faces, and the reproach of his people will he take away from all the earth, for the Lord has spoken. [Isaiah 25:8]

I always wished that it were so. I desperately wanted it to be so. I wanted to believe that the Lord God of Israel would indeed swallow up death forever and wipe away all tears, but in the depths of my being I knew it wasn't so, that mother earth alone was the giver and the receiver, that all of the efforts of my ancestors to proclaim that the father would be victorious over the mother were expressions of the same futile, pathetic but inevitable hope I experienced every time I conducted a funeral. As I looked into sorrowing eyes, I knew that the people I served felt as I did. They too were humbled by the finality of earth's victory. It was in their eyes. They had given themselves over to a masculine sky and thunder god in the hope that he would save them, knowing all the while that there was only one divinity, she who had given birth to us, she who had clothed us with her living substance, and she who would finally take us back to herself.

When I saw the bodies of men and women I had come to know lowered one after another into the grave, I could not deceive myself. They were going into their private black holes. They were the human vanguard of an irreversible cosmic movement. Astronomers sometimes speak of the origin of all things as a cosmic black hole so densely imploded that even light waves cannot escape its gravitational pull. The same astronomers also regard the cosmic black hole as the end of all things, when all that was, is and shall be finally implodes into the source-from-whence-it-came. The astronomers unwittingly bear witness to the truth of the living god. God is mother night, the cosmic black hole, which alone is the ground of being of which theologians and mystics have written. Whenever I committed someone to burial, I felt that I was committing that person to his or her journey back to the cosmic black hole.

It was impossible to conduct funerals without being affected by the experience. Funerals influenced every aspect of my life. My dreams were affected by them. In periods when I had to conduct them with extra frequency, my feelings were glazed over with a coating of depression. From time to time I experienced a certain shuddering which could only be relieved by uttering a desperate animal cry. This shriek would have been altogether out of character had anybody heard me. The best place for those cries was when I was driving along a crowded highway, such as Route 9 from Natick to Boston, with the windows of my car securely shut. So much for the power of the priest! This was the other side of the coin.

Nor did my lack of faith in life beyond the grave cause me to look down upon those who held fast to such a hope. We were all afflicted by the same terrors. I saw the believer's faith as a reflection of the dread we

143

shared. I envied Christians their Easter faith. I hoped that they could really believe it. I knew that some did. I also knew that even among those who uttered the words of faith there were many like me.

In addition to the shuddering sense of anxiety, I also experienced a sense of relief bordering on triumph every time I conducted a funeral: I was still alive. I had survived to live another day. In my fantasy, I sometimes wondered whether I might ultimately beat the odds.

To some people in the congregation, I had almost become the angel of death. If a man were dying, it was not wise to summon the rabbi too quickly. When he came, he might be taken as the dark herald himself. Sometimes people had mixed feelings about my role. They were grateful that I had offered whatever consolation the rituals of leave-taking and mourning could express, yet I was the one who had finalized the eternal separation. For those who were looking for someone to blame, and there were some, I was the most convenient target. I had to take it. There was no way I could hit back, and they knew it.

The funerals also affected my social relations. When I arrived in Brockton, I hoped to develop a core of friends within the community. I had no idea of how great a barrier the clerical office can be to the formation of unselfconscious friendships. Those who might turn to me in moments of extreme anguish had little choice but to regard me as someone set apart. It was built into the nature of the relationship. The Catholic Church insists upon clerical celibacy and makes no pretense about the profound separation between clergy and laity. Both Jews and Protestants are somewhat ambivalent. They want their clergymen to be family men, yet they too are compelled to set them apart. Few men are really prepared for the altered character of their social relations when they enter the ministry. No seminary course in pastoral psychology can prepare a man for what experience alone must teach—the experience of being utterly isolated, the experience of being constant witness to the ever repeating cycle of infirmity and mortality—in short, the experience of being a holy man.

Although I liked to preach, with the exception of one or two crucial sermons, my role as preacher and educator was subordinate to my priestly role. Officially, rabbis are not priests. The hereditary priesthood lost its religious authority two thousand years ago. Yet, the holy man in Israel remains indelibly a priest. Rabbis are, in fact if not in law, the priestly order which supplanted the old priesthood after the fall of Jerusalem.

The overwhelming importance of the priestly aspects of my office was contrary to what I have been taught in the rabbinical schools. I had been trained to stress my ability as a preacher and teacher. When I came to Brockton initially, I saw myself as a teacher of American-born Jews. I envisaged a kind of intellectually oriented rabbinate. I saw the sermon primarily as a pedagogic instrument. Eventually in my sermons, I came to discuss Freud, Kierkegaard, Kafka, psychoanalysis, and existentialism. (Marx was taboo in the McCarthy period.) I wanted to show the relevance of Judaism to the contemporary cultural and intellectual scene. My congregants were not entirely disinterested. In general, they were tolerant, but they had not hired me to be an intellectual leader. The synagogue was neither a college nor a university. The congregants wanted the sermons to be interesting, but basically they required a priest. If I was to do any teaching that mattered, it was with the children. I was really needed for weddings, funerals, circumcisions, and bar mitzvahs. When the seasons changed, I was expected to preside over the changes by officiating at Israel's great seasonal festivals and Holy Days. It was also my responsibility to turn public meetings and banquets into semi-sacred occasions by my invocations and benedictions.

I often experienced the greatest conflict when called upon to conduct weddings. Many of the ceremonies were the source of genuine gratification, especially when I knew the principals. Nevertheless, in view of the wreckage of my own marriage, it was often impossible for me to feel at ease when I officiated. I was, for example, always fearful that I might forget the names of the bride and groom as I was about to say: "Do you, so and so, take so and so to be . . ." I protected myself by writing the names on a card which I carried in my manual. Largely because of my own difficulties, I became acutely aware of the emotional interchanges between the men and women who came to me as they prepared for marriage. I always insisted on at least one pre-marital interview in order to get to know the couple and diminish the impersonal nature of the ritual. Unfortunately, it was all too easy for me to detect the latent antagonisms and the unrealistic expectations of bride and groom at those sessions. I beheld in wonder the variety of motives, both realistic and fantastic, that impelled men and women to link their lives together. At times I wanted to scream out: *For God's sake, don't go through with it! You'll destroy each other—and your unborn children. You don't love each other. You're seducing each other so that you can have a life-long partner in combat. Get help! You need it!* I never uttered a word. I kept my thoughts to myself. I knew the limits of my role. I was neither an analyst nor a marriage counselor. I was

145

asked only to ratify a decision which had been made long before I was consulted. I did my best to conceal my unease as I conducted marriages I knew to be doomed in advance.

The priestly role was also more acceptable to my congregants than that of the prophet or social critic. I heard more about the rabbi as a prophetic figure in Reform than in Conservative Judaism. The Conservative movement was inherently more priestly because of its greater emphasis on ritual. When I entered the rabbinate, I was painfully aware of the obvious injustices of race, class, and economic oppression in American society. I wanted to do what I could to bring about a saner and a healthier society. I came to understand that I could always speak out on issues in which the congregation's leaders had no direct interest. It was, for example, quite acceptable for me to denounce segregation in Little Rock, Arkansas, Selma, Alabama or Albany, Georgia, but I would have been in serious trouble had I taken a controversial political stand on matters affecting the Boston area. To the best of my knowledge, no houses were sold to blacks in the newly constructed suburban developments of Natick or Framingham from 1954 to 1956, the years I served those communities. The developer had turned empty fields into huge middle class suburbs. He was nominally a member of my congregation. He was immensely wealthy and powerful. Had I taken realistic action to desegregate the community, I would have been out of a job in no time.

It was obvious to me that few ministers serving local churches or synagogues could be effective instruments of social change in the real world. The pulpit gave me the illusion that I was influencing people's political attitudes. It was an illusion that could be maintained only by a strong dose of self-deception. One of the reasons why I eventually became a university professor was that I was far freer to write and say what I believed as a professor than as a clergyman. If one wishes to be politically effective, one must command great financial resources, have access to the communications media, or enter politics. As long as I remained a "servant" of the congregation, I was compelled to stick to religion. And, for my people, religion meant priestly religion. I am convinced that men who "stick to religion" perform a good and an indispensable service. Nevertheless, there is far more to religion than "sticking to religion."

I had sought the rabbinic office very largely because of the priestly magic and charisma I imagined I would acquire. My actual experience as a rabbi was humbling. My frequent visits to the hospital and the cemetery put all pride and ambition, my own included, in proper perspective. It was impossible not to be moved by the constant reminders of human frailty and transience. The impersonal requirements of the rabbinic office were infinitely more important than the rabbi's personality or his intellectual ability. In the language of Max Weber, personal charisma had long ago been routinized and displaced by the charisma of office.

Nature provided the foundation for the calendar and its cycle; it also provided the occasions for the rituals of the life cycle. It is the order of nature that men are born, grow to mature estate, and die. When they reach the crucial turning points of life and death, appropriate rituals are in order. There is a strong element of passivity in being a priest. I was summoned to recite the fixed, age-old formulae when the proper time came. All my other roles were peripheral. I was not expected to initiate novelties of opinion, value, lifestyle or belief. Nor did it matter that it was I who performed the ritual. Rabbis are essentially interchangeable. Any rabbi with a minimum of intelligence and sensitivity to human need could do it just as well. The words of ritual remained essentially unchanged no matter who pronounced them. Within certain limits, it made little difference who said them.

My rabbinic education as well as my interest in theology, pastoral counseling, and politics were largely irrelevant on those occasions when my congregation really needed me. Even the most non-believing congregants did not let their doubts trouble them when a parent died, a daughter was married, or a son had a bar mitzvah. The important thing was that the appropriate ritual be performed. I had trained for years in rabbinical schools only to discover how little relevance most of what I had learned had for the actual work I was required to do. It was also apparent that there was very little to distinguish one rabbi from another, save the greater experience and maturity of the older men. We were all men set apart. What was of fundamental importance was our willingness to subordinate our personalities to the ebb and flow of nature's inevitabilities as they were dealt with in Jewish tradition.

147

9

TILLICH
AND HARVARD

I entered Harvard in 1952 at the beginning of the Eisenhower era. It was impossible for me to complete my doctoral studies within the normal three to five year period because of my other responsibilities. In 1956 I left the Natick congregation to become Interim Director of the Hillel Foundation and Chaplain to Jewish Students at Harvard. I remained in residence at Harvard until August 1958 when I accepted an appointment as Director of the Hillel Foundation at the University of Pittsburgh. I did not receive the Ph.D. until June 1960 at which time I was thirty-six years old.

At Harvard I was a participant in an intellectual banquet of unparalleled richness and variety. My initial experience in Cambridge was one of unprecedented intellectual liberation. During the five years I had spent at Chaim Berlin and the Jewish Theological Seminary, I had no formal involvement with learning outside of the Jewish sphere. Although some seminary students took work concurrently at Columbia, it was impossible for me to do so. The years at the seminary were a period of learning about Judaism from the inside. At Harvard I was to discover that there was another way of understanding Judaism.

149

The initial intellectual liberation was the result of the altered perspective Harvard gave me on my rabbinical studies and my professors at the seminary. The seminary professors were undoubtedly men of extraordinary scholarship, but their horizons seemed far more limited in Cambridge than in New York. Biblical studies were an especially glaring example. Although the Jewish Theological Seminary had on its faculty at least one biblical scholar of preeminent international reputation, H. L. Ginsberg, no formal course was offered in the five books of Moses. No explanation was ever given for the omission, but it was said that the seminary faculty was trapped by a theological dilemma characteristic of some of the wider conflicts of Conservative Judaism. The faculty could not permit the Torah to be interpreted in the light of contemporary biblical scholarship which asserted that the Torah was an edited compilation of a number of documents, most of which could not possibly be of Mosaic authorship. To do so would have involved an unacceptable breach with Orthodoxy. It was also impossible to present the Torah from an Orthodox point of view with its insistence on the divine inspiration, Mosaic authorship, and unitary character of the document. Unable either to break openly with Orthodoxy or to reject modern biblical scholarship, the faculty simply ignored the most important single document (or collection of documents) within Judaism. It was assumed that the students would make up the deficiency on their own. Unfortunately, most students were too busy to do so.

When I arrived at Harvard, I was informed that I would be required to pass an examination on the history of the Old Testament. I consulted with Professor Robert H. Pfeiffer about meeting the requirement. Pfeiffer agreed to take me on for a year-long reading course. I was immediately struck by the open, unhedged way Pfeiffer approached the study of the Bible. I did not share all of his conclusions, but I was impressed by the fact that Pfeiffer's interest was historical and scientific rather than theological. He wanted to know how the Bible had come into being during Israel's long history. He was not interested in whether or not his findings were in harmony with any religious community's doctrine of scriptural revelation. Naturally, his perspective was influenced by his Christian background, as mine was by my Jewish background, but he sought to subordinate the claims of theology to impartial historical scholarship.

When I began to study with Pfeiffer, I was still extremely Orthodox. I had almost convinced myself that Moses was the author of the Torah, save for the concluding verses of Deuteronomy, and that the laws and traditions of Judaism were ultimately of divine inspiration. I was almost convinced that I was literally obeying God's will by my religious behavior.

That conviction was being shaken by my personal difficulties and my analysis. Intellectually, it could not survive a year of intensive study with Pfeiffer. At no point did Pfeiffer enter into theological questions of whether Scripture rested ultimately upon divine inspiration. He was concerned with the analysis of the biblical documents in the light of literary criticism, archaeology, and ancient Near Eastern History. Once I had become convinced by Pfeiffer's teaching that Scripture was the record of a diversity of often conflicting Israelite religious perspectives, it was impossible to remain an intellectually convinced Orthodox Jew. For a number of years I continued with diminishing enthusiasm to observe those aspects of Jewish law, such as the dietary laws, that were a matter of public notice. However, I did so more out of fidelity to the requirements of the rabbinic office and respect for the inherited traditions of my people than out of any conviction that I was obeying God's will. In time, my personal observance became minimal.

Another memorable professor was Harry Austryn Wolfson, Harvard's great Jewish scholar. Wolfson was a Lithuanian Jew who came to Harvard as an undergraduate and remained there all of his life. His background was similar to Rav Hutner's and Aaron Kleinman's. As a young man in Lithuania he received the unexcelled rabbinic and Talmudic training for which the Lithuanian Yeshivoth or Talmudic academies are justly famous. Wolfson applied his incredible mental ability and verbal competence, which had been sharpened in the Yeshivoth, to the life-long study of medieval Jewish philosophy. His most famous published works dealt with Spinoza, Philo Judaeus, and the church fathers. He was a master of Greek, Latin, and Arabic as well as Hebrew and Aramaic. He had a first-hand knowledge of the great medieval Jewish, Christian, and Islamic philosophers, all of whom he studied in their original languages. No man of the period of his most productive years could discern with greater precision the intellectual relationships between the great medieval thinkers than Wolfson. During my first year at Harvard, I took a year-long seminar with him. We studied the most important document of medieval Jewish philosophy, Moses Maimonides's *The Guide to the Perplexed*. Wolfson's approach was intensive rather than extensive. We would often spend hours discussing the meaning of a single crucial Hebrew philosophic term. Wolfson showed us why that term and not another had been chosen as well as how the term was used by other thinkers writing in Greek, Latin,

151

or Arabic. Wolfson's discussions were lessons in high scholarship. He had the kind of command of the texts and documents of medieval philosophy that Kleinman had in the field of Talmud.

There was, however, a side to Wolfson that I found less appealing. More than any other Harvard professor, he reminded me of Aaron Kleinman. While Kleinman was undoubtedly an extraordinarily learned scholar, his commitment to scholarship apparently took precedence over all other activities. There is, of course, nothing intrinsically wrong with such an ordering of personal priorities. Nevertheless, by the time I entered Harvard, I could no longer choose that hierarchy of values.

Wolfson's commitment to scholarship was even more total than Kleinman's. Kleinman was married. Wolfson remained a life-long bachelor. His real home was his study in Widener Library. His life had been given over selflessly, perhaps monkishly, to the pursuit of scholarship. No family man could possibly have done justice to his household responsibilities and achieved Wolfson's level of scholarly excellence.

Wolfson also had a reputation for keeping his students with him for a very long time before permitting them to receive the Ph.D. When I came to Harvard, I thought it a good idea to expose myself to the great master, but I had no intention of enrolling in the doctoral program under Wolfson. I enrolled in the joint Divinity School–Graduate School program in the History and Philosophy of Religion. Influenced by Heschel's seminar and the existentialism which was very much in vogue, I wanted initially to write a doctoral thesis on Sören Kierkegaard. This did not please Wolfson who felt that I ought to concentrate on Jewish studies. Although I was greatly impressed, perhaps even overawed, by Wolfson's learning, I had not come to Harvard to continue on the same track I had pursued at the seminary. Throughout my intellectual career, I have hovered between two poles, one of intense interest in Jewish learning, the other of involvement in the wider concerns of contemporary culture. At Harvard, the time had come to turn to the wider concerns once again.

One evening sometime in the winter of 1952, a local rabbi, a distinguished alumnus of the Jewish Theological Seminary who had received his Ph.D. under Wolfson, took me aside at a party to discuss my scholarly plans. He told me that I had an extraordinary opportunity to do my Ph.D. under a scholar of Wolfson's stature, and added that I would be most unwise were I to fail to take advantage of the opportunity. Wolfson, he said, felt that my knowledge was such that there was reasonable assurance that I might eventually become a competent scholar in medieval

Jewish philosophy. He was, however, opposed to my continuing my work at the Divinity School on Kierkegaard. I told the rabbi that I appreciated Wolfson's confidence but that I did not want to change my course. It was suggested that I talk things over with Wolfson.

Several days later I dropped in on Wolfson. He had been informed of my response. He looked up at me from his desk and said, "Mr. Rubenstein, I have only one question to ask you: Do you want to become a scholar or a Ph.D.?"

I had heard that some men had trained under Wolfson for almost ten years before he regarded them as qualified. I was fearful that such might be my fate. I did not see myself spending my life pouring over Greek, Latin, Arabic, and Hebrew manuscripts. Wolfson's question was not unlike an invitation to join the Castalian order so well described by Hermann Hesse in his novel *The Glass Bead Game*. Surrounded by books and manuscripts crammed in every corner of his office from floor to ceiling, Wolfson was inviting me to begin my apprenticeship for the Glass Bead Game in earnest. Playing that game involved a lifetime of abstract mental achievement, far removed from the passionate concerns of ordinary men. If I accepted the invitation, I might spend eight to ten years poring over medieval manuscripts. This activity would become the center of my life. The approval of the great master would supplant all other tokens of worth. I would earn a living only as a necessary evil which would permit me to further my studies. My marriage would collapse completely. There would, of course, be as little room for erotic relationships in this Castalia as in Joseph Knecht's. Then, some day if I worked diligently, I would publish my first critical edition of a hitherto unknown medieval Hebrew manuscript. It would be said that I was Wolfson's pupil and that I had done well for a beginning. Perhaps by the time I was fifty and, divested of all diverting emotional relationships, I would bring out an authoritative interpretation of some little known philosopher, who would, thanks to my scrupulously careful research, be revealed as a more important figure than the scholarly community had hitherto assumed. At this stage of the Game, I would have students of my own who would wonder whether they could ever achieve my great learning. In spite of my students' admiration, I would never forget how little I knew in comparison with my great master. A whole life could have been spent in that fashion. As much as I respected Wolfson, I knew that such a life was not for me. I looked straight at Wolfson and said, "I want to be a Ph.D., professor. I'll take my chances on the rest." It was not the answer he wanted. His features reminded me somewhat of my father's. Perhaps some common Lithuanian ancestor had given them both their features. His face tightened slightly. He was displeased but said nothing. The interview was over. I completed the course on Maimonides. He gave me an A — for the second term. He had given me an A for the first. I took this to be a sign of his displeasure. Although I often chatted with him whenever I met him at Widener Library, I never again took a course with him.

Even before coming to Harvard, I was deeply impressed by Paul Johannes Tillich, perhaps the most influential Protestant theologian to teach in America in the twentieth century. Of all the courses I attended at Harvard, Tillich's course on classical German philosophy was the most memorable.

Tillich's interpretation of nineteenth century German thought was greatly influenced by Karl Löwith's *From Hegel to Nietzsche*. In that seminal work, Löwith demonstrated how most of the crucial issues of modern religious and social philosophy stem from the breakdown of the great Hegelian synthesis. Hegel argued that all of the diverse manifestations of art, religion, and philosophy throughout human history are expressions of one underlying unitary process. For Hegel the immense sweep of world history in all of its variety is the expression of a single, evolving, self-differentiating metaphysical reality which Hegel designated as *geist* or spirit. Hegel regarded *geist* as the ultimate reality. He was convinced that *geist* is both dynamic and inherently rational. Hence, he described *geist* as the process of reason at work in history. For Hegel the entire history of religion from its earliest beginnings in magic and animism to its fulfillment in Christianity was an inherently rational, unitary process that finally yielded its ultimate truth, the reconciliation of God and man in Christ. Thus, reason and religion are not in opposition; nor are God and man. They are all expressions of the same process. However, it was Hegel's conviction that even what he regarded as the highest and final stage of religion, Christian revelation, could not fully comprehend its own intrinsic rationality. Even the highest religion expressed imperfectly what only philosophy, in fact only Hegelian philosophy, could express with perfect clarity and consistency, the self-unfolding of *geist* in the course of world history. According to Hegel, it is the task of philosophy rather than religion finally to proclaim "the eternal kingdom of God." In Löwith's phrase, "the Holy Spirit lives on in the congregation of philosophy."

Viewed from one perspective, Hegel's philosophy brings to an end the age-old tension between reason and revelation insofar as philosophy validates religion. From another perspective, Hegel dissolves religion into philosophy. According to Hegel, religion expresses in anticipatory images truths that are expressed in full only by philosophy. The survival of cult and worship are necessary only for those who are insufficiently enlightened to incorporate religion into the philosophy of religion.

Even Hegel intuited that his daring reconciliation between reason and faith was "a destroying reconciliation." According to Löwith, Hegel's philosophy of religion is "a final step before a great turning and break with Christianity." In 1843 the German thinker Michelet wrote that "the goal of [Hegelian] history is the secularization of Christianity."

Undoubtedly, Hegel's most influential theological critic in the nineteenth century was Sören Kierkegaard. Kierkegaard took especially strong exception to Hegel's claim that history was a rational process immanent in the order of things. Kierkegaard was acutely aware of the fact that in his time the historical process had brought forth European bourgeois society and the beginnings of mass social and intellectual conformity. Kierkegaard saw no way to equate the bourgeois "Spirit of the Age" with the truth of Christianity which had expressed itself uniquely and finally in Christ's self-sacrifice on the cross. Kierkegaard made a radical distinction between Christianity and Christendom. According to Kierkegaard, the Christian Church mocks its founder with its unavoidable compromises with the bourgeois world. For Kierkegaard, it was impossible to follow Christ and still participate in the institutional structures of the nineteenth-century church. The way of the Christian was the solitary pilgrimage of the one who takes Christ as his model. Where Hegel insisted on the crucial importance of the historical process, Kierkegaard insisted that *nothing* of any spiritual consequence had happened for the Christian in history since Calvary and the first Easter. The Christ event was unique, singular, and without historical or philosophic analogue. It was certainly not an anticipatory image whose meaning had been fully comprehended by Hegelian philosophy.

Hegel's reconciliation of reason and faith was unacceptable to Kierkegaard on Christian grounds. Kierkegaard insisted that one could affirm *either* the truth of philosophy, which dissolved and secularized Christianity, *or* the truth of the Christ event, which confronted the believer with a reality neither reason nor philosophy could ever comprehend. After Kierkegaard, no believer could ever attain the kind of philosophic certainty claimed by Hegel. The believer would always be a man inwardly torn by the knowledge that his faith could never be reconciled with reason and philosophy. Henceforth, faith would be forever imperiled by a "sea of doubt twenty thousand fathoms deep." Kierkegaard's faith always hovered very close to the borders of atheism. Like Tertullian, Kierkegaard saw the difficulty of harmonizing the insights of Athens and Jerusalem. He chose faith largely because he perceived despair and hopelessness as the only alternative. Those who were unable to follow Kierkegaard in his desperate leap of faith might easily agree with such critics of Hegel, as Ludwig Feuerbach, Karl Marx, and Friedrich Nietzsche, all of whom rejected religious faith as a viable intellectual possibility.

Tillich's lectures on German philosophy were a veritable introduction to the intellectual origins of contemporary culture. One of the most important issues dealt with by Tillich was the *objectivity of God*. He did so in connection with his lectures on Hegel's *Early Theological Writings*. The English word object does not carry the full impact of the corresponding German word, *Gegenstand,* that which stands over against. An objective God is one who stands over against man. This was the way both Tillich and Hegel regarded the transcendent, commanding God who confronts man as an all-powerful other. This conception is in contrast to Tillich's own idea of God as the source or ground of being. In the *Early Theological Writings*, Hegel asserted that the idea of the God who stands over against man was conceived originally by the patriarch Abraham. Hegel offered a sociological interpretation of Abraham's faith which foreshadowed both Marx and Nietzsche. According to Hegel, "Mastery is the only possible relationship" in which Abraham could stand up to the world about him. Abraham was, however, unable to achieve the dominance he sought. Rather than renounce it altogether, he ceded it "to his Ideal," a divine being who was outside of and alien to the order of nature. Anticipating Nietzsche, Hegel argued that the God of biblical monotheism originated as an idealized, compensatory projection of Abraham's inability to realize his will-to-power in the world of actuality.

Hegel's analysis has been attacked as anti-Semitic. It is certainly not generous in its evaluation of Judaism. Nevertheless, Hegel's suggestion that Abraham's faith expresses in religious images the estrangements of a wandering, nomadic social order sheds much light on both Judaism and American Protestantism. It was Hegel's conviction that the religion of Abraham and his progeny, that is biblical monotheism and its successor, rabbinic Judaism, is the religious ideology of the nomadic stranger who is unable or unwilling to call any corner of earth home. This is evident in his harsh description of Abraham:

> With Abraham, the true progenitor of the Jews, the history of this people begins, i.e., his spirit is the unity, the soul, regulating the entire fate of his posterity. . . .

> Abraham . . . had in youth already left a fatherland in his father's company. Now, in the plains of Mesopotamia, he tore himself free altogether from his family as well, in order to be a wholly self-subsistent, independent man, to be an overlord himself. He did this without having been injured or disowned. . . . The first act which made Abraham the progenitor of a nation is a disseverance which snaps the bonds of communal life and love. The entirety of the relationships in which he had hitherto lived with men and nature, these beautiful relationships of his youth he spurned.

The same hostility to his surroundings which moved Abraham to forsake his place of birth was manifest, according to Hegel, in his wanderings:

> With his herds Abraham wandered . . . over a boundless territory without bringing parts of it any nearer by cultivating or improving them. Had he done so, he would have become attached to them and adopted them as parts of *his* world. . . . The groves which often gave him coolness and shade he soon left again. . . . He was a stranger on earth, a stranger to the soil and men alike. . . .

Abraham's rejection of fellowship and fixed habitation is the earthly counterpart of his God's dreadful exclusivism:

> . . . in the jealous God of Abraham and his posterity there lay the horrible claim that He alone was God and that this nation was the only one to have a god.

If the young Hegel was hostile to Judaism, he had almost as little regard for Christianity. Walter Kaufmann has observed that the *Early Theological Writings* are inappropriately named. Unlike Hegel's later writings, they are actually anti-theological. Although both Jews and Christians regard Abraham as worthy of great esteem for his willingness

157

obediently to forsake his home that he might serve the one true God, Hegel condemned Abraham for "spurning the beautiful relationships of his youth." When Christian historians attributed the victory of Christianity over the pagan gods of antiquity to "intellectual enlightenment," or Christianity's "divine origin," Hegel bitterly defended the superiority of paganism:

> . . . in everything great, beautiful, noble, and free they [the Greek and Roman heathens] are so far our superiors that we can hardly make them our examples but must rather look up to them as a different species at whose achievements we can only marvel.

Pagan religion was for Hegel the religion of free men:

> As free men the Greeks and Romans obeyed laws laid down by themselves . . . gave their property, exhausted their passions and sacrificed their lives by thousands for an end which was their own.

According to Hegel, the Greeks and Romans became Christian only after they had ceased to be free men. Anticipating Nietzsche's analysis of Christian morality as an expression of the *ressentiment* of slaves, Hegel wrote:

> Greek and Roman religion was a religion for free peoples only, and, with the loss of freedom, its significance and strength, its fitness to men's needs, were bound to perish.

In his lectures, Tillich pointed out that the Greeks and Romans could represent their gods anthropomorphically because, as free men, their relationship to the gods was one of fellowship. By contrast, the aniconic followers of the God of biblical monotheism could only relate to their God as slave to master. I cannot stress strongly enough the profound sense of both shock and illumination I gained from both Tillich's lectures and Hegel's writings. And, it must be remembered that Tillich spent more time on what Kaufmann called the *anti-theological* writings of Hegel than the later, more Christian writings. Until I studied Hegel with Tillich, I had regarded the keen sense of estrangement which I had experienced since earliest childhood as primarily a personal and psychological phenomenon. Tillich helped me to appreciate the social and historical dimensions of my experience. Admittedly, all men must endure some irreducible element of alienation insofar as we are creatures of divided conscience and unfulfilled desire. Nevertheless, I began to perceive that my abiding sense of alienation and the problems which attended it had been intensified by the fact that my ancestors had been wandering nomads who had been defeated in war and expelled from their own country. Had my people found a grove which gave them coolness during their wanderings, it would have been disastrous for them to have attempted to strike roots upon it. Having no secure land tenure anywhere, any attachment to a place would only have aggravated the stress of dislocation when the inevitable expulsion took place. Being without place, they could only worship a placeless deity to whom they ceded all power. There was no viable alternative. Furthermore, if they had not believed that their God had the power to reverse their continual defeats, they would have been utterly without hope and reduced to despair. This fact was brought home to me when I visited a group of Catholic intellectuals in Kraków, Poland in 1965. In our conversations, I told them that I regarded hope as at best a problematic theological category. Almost to a man, they replied that hope may be problematic for those living securely in America, but it was all they had left. They asked me if I realized what their lives would be like if they felt they had no hope of ever being liberated from foreign domination. Without hope that Israel's placeless, all-powerful deity would eventually reverse their fortunes, my people would have perished long before Auschwitz.

Nevertheless, there is another side to the story of Judaism that neither Tillich nor Hegel could see, although I am indebted to both thinkers for what they helped me to understand. According to Hegel, Abraham's alienated, wandering existence was undertaken *voluntarily*. Hegel saw both Jewish nomadic existence and belief in the omnipotent God which attended it as a fate *willed* by Abraham and his progeny. Had Hegel been better acquainted with Jewish prayer, he might have encountered a radically different interpretation of Jewish exilic existence, exile as catastrophe. Three times a day, traditional Jews pray that their nomadic existence may be terminated. The Jewish reality is infinitely more complex than either Hegel or Tillich indicated in their analyses, perceptive though these were. I can never forget the Palestinian earth my maternal grandmother had treasured for years in a brown paper bag and which was cast upon her coffin by her oldest son as she was lowered into her final resting place. It was her way of saying, "I don't want to be a wanderer

159

forever. I want to go home." Nor can I forget the prayers of restoration to Zion which I had recited daily for years, such as:

> Sound aloud the great horn for our freedom; lift up the banner to gather us from the four corners of the earth. Blessed art Thou, O Lord, who gathers the banished ones of thy people Israel.

For my ancestors, nomadic existence was the result of a catastrophe they hoped would ultimately be reversed. They were no different than other men. They too wanted to plant vineyards and rest in the cool of a grove; they too wanted to say, "This place is mine; this is where I belong."

They were unable to do so because their ancestors had lost two wars against the Romans in 70 and 135 C.E. Hegel was clearly mistaken about the voluntary character of Jewish nomadic existence. Nevertheless, in Hegel's discussion of Abraham, it is possible to discern a rudimentary sociological analysis of Jewish religious idelogy. Hegel's analysis anticipated Marx's assertion that the superstructure of religious belief and practice evolves out of the substructure of concrete conditions of actual life of the believing community. Thus, hunting societies develop a very different kind of religious life than agrarian communities. Furthermore, a significant shift in a community's concrete social relations would sooner or later be reflected in altered forms of religious consciousness. In highly developed societies, the ideologies and institutions of one era might congeal and be resistant to further change. Nevertheless, even congealed religious institutions would eventually be affected by social change. If monotheistic Judaism was a reflection of the nomadic existence of the wandering Jew, I reasoned, then a reversal of Jewish nomadism, such as has occurred in modern Israel, would in all likelihood be followed by abandonment of faith in the placeless God of the Bible by those Jews who were once again able to say of their habitations, "This place is mine. This is where I belong."

Even in the biblical period, the Jews were not always believers in one God. In the opinion of many scholars, monotheism did not prevail until the time of the Babylonian exile. My ancestors were nomads who required an alien God. A mode of existence that ceased to be nomadic might require other gods. This was a sociological commonplace. Another sociological commonplace was that congealed religious institutions were bound to resist changes in religious ideology. Nevertheless, the pagan gods of ancient Canaan had never entirely lost their power within Judaism. The

Bible records that whenever Abraham's progeny struck root in Canaan, they offered their reverence to the gods of that land. After the holocaust, the Jews of Europe had no alternative but to return to the place from which their ancestors had come and to put to an end their exile. Zionism seemed to be the only ideology that had any degree of practical realism for Europe's Jews in the aftermath of World War II. Certainly, few Jews were prepared once again to entrust their destinies to their European hosts. However, Zionism was destined to have unforseen consequences, such as the transformation of the passive Jews of the Diaspora into a military force. Sooner or later, I was convinced, there were bound to be religious transformations as well. In spite of the official status of Orthodox Judaism in Israel, the most important single theological consequence of Zionism might be a revival of earth paganism and the displacement of biblical monotheism by some form of renewed Canaanite earth religion. At the level of folk religion, it was evident to me that a transformation was already in process. Even in the biblical period, the Israelites were not always believers in one God. The millennial reign of the God of time seemed to be giving way to a return of the gods of earth and place in Israel.

More than any other aspect of Tillich's lectures, his sympathy for paganism both shocked and enlightened me. I remember one unforgettable lecture in which Tillich referred to the abiding power of the old pagan divinities. He related to us how he had stood one day at the site of an ancient Greek temple and had experienced the abiding sacred power of the gods of that place. I was amazed. Was this America's leading Protestant theologian or a pagan mystagogue who stood before us? There was reverence and awe in his voice as he spoke of the sacred reality he had encountered in Greece.

I later concluded that Tillich was both pagan and Christian. Where others saw gaps in the religious life of mankind, Tillich saw continuities. Like Hegel much of Tillich's labors had been motivated by a desire to integrate, correlate, and reconcile diverse and often apparently contradictory realms of human experience. Instead of regarding the powers he had experienced in Greece as a challenge to Christianity, Tillich saw them as part of a larger, complex, sacred totality of which Christ was the unique center. He had no doubt of the singular and decisive role of Jesus as the Christ, but he was unwilling to deny the experience of the sacred of pre-Christian men and women.

There was another aspect of Tillich's thought that linked him with

161

paganism while he remained at all times Christian. Thomas J. J. Altizer and William Hamilton have called Tillich "the father of radical theology." Shortly before his death Tillich rejected the ideas of Altizer and Hamilton, but, more than any other theologian at work in the fifties, Tillich's writings and lectures made it inevitable that the generation of religious thinkers that followed him would include men and women for whom the transcendent God of the biblical tradition was 'dead'. It was Tillich himself who dared us to follow the logic of his position to its radical conclusion when he wrote in *The Courage to Be*:

> The God of theological theism . . . appears as the invincible tyrant, the being in contrast with whom all other beings are without freedom and subjectivity. He is equated with the recent tyrants who with the help of terror try to transform everything into . . . a cog in the machine they control. . . . This is the God Nietzsche said had to be killed because nobody can tolerate being made into a mere object of absolute knowledge and control.

The "God of theological theism" to which Tillich referred is, of course, the all-seeing, all-knowing, all-powerful God of the biblical religions. Tillich's observations about the tyranny involved in serving such a God were constantly reiterated in the substance of his Harvard lectures until his call for revolt became irresistible.

Tillich used the terms "Being Itself," "Ground of Being," and "Source of Being" to designate the God he did affirm. These terms suggest a feminine, maternal imagery which contrasted with the decidedly masculine character of the God of biblical theism he rejected. This corresponded to my own inner experience in which my mother was always more dominant than my father. One comes forth from the source or ground as the infant comes forth from the maternal source. One is restored to unity with the ground when the travails of finitude are put aside. The imagery is admittedly imprecise. Tillich wanted at all times to affirm that men can be individuals with fully developed selves distinct from their ground in which they nevertheless remain at all times immersed. He conveyed this idea best when he spoke of God as "Being Itself."

Tillich's conception of God is, I believe, more indebted to the religious conceptions of German mysticism than to the biblical tradition. Both Jewish and Christian mysticism, insofar as they stressed God as ground and source, preserved feminine images of God which were ultimately derived from the earth paganisms of the ancient Mediterranean world. The mystical traditions and their conception of God can be seen as an indication of the inability of the monotheistic, patriarchal religions entirely to obliterate a far older reverence for the Great Mother which has persisted as an underground current in both religions.

If I were to summarize briefly the substance of what America's greatest Christian theologian of that era taught me, it would be that he taught me how to express and conceptualize the deeply pagan instincts I had been suppressing during my years of rabbinical study. He also taught me not to be afraid to be a pagan. I had been driven to affirm and serve the masculine sky god of biblical and rabbinic Judaism largely because of my fear of chaos, meaninglessness, and death. I had come to see in my own life how self-defeating my attempt to accept biblical faith had been. Tillich offered me an intellectually and emotionally satisfying alternative which was in harmony with my own experience. My practical experience as a clergyman had convinced me that in spite of all pretense of serving a male sky god, the religion I and my community were actually practicing was a pagan cult rooted in the vicissitudes of earthly, biological existence. Tillich's lectures taught me to recognize it as such. Although it was hardly his intention, he also helped me to understand that it is possible to be both pagan and Jewish at the same time. Most of my congregants were unconsciously pagan. I was becoming consciously pagan.

While I attended Tillich's lectures, my psychoanalysis was proceeding. In my analytic probing I was involved in the process of *demystifying* my faith in a commanding sky god, my role as a rabbi, and my vaunted cosmic aspirations. I was enabled to see that the pretentious mythic and ideological superstructure I had erected was largely based upon the substructure of my own childhood conflicts and longings. Tillich, especially through his lectures on Hegel, Marx, and Nietzsche, helped me further to enlarge the process of demystification. My analyst was not professionally or intellectually equipped to take me beyond problems arising out of the psychological stresses of the nuclear family. But, my parents did not exist in a social vacuum. They too had parents whose personalities were largely shaped by the political and social realities with which they had to cope. *Personal* psychoanalysis was insufficient to yield an understanding of the full psychological complexity of my situation. My personal history might yield much helpful information. Nevertheless, I was compelled to inquire about my people's social history in order to really understand myself. As I had attempted to identify the dimly recollected emotional trauma in my own past that had had so great an influence on the development of my personality, I now searched for the decisive trauma in my people's past that had shaped their distinctive beliefs, personality structure, and social organization.

It was not difficult to locate the traumatic event *par excellence* in the history of the Jewish world. It was, as I have written, the overwhelming defeat of the Jews by the Romans in the Judaeo-Roman War which ended in 70 C.E. That trauma was followed shortly thereafter by the second Judaeo-Roman War in 132–135 and the confirmation of the first defeat. As a result, the lives of my ancestors were decisively altered. They were condemned to wander over the face of the earth, always as unwanted guests in other people's houses, always on sufferance, never certain of the duration of their tenure.

At times Tillich's influence was more suggestive than direct. As my interest in the sociology of religion expanded, I began to wonder whether the distinctive complexities of male-female interaction among Jews might be as much an expression of their powerless, nomadic existence as was their official creed, their belief in an alien monotheistic sky god. My own marital difficulties were far more aggravated than most, but there was a historical and a sociological dimension to our family's problems. Like so many other Jews in every age since the fall of Jerusalem, Ellen had had to flee for her life. Ellen's personality was profoundly affected by this fact. I was subject to all of the emotional complexities of being a male in a community without power. My masculine identity had not even received the tenuous support Jewish religious culture normally makes available in the bar mitzvah ritual. Masculine identity is especially problematic in societies and social classes devoid of power. The men cannot protect the women from physical assault or sexual abuse. In the Jewish communities of Europe, pogroms meant rape and other forms of sexual abuse in addition to wanton slaughter. The sexual aspects of Jewish powerlessness have seldom been more tellingly described than by the Hebrew poet Hayyim Nahman Bialik after the Kishinev massacres in Russia in 1903:

> Descend then, to the cellars of the town,
> There where the virginal daughters of thy folk were fouled,
> Where seven heathen flung a woman down,
> The daughter in the presence of her mother,
> The mother in the presence of her daughter,
> Before slaughter, during slaughter, and after slaughter! . . .

Note also, do not fail to note
In that dark corner, and behind that cask
Crouch husbands, bridegrooms, brothers, peering from the cracks,
Watching the sacred bodies struggling underneath
The bestial breath,
Stifled in filth, and swallowing their blood!
Watching from the darkness and its mesh
The lecherous rabble portioning for booty
Their kindred and their flesh!
Crushed in their shame, they saw it all;
They did not stir nor move;
They did not pluck their eyes out; they
Beat not their brains against the wall!
Perhaps, perhaps each watcher had it in his heart to pray:
A miracle, O Lord,—and spare my skin this day!
They crawled forth from their holes, they fled to the House of the
    Lord,
They offered thanks to Him, the sweet benedictory word.
The *Cohanim** sallied forth, to the Rabbi's house they flitted:
Tell me, O Rabbi, tell, is my own wife permitted? . . .†

Western readers have been impressed by Martin Buber's accounts of
the Hasidim and Abraham Joshua Heschel's nostalgic reminiscences of
Eastern European Jewish life. Bialik's bitter poem helps to achieve a more
balanced picture. Powerlessness had disastrous emotional consequences
for Jewish men and women.

In spite of the inability of Jewish men to protect their women, the
women were at all times socially and economically dependent upon them.
The men could only assert, and truth to tell, exaggerate, their masculine
prerogatives *within* the community, never in the larger world. All of the
masculine bias which Jews had inherited from ancient Palestine was
intensified in the Diaspora. The Jewish God was a masculine God. The
Jewish religion stressed the prerogatives of the male in two domains of
fundamental importance over which Jews had any measure of independ-

---

* The *Cohanim* are the hereditary priests who had to maintain special ritual purity. Their
inquiry concerned the question of whether they would be required to divorce their wives after
the violation.
† Hayyim Nahman Bialik, *Complete Poetic Works,* trans. A. M. Klein. (New York, 1948), pp.
133–134.

ence, worship, and learning. Only men were normally expected to participate fully in religious worship. At daily services the synagogue was something of a men's club. Only men were normally given training in religious learning. Even the insistence on the beard was, I believe, a pathetic attempt on the part of powerless men to assert their threatened masculinity in whatever way they could.

And all the time, the Jewish family was threatened by the fury of drunken peasants and a rapacious nobility. It is an old story; American blacks know it well. The powerful could always preempt more than the possessions of the powerless. The very center of Jewish emotional security, the family, was forever threatened by the powerlessness of the head of the household.

When the sexual assaults did take place, it is not difficult to imagine the subsequent emotional complications between husband and wife. Would not the man be likely to wonder whether the woman was really forced during the outrage? Would he not wonder whose child came forth nine months later? Even though it was hardly likely that a woman would enjoy that kind of molestation, was it not possible that the husband, perhaps against his conscious intent, felt impotent rage against the violator which could only be expressed as silent resentment toward the wife? Nor could the wife have been without troubled feelings toward the husband. How much respect could the women described in Bialik's poem have had for their peering, cringing husbands impotently watching the scene? Can the situation described by Bialik have been conducive to genuine sexual harmony?

There was also the problem of rage. My analytic probing had persuaded me that one of my most pressing motives for accepting the disciplines of Jewish law had been the desire to contain my own rage. At Harvard, my readings in the sociology of religion convinced me that the voluntary acceptance by the Jewish community of the same behavioral constraints for almost two thousand years had been similarly motivated. After the fall of Jerusalem Jews could no longer hit back. They had to contain their rage. The necessity was so great that they were trained to distrust emotional spontaneity from earliest childhood. They were indeed fortunate that their religion compelled them to an extremity of behavioral discipline few other peoples have ever had to endure.

Perhaps no contemporary novelist has examined the problem of bottled-up emotions among Jews as unsparingly as Philip Roth. Some people have called *Portnoy's Complaint* a black comedy. It is in reality a

166

tragic description of Jewish rage and impotence. Much of the humor of the novel concerns the inability of Portnoy's father to rid himself of his solid wastes. He sits for hours upon the toilet, but hardly anything comes forth. The man is so bottled up that he cannot even eliminate his own waste. When we look at his life situation, it is not difficult to understand why: He is a typical marginal Jew doing the kind of cast-off dirty work few non-Jews would want. He works for a White Anglo-Saxon Protestant insurance firm collecting the minuscule premiums paid by impoverished blacks in Newark's ghetto for burial insurance and small life insurance policies. The work is thankless and dangerous. As the visible representative of an anonymous corporation, he is the only concrete object of his clients' resentment. He is constantly in danger of assault by petty thieves. Should his accounts be short, he must make up the difference out of pocket.

In spite of his marginal position, he performs faithfully hoping that the insurance company will recognize his services and offer him a better position, but he knows that his hope is illusory, that as a Jew he has no chance for advancement in the company. He is locked into an anger-producing job, but he must contain his anger. He cannot express his feelings to the clients who use him as a target of their rage or against the company which uses him as an expendable shield. His constipation is symbolic of his emotional predicament as a marginal Jew in a non-Jewish world.

The actual narrative of *Portnoy's Complaint* consists of Alexander Portnoy's monologue on the psychoanalytic couch. The son is also afflicted with an inability to let go. His complaint is that he can never enjoy sexual release in normal heterosexual relationships. He spends long hours masturbating. Occasionally, he achieves some release through perverted relationships with non-Jewish partners. He is as locked up emotionally as his father. He is too frightened by interpersonal relationships to be able to let go even in the privacy of the bedroom with a partner who seeks not to harm him but to join him in pleasure. When I read Roth's novel, I saw the inability of both father and son to let go as prototypical of some of the deepest problems faced by Jewish men since the fall of Jerusalem. The feeling side of life had to be rigidly controlled. The mind could be developed, even over-developed, but feelings, especially feelings of release, had to be contained. One had always to be on one's guard.

And, I knew my ancestors had no alternative and that I owed my existence to their exercise of self-control. I shall never forget my reaction

167

when I saw a drunk weaving about at a railroad station in Lublin, Poland in 1965. As I saw that peasant, I thought to myself that in all the centuries Jews lived in Poland, they never had the security to let down their guard the way that drunk did. The drunk knew he could safely let go. The worst that could happen was that an indulgent policeman, who knew about the necessity of occasional self-forgetfulness, would take him to jail to sober up overnight.

My ancestors bottled up their rage, and much more besides. If one feels compelled to control rage, it is best to be on the safe side. So, from cradle to grave, Jews were trained never really to let go. Mental energy and calculating rationality, the kind in which Lithuanian Talmudists excelled, took priority over the body and its urgencies. The marital results were disastrous in spite of the romanticized accounts of the beauties of Jewish family life. Men and women who were trained from earliest childhood that it was dangerous to let go could hardly lose themselves in sexual passion. There is something awesomely symbolic about the fact that the Jewish male encounters the full force of his religious culture for the first time in the rite of circumcision.

Food was safe. Food could be equated with love, especially when other forms of love were so problematic. There is much sadness in all those jokes about chicken soup and overprotecting Jewish mothers. Nor is it accidental that food and maternal overprotection figure so largely in *Portnoy's Complaint.* Unable to get adequate emotional supplies from the bottled-up husband, the wife would often invest excessive feelings in the son, thereby intensifying the son's attachment to mother and diminishing his capacity fully to turn to an adult female later on. The excessive mothering intensified the sons' inhibitions with their wives who then invested their emotions in their offspring, thus perpetuating the cycle from generation to generation. It is not surprising that Sigmund Freud stressed the Oedipus complex as the nuclear component in neurosis. The families he knew best were Jewish.

Obviously, Jewish families are by no means the only ones that are sexually disturbed. All civilizations have their own characteristic forms of sexual repression. Nevertheless, the Yiddish language has made a distinctive contribution to the lexicon of masculine inadequacy with the term *schlemiel.* Although the figure of the schlemiel has recently been romanticized in the character of Tevya in *Fiddler on the Roof,* it is doubtful that the schlemiel was any more adequate as a lover than as a manager of his family's affairs. The simple fact is that the hazards of Jewish existence materially augmented the emotional difficulties between Jewish men and women.

I was coming to understand to my horror and amazement that many of my own sexual conflicts had roots that were at least two thousand years old. Some, I was to discover later, were even older. Ten years had passed from the time I entered rabbinical school to the time I was ordained. On no occasion during those years did I ever hear any professor suggest that the conditions under which Jews had lived in the Diaspora had had disastrous consequences for their sexual and emotional well-being. Such issues were ignored. Instead, we were often told that our real problem was our insufficient understanding of our religious tradition. We were assured that, were we to study diligently, we would eventually come to understand the tradition and its wisdom. Then, all would be well.

In the secular world social theorists have long understood that a social system can have a decidedly pathogenic effect on its members. All societies place painful limitations on the individual. Unfortunately, some societies are more restrictive than others. In the world of rabbinical schools, no one even raised the question of whether the broken Jewish culture of the post-medieval world might itself be deeply pathogenic. But then, how could our professors have questioned the only way of life about which they had any knowledge? By training and experience they were committed to perpetuating rather than examining that way of life. The entire scholarly enterprise at the rabbinical schools was designed to promote rather than to ameliorate the dis-ease.

Above all, I was horrified by the growing awareness of my own involuntary complicity in perpetuating the dis-ease every time I served as a model of fidelity to the commandments of the sky god and every time I ascended the pulpit to persuade people, in a guilt-inducing manner, to "live good Jewish lives." Nevertheless, I felt compelled for the time to keep silent. I was still too unsure of myself to break with the patterns of belief and life style which, as a rabbi, I felt obliged to foster. Having no viable alternative to offer, I reasoned that a pathogenic culture was better than none at all. I began to identify very strongly with Dostoevski's Grand Inquisitor who was convinced that his flock required miracle, mystery, and authority but could not tolerate freedom and truth, especially the truth about themselves.

10

RABBI YOCHANAN'S
BARGAIN

I left Cambridge in September 1958, before receiving my doctorate, to become the Director of the Hillel Foundation and Chaplain to Jewish Students at the University of Pittsburgh and Carnegie Institute of Technology, now known as Carnegie–Mellon University. During my first two years in Pittsburgh I spent every free moment in my basement study completing my thesis. Gordon Allport, the distinguished Harvard psychologist, was my thesis adviser. Although not a Freudian, Allport was willing to guide me in a dissertation in which I attempted to interpret the myths and legends of rabbinic Judaism in the light of Freudian psychoanalysis. The thesis was subsequently published in revised form as *The Religious Imagination.*

My thesis research was an extension of my personal psychoanalysis. In the personal analysis I had sought to uncover the disturbances within my early childhood that had so disastrously affected the development of my personality. Largely as a result of my encounter with Tillich, I had come to understand that my personal psychoanalysis would be incomplete were I to ignore the decisive events that had defined the way my parents and forebears had experienced their world. It was increasingly clear that my life had been decisively influenced by the Fall of Jerusalem to the Romans in 70 C.E.

When my ancestors revolted against Roman rule in 66, there was every likelihood that their rebellion would be speedily subdued. The inevitable outcome was unexpectedly delayed far longer than the Romans anticipated. The delay multiplied the cost in blood. Practically every town and village from Galilee to Jerusalem inhabited by Jews became a stronghold. The Romans had to contend with the kind of defensive fighting in which Palestine's Jews excelled. As the Romans finally subdued the rebels, they leveled their habitations and put the people to the sword. Rapine, famine, and desolation were the order of the day. The Talmud records that for seven years after the fall of Jerusalem "the nations of the world cultivated their vineyards with no other manure than the blood of Israel."

In the wake of the catastrophe, some order had to be brought out of the almost total breakdown of the Palestinian Jewish world. Only one group was capable of meeting the challenge of spiritual and political reconstruction, the Pharisees under Rabbi Yochanan ben Zakkai. Yochanan had opposed the rebellion against Rome in the first place. According to Talmudic tradition, he counseled that the Romans be given the tokens of submission they required. His counsel was bitterly opposed by the Zealots who were convinced that God alone was king over Israel and that no foreign sovereign had any right over his Holy Land. If the Jews were to offer tokens of submission, they were to be given to the Lord God of Israel alone.

The Zealots were deluded in their faith. They were convinced that, weak as they were, God would enable them to defeat the world-conquering foe. Yochanan and the Pharisees were more realistic. They understood that it was impossible for the Jews to overcome Roman power. Furthermore, they saw no pressing reason why they should. According to the Pharisees, Jewish dignity and integrity were not dependent upon martial victory. The proper task of the Jew was reverent obedience to the creator's law in the home, the school, the synagogue, and the market-place. When Yochanan learned of the destruction and desecration of the Temple, he wept bitterly, yet he consoled Israel with the words: "We have a means of atonement as effective as the Temple; it is doing deeds of loving kindness."

Yochanan taught his community how to remain intact after they had been stripped of the Temple cult, their sovereignty, and all control over

172

their political destiny. As terrible as was the war of 66–70, it was not the intention of the Romans to exterminate the Jewish community in Palestine or throughout the empire; nor did the Romans seek to extirpate Judaism as a religion. In the words of the distinguished historian, Jacob Neusner, the postwar policy of the Romans toward the Jews was to "reconstitute limited self-government through loyal and nonseditious agents." Their policy was "not persecution, but tolerance and scrupulousness."

The Romans found their "loyal and nonseditious agents" in Rabbi Yochanan ben Zakkai and his followers. Every rabbi has had engrained in his consciousness the story, perhaps somewhat apocryphal but no less psychologically true, of Yochanan's meeting with the Roman commander and soon-to-be Emperor Vespasian outside the walls of besieged Jerusalem. Because it was forbidden to hold the dead in Jerusalem for even one night, Yochanan's disciples were able to carry their master out of the stricken city by placing him in a coffin and pretending that he was dead. According to tradition, Vespasian knew that Yochanan had opposed the rebellion. He was therefore willing to receive the rabbi. When the future emperor in effect asked Yochanan what were his terms, Yochanan replied: "I ask nothing of thee save the [rabbinical academy at] Yabneh where I may go and teach my disciples and there establish a [house of] prayer and perform all the commandments." In the face of overwhelming power, Yochanan wanted only a spiritual center.

And so it came to pass that the Romans chose the Pharisees as their instrument to serve as the political and religious leaders of the Jews. A bargain was struck. The Pharisees under Yochanan gave the Romans the tokens of submission they demanded, foreswearing all resort to power in their dealings with their overlords. The Romans permitted the reconstituted community internal autonomy. Henceforth, the Jews would be obedient neither to their own princes nor to the priests of the destroyed Temple. With the backing of Rome, the rabbis assumed leadership over Israel. In later generations real power would pass to the monied classes, but the bargain would be kept. The Jewish communities in the Diaspora would be governed by "loyal and nonseditious agents."

A tale is told that, after the fall of Jerusalem, many were reduced to the most painful extremities of hunger. One day on the road to Emmaus, Yochanan saw a Jewish girl extracting the barley-corn out of the excrement dropped by an Arab's horse in order to secure something, anything, to eat. Referring to the incident, Yochanan told his disciples:

173

> Because you did not serve the Lord your God when you had plenty, therefore you shall serve him in hunger and thirst. . . . Because you did not serve the Lord . . . by reason of abundance of all things, therefore you shall serve your enemy in want of all things. . . .

Yochanan's theology of history was very similar to that expressed to me by Dean Grueber in Berlin in 1961. Whatever its merits, Yochanan did offer a way to endow with meaning the disaster that had befallen his people. At the same time, he gave them the only program for improving their lot that was realistic in their situation. Yochanan's program radically transformed the Jewish people. Instead of an altar of stone upon which bloody offerings were slain, Jewish religious life focused exclusively on bloodless worship and a bloodless Book. Instead of seeking bloody revenge against the Romans, my ancestors were taught to turn inward and, through a life of religious study, to become reconciled with the true and righteous author of their desolation. Yochanan and his followers taught the people that their happiness, their joy and their wisdom were to be found nowhere save in the Book, a book of memory and hope. And so it came to pass that a brave and warlike people that had dared to enter into combat with the world's greatest power foresook the sword for the Book.

The bargain suited the Romans. Jews were to be found throughout the empire. The Romans wanted to avert an ethnic revolt that might have caused them to withdraw troops from their far-flung frontiers. The rabbis were able to assure the Romans that, under their leadership, the Jews would be docile and submissive subjects. Only once again did the Jews wage war. In the time of Bar Kokba (132–135), the Romans seemed to renege on their willingness to permit the Jews religious if not political autonomy. The latent enmity exploded in open warfare. Once again the Jews lost a bloody war; once again the same bargain was struck. This time it was more or less kept.

Every Diaspora rabbi for almost two thousand years has been the heir of Yochanan and his bargain. Every rabbi has been trained to help his people to develop those traits of character that would enable them to foreswear the utilization of power and violence in their relations with their overlords. It was, of course, a gamble. Yochanan had committed his people to a way of life in which defenselessness was their only defense. They were despised, abused, and slaughtered, but, somehow, a remnant managed to survive, because even killers get bored with homicidal passion

174

after a while. Furthermore, despised as they were, the Jews were nevertheless needed before the age of universal literacy to perform tasks that were beyond the competence of the peasantry and beneath the dignity of the nobility.

Yochanan's bargain was a good one, if for no other reason than the fact that the alternative was group suicide. It worked until the twentieth century because it was almost never the intention of those who dominated the Jews to exterminate them. Neither the Romans nor their successor, the Roman Catholic Church, had a program of genocide. Even the Catholic monarchs, Ferdinand and Isabella, permitted the Jews to depart when they decided to rid Spain of its Jewish population in 1492. Certain elements in Christian doctrine could have led to genocide. Their potency was blunted by the moral restraints the Church imposed upon itself in its dealings with the Synagogue. The Church was harsh but never genocidal.

Undoubtedly Yochanan understood the obvious risks of his bargain. He probably had some idea of the cost involved in the path he had chosen, but he saw no viable alternative. The bargain finally broke down in the twentieth century when that other enemy of Imperial Rome, the Germans, changed the rules. The world of the twentieth century had been transformed by technology and bureaucracy. It was no longer necessary to employ passion to murder people. Technologically competent bureaucracies were able to keep the impersonal business of manufacturing corpses going long after the enterprise had lost its initial charm. The Germans of the twentieth century were not interested in keeping the Jews in their place. The Germans had become far too literate and far too skilled in doing the sort of things the Jews had been doing for centuries to have any further need of them. The Jews had become a surplus population. With impeccable logic but no humanity, the Nazis understood that there could be a "final solution" to the problem of riddance of an unwanted population, extermination. From the moment Hitler wrote in *Mein Kampf* of eliminating Jews like insects to the time the Germans used an insecticide, Cyklon B, to rid Europe of its Jews, the train of events was inevitable.

Europe had changed; unfortunately, the Jews hadn't. Confronted with the Nazis, most of them behaved as if Yochanan's bargain still held. The Jewish community did not understand, many still do not understand, that they could not keep Yochanan's bargain by themselves. They were so fixated on past experience that they could not distinguish between persecution and extermination. As a result, they became the unwitting accomplices in their own undoing. The work of the exterminators was almost effortless. Defenselessness was no longer a defense. It had become an invitation to Auschwitz.

When I came to understand that fidelity to Yochanan's bargain had become an invitation to genocide after the Nazis changed the rules, I concluded that the greatest disservice I could do to my people would be to encourage them to continue in the religious way of life which was the direct consequence of that bargain. In the previous chapter I wrote of my horror when I realized my complicity in fostering a religious culture that had a deeply pathogenic effect on my people. In this book I have described some of the emotional disorders that were the inevitable consequence of the culture created by Yochanan's bargain in modern times. Nevertheless, there was nothing pathogenic about the culture Yochanan fostered as long as it was reasonable to expect that the bargain would be kept. The repressions of sexuality, artistic imagination, and normal aggression that were an integral part of traditional Jewish culture were the emotional costs Jews had to pay to stay alive in an alien and hostile world.

Yochanan probably met with the Romans in 67 or 68. When it became apparent that Jerusalem's fall was inevitable, another group of Jews, the Zealots under the leadership of Eleazar ben Yair, decided to leave the besieged city, withdraw southward to the Dead Sea, and make their last stand at the mountain fortress of Masada. When they arrived at Masada they found immense stores of oil, wine, corn and dates that had been deposited there a hundred years before. They were determined never to surrender to the Romans. There the Zealots held out until May 73. When it became evident that the Romans would overwhelm the fortress, Eleazar ben Yair exhorted his followers "never to serve the Romans nor any master other than God who alone is the true and just Lord of mankind." There would be no surrender. Eleazar rejected the powerlessness and submissiveness that were to become sanctified as God's way for the next two thousand years. When a few of his followers indicated their reluctance to follow him, Eleazar is reported to have declared in a speech that his band had refused to surrender at the time of the fall of Jerusalem because of a "not ignoble hope that we might possibly be able to avenge her on her foes." Eleazar recognized that the hope "is now vanished forever." All that remained in their power was the possibility of an honorable death as free men. Anticipating the horrors of powerlessness

176

that were only to be fully realized in the twentieth century, Eleazar is reported to have said:

> Let us take pity on ourselves, our children and our wives while it is still in our power to show pity. For we were born to die, as were those whom we have begotten; and this even the fortunate cannot escape. But insult and servitude and the right of our wives being led to infamy with their children, these among men, are not natural or necessary evils, though those who do not prefer death, when death is in their power, must suffer even these because of their cowardice.

For Eleazar, the way chosen by Yochanan, the way my ancestors lived under the tutelage of Yochanan's heirs, was the way of cowardice and submission. Almost two thousand years before Hayyim Nahman Bialik wrote his bitter poem about the Kishinev pogrom, Eleazar anticipated the inevitability of the degradations depicted in that poem. Eleazar would have none of it. There was a point beyond which life was simply not worth another breath. As Eleazar continued his exhortation, he played the role of prophet of a Jewish future he could never accept:

> Elated with courage, we revolted against the Romans, and when bidden to assent to an offer of safety, would not listen to them. Who then, if they take us alive, does not anticipate their fury? Wretched will be the young, whose strong bodies can sustain many tortures; wretched, too, the old, whose age cannot endure afflictions! One man will see his wife dragged away by violence, another hear the voice of his child crying to a father whose hands are bound.

> But ours are still free and grasp the sword. While they are so free, let us die unenslaved by our foes, and, blessed with freedom, depart, together with our wives and children, from this life. . . ."

The historian Josephus relates that, with the exception of five children and two women, all nine hundred and sixty defenders died by their own or a beloved's hands.

Recently, the Israelis have been accused of having a Masada complex. For almost two thousand years very little was said about the story of Masada within the Jewish community although the tale was never forgotten. Yochanan's story was retold in every generation because it was the story a dominated people needed to hear. Today, Masada's story has again become the story that must be told. It is sometimes said that Arab threats to exterminate the Israelis are mere hyperbole. After Auschwitz, no Jew can ever take such a threat lightly. Every sane Israeli must at least face the possibility that, were the Arabs ever to defeat them decisively, they would tolerate no such bargain as that made by Yochanan and Vespasian; nor would most Israelis accept a repetition of the cycle of powerlessness that led to the death camps. It is earnestly to be hoped that peace can come to the Middle East. An indispensable element in such a peace must be assurances of genuine credibility that Arab threats of extermination are in fact hyperbole rather than an actual statement of intent. Until then, the Israelis will have no choice but to assume that those who refuse to recognize the State of Israel anticipate a Middle Eastern Auschwitz. Should the Arabs ever have real dominion, it is questionable that the oil-rich victors would be prevented from doing what they will.

Under the circumstances, it is not surprising that Masada not Jabneh, the place of Yochanan's rabbinical academy, has captured the symbolic imagination of the Israelis. Masada is a liberating symbol. When one faces the possibility, as do the Israelis, that one's enemies may kill if they have the power, it is no longer necessary to predicate one's life on an appeasing servitude to the expectations of others, whether those others be human or divine. When Masada is an ever-present possibility, there can be no second Auschwitz. Eleazar ben Yair would never have submitted to the Nazis. Like the defenders of the Warsaw ghetto, he would have found a way to resist. Before submitting to the Germans, he would have killed himself and his family. The *Judenräte,* the Jewish councils that cooperated with the Nazis in the elimination of their own people, behaved toward the Nazis as Yochanan had counseled Jews to behave toward the Romans. They gave the Nazis the requisite signs of submission. In fairness to Yochanan, it must be repeated that he was dealing with a master who was infinitely more humane though not necessarily more truthful. As Elie Wiesel has observed in his memoir *Night,* it was not God but Adolf Hitler who alone kept his word to the Jews. Yet, in spite of Hitler's candor, the Jews were so fixated on Yochanan's bargain that they did not take the dictator at his word.

It is a mistake to regard Masada primarily as a symbol of national suicide. The real message of Masada is that *only a free life is worth living.* The defenders of Masada faced death and endured hardships of great intensity, but they did so willingly. They wanted to survive but only as free

178

men. When they could no longer do so, they simply recognized that their time had come.

I am not sure when the image of Masada became a controlling symbol in my own mind and heart. I believe it happened during the Sinai campaign against Egypt in 1956. During the campaign I heard a lot of talk at the Harvard Faculty Club, where I often took lunch, about how mistaken the Israelis had been to take on the Egyptians. In the initial stages of the campaign, someone suggested that the Arabs might yet turn the tide, overwhelm the Israelis and inflict a second Auschwitz upon them. I mentioned the conversation to Ellen that evening. She replied: "I'm really not worried. I have no idea of what is going to happen to the Israelis, but I am certain that, whether they live or die, they will do so as free men." Ellen and her family had been close enough to the threat of Auschwitz to have learned its lessons. The time might come when the Israelis might be compelled to choose a nuclear Masada; a second Jabneh is no longer a possibility; they could never tolerate another Auschwitz.

When I arrived in Pittsburgh in 1958, all that remained for me of Jabneh and the culture it had engendered was a servile consciousness I had no desire to perpetuate. Out of the wreckage and the rebirth of my time, I was determined to create a religious life for myself, rather than conform to other men's conceptions of what that life ought to be.

During the time we lived in Cambridge and the first two years in Pittsburgh, Ellen and I got along fairly well. Our youngest child, Jeremy, was born in Boston on June 4, 1958. However, by 1963 we realized we no longer had a real marriage to bind us. We were irrevocably bound to each other by our shared years and our children, but it was best for both of us that our difficult marriage was finally terminated.

The divorce from Ellen was the first of two related divorces. The second was a divorce from an increasingly difficult vocational situation. Neither sexually nor aesthetically was it possible for me to live the kind of repressed existence the Jewish community expects of its rabbis. I do not have a sensational sexual story to tell. What happened was rather simple. As a result of analysis, it became possible for me to slowly overcome my worst fears and uncertainties with women so that I could genuinely enjoy their company and delight in the act of love. I also had become sufficiently aware of myself to know that I could not fully share the act of love without becoming deeply involved with my partner.

179

I was extraordinarily fortunate to meet my second wife, Betty Rogers Alschuler, shortly after Ellen and I were divorced. Betty had also recently been divorced. We discovered that emotionally, aesthetically, and intellectually we shared the same world. We delighted in each other's company and wanted to share our lives together. We were married on August 21, 1966. Together with Betty's daughter, Lucy, and my children, Aaron and Hannah, we settled into a home in the Shadyside section of Pittsburgh. Jeremy remained with Ellen, and Betty's older children, John and Jean, were at school and married respectively. After seven years of marriage, the delight and excitement we shared as our marriage began has deepened and intensified.

Betty had been a member of the board of trustees of a Reform congregation in Chicago's northern suburbs. She had a very good understanding of the way power was distributed within the Jewish community. After we were married she saw things on the other side. She became convinced almost immediately that I had to get out of the rabbinate. She also saw that I had to be true to myself until I did. Getting out was to prove far more difficult than we anticipated. My theological writings were receiving a thoughtful reception in the academy if not within the Jewish community. In the course of a few years I was invited to lecture at over one hundred and fifty colleges, universities, and theological seminaries in the United States, Canada, and Europe. However, my visibility diminished my chances of finding suitable academic employment. As I have indicated, few religion departments were willing to risk hiring a Jew who was regarded with hostility by important segments of the Jewish community.

It was possible for me to remain a Hillel director and university chaplain largely because of the loyalty of the men and women who had brought me to Pittsburgh. They were of middle class and Eastern European origins. They had their own reasons for distrusting those with real power in the community. They were apparently determined that I be left alone to write and lecture without interference. Nevertheless, I knew that sooner or later the small, loyal group that stood behind me would be unable to resist the pressure of those who were determined to get rid of me. For many years those with power in the Jewish community had regarded work with college students as unworthy of their attention. They ignored the Hillel Foundation and were content to permit those whom they regarded as socially and financially beneath them to run it. In the mid-sixties, the rise of student activism compelled them to change their minds. Too many of the visible activists were Jewish. There was always the possibility that campus explosions might lead to the kind of heightened anti-Semitism that might affect them. For years the Pittsburgh United Jewish Federation had ignored the Hillel Foundation. In the late sixties, they were determined to control it.

As soon as the Federation became interested in the Hillel Foundation, the possibility that many of my supporters could achieve greater status within the Jewish community became open. Recognition by the Federation meant heightened status. As long as the Federation ignored them, my opposition to the Federation was welcome. As soon as the Federation took cognizance of them, I became a liability. They were good people. They did not want to recognize the change. Since my career was at stake, the altered circumstances were more immediately obvious to me than to them.

There was, however, an important difference of opinion between me and those with whom I worked concerning the nature of my role. Over the years, I found myself increasingly disinterested in a narrowly sectarian conception of the chaplaincy. When I first came to Pittsburgh, I tried very hard to encourage large attendances at the Sunday bagels and lox brunches that are traditionally a central part of any Hillel program. I also offered foundation-sponsored noncredit courses in Jewish religion, literature, and history. These courses were usually poorly attended after the third or fourth week at Pitt as they were throughout the country. Invariably, noncredit courses start out with fair enrollments, but students tend to drop out as the pressure of regular work builds up. It was obvious that if I wanted to reach students at any level other than feeding them, I would have to do so through the normal curriculum.

Furthermore, I had no interest in making the students feel "at home" in the American Jewish community as it was constituted. I wanted to help them to achieve a measure of insight into the nature of their religious and personal existence so that they might create something of integrity for themselves. I believed I could serve best as a counselor and by working hard at my university teaching. I felt that my academic training in psychoanalytic theory and my personal psychoanalysis were a help in that work, especially as I tried at all times to respect the limits of what a nonpsychiatric counselor might achieve. My courses at the university proved popular. In the last few years in Pittsburgh, five hundred students were enrolled in each. Nevertheless, because many of my students were non-Jewish and I was obviously not interested in doling out bagels and

181

lox, people in the Jewish community complained that I was not reaching Jewish students. It was clear that my vision of a university chaplaincy was radically different from what the community was prepared to accept. I sought to transform a pervasive servile consciousness by insight; the community had no idea of what I was about.

After the publication of my third book, *Morality and Eros,* one of the national leaders of B'nai B'rith who lives in Pittsburgh told me that there was a lot of discontent about my writing books. She asked me not to write any more books or accept any more invitations to lecture at universities for at least a year, in order to prove to people that I really wanted to be a good Hillel rabbi.

"The way things are now," I replied, "I know that at least one person thinks I'm doing the job the way it should be done. If I follow your advice, there'll be none."

There was no point in arguing. She was a good woman who was honestly trying to be helpful. She had stood by me many times in the past. She clarified as well as anyone could the chasm between my conception of a college ministry and my community's.

It is not without irony that as the lay community found it more difficult to accept me, my fellow rabbis in Hillel service came to trust me and to seek my leadership, although most disagreed with me theologically. During the fourteen years that I was a Hillel rabbi, I came to value very greatly the fellowship of my colleagues who served as chaplains at colleges and universities throughout North America. Of all the honors I received during the sixties, none meant more to me than one they bestowed upon me. In 1969 I became first vice president of the National Association of Hillel Directors. It was understood that I would become the next president, but I left Hillel service before my term as vice president expired.

Another source of support and encouragement came from Charles E. Merrill, Jr. of Boston, the headmaster and founder of a Boston prep school called the Commonwealth School. His father had been the founder and senior partner of the brokerage firm of Merrill, Lynch, Pierce, Fenner and Smith. When the senior Mr. Merrill died, his will provided for the establishment of the Charles E. Merrill Educational and Charitable Trust. Charles told me of the establishment of the trust in the late fifties while I was at Harvard. He asked me for suggestions as to how the trust might help Jewish philanthropic and educational institutions. The Merrills are Protestant, but Charles's father stipulated in his will that Catholic and Jewish as well as Protestant institutions were to receive support from the

182

trust. Over the years Charles's friendship has been of great importance to me. While I was at Pitt, he made it possible for me to become the Charles E. Merrill Lecturer and then the Charles E. Merrill Adjunct Professor in the Humanities. While the power structure within the Jewish community sought to deny me any platform whatsoever, often by means that can with charity only be described as underhanded, a Protestant layman made it possible for me to begin university teaching. The grant to Pitt was designed so that the university took over the costs involved when the program became established. In 1965 Charles made it possible for me to lecture at the Catholic University of Lublin as well as to Catholic intellectual circles in other parts of Poland. Charles had a number of contacts among Polish Catholic intellectuals. He wanted them to become acquainted with me and I them. While in Poland, I visited Auschwitz. Shortly thereafter I had to choose a title for my first book. The title *After Auschwitz* was inescapable.

In 1969 it became evident that the Hillel Foundation at Pitt required new sources of financial support. This meant turning to Pittsburgh's United Jewish Federation. As in every American city of any magnitude, the Federation is ostensibly the fund-raising institution of the local community. By virtue of the fact that it is also the disbursing agency and its allocations can mean the difference between growth and atrophy for its beneficiaries, it is the locus of whatever real power exists in the Jewish community. In Pittsburgh as in most American cities, the Federation is dominated by extremely wealthy German and imitation German Jews. I knew that the price of financial support for Hillel from the Federation would be simple: Get rid of Richard Rubenstein.

I was assured by my trustees that they could both receive Federation financial support and retain me. The Federation made similar noises in the initial stages of the negotiations. I had no illusions. Shortly before formal negotiations began, I invited Rabbi Oscar Groner, of the national Hillel staff, and key members of my local board of trustees to dinner at my home. Most of the people who accepted my invitation were good men and women who never dreamed when they hired me in 1958, that their Hillel rabbi would take issue so visibly with established patterns. They were basically decent, theologically uncomplicated people. They certainly had no idea of the extent to which I questioned their traditional faith. Nevertheless, when my views became a matter of controversy, they stood behind me as they stood behind me when Ellen and I parted. But despite contrary assurances, I knew there was a limit to their backing in the face

183

of pressure from the lay and professional leaders of the Federation. The Federation leaders were unwittingly the heirs of Yochanan's bargain, save that they lacked the inner dignity and the moral integrity of Yochanan's honest religious faith. To his last breath Yochanan feared God far more than any king of flesh and blood. Yochanan could counsel his people to submit to an earthly sovereign, confident that the submission was part of God's providential design. Most of the really powerful men who led my community had faith in their wealth and little else. Because they had little real power in comparison with Pittsburgh's Protestant élite, their consciousness was servile to an extent and for a cause that Yochanan and his spiritual heirs would have regarded as unworthy. Had I submitted to such men, it would have been difficult for me to contain my self-contempt.

At the dinner, after we had gone through the preliminary pleasantries, I said what I had to say: "I know that the Hillel Foundation needs money. Realistically, the Federation is the only source to which we can turn. I want to urge you to come to an agreement with the Federation. I strongly favor such an agreement, but there is one thing you must know: When you come to terms with them, you will have another Hillel Rabbi. I will not and cannot work with those people."

Men with a servile consciousness unredeemed by religious faith, no matter how wealthy or highly placed, can never be trusted. In Pittsburgh, the highest ambition of the very wealthiest men who dominated the Federation was to gain admission to the top-status, formerly all-Christian Duquesne Club. At the time I left Pittsburgh, there was said to be an informal quota of about six token-Jews a year. In spite of their extraordinary wealth, when permitted to do so, these men behaved toward those with real power in Pittsburgh, such as the late Richard King Mellon, after the fashion of flattering lackeys at the court of an absolute monarch. In order to achieve the miserable token of bestowed status, they were quite willing to betray their own people if necessary. For example, the leaders of the Jewish community publicly supported policies that had the effect of barring less affluent young Jews from admission to the University of Pittsburgh. As men of great resources, they had little difficulty in placing their own sons and daughters in the better eastern universities and professional schools. Nevertheless, they actively supported preferential quotas for blacks and other minority groups, quotas that guaranteed that a certain proportion of those admitted to school or hired by the faculties be black. As a result, in Pittsburgh, there was a rapid decrease in the number of Jews admitted to the law, medical, and dental schools of the university as the number of far-less qualified blacks increased. I cannot fault blacks for seeking this means of righting an historical injustice. Unfortunately, Jewish leaders had no comparable concern for their own people. Weak men cannot tolerate those who refuse to be bound by their submissions. Were I to work for such people, all the anger and contempt I felt toward them would have had to be internalized. And, I didn't even have a helpless, financially dependent rabbi upon whom I could take out my rage. Regrettably, some Jews need scapegoats as much as some non-Jews. The Gentiles can use Jews; all too often the Jews use their own rabbis. I had no intention of becoming a target the men of the Federation could hit without fear of retaliation. As I have reiterated throughout this book, I had seen too many good rabbis emotionally assaulted to have any illusions. The aggression directed against me would have been psychic rather than physical. It would often have been disguised. Sooner or later, it would have been effective, had I played the game. There are many causes worth dying for. My employers' appetite for scapegoats was not one of them.

The trustees were shocked when they realized the import of my words. Our relationship of almost twelve years was coming to an end. Sammy Silverman, who was the object of the murderous Yom Kippur fantasy, which I describe in Chapter Two, broke the silence. He was the only member of the Hillel board who was a Federation leader.

"Rabbi," he said, "you can't mean what you've just said. If you can't work for the Pittsburgh Federation, there's not a place in America where you can get a job."

Silverman was correct. If my profound distrust of the Federation became known, I would be the object of a national blackball system that required nothing more than a telephone. I had already experienced the blackball system when I sought an academic post. Silverman was warning me that my chances of finding further work as a Hillel director were in jeopardy. Technically, I had tenured status, but that would prove no real protection. Both Silverman and I knew that Hillel rabbis were generally paid far less than rabbis with comparable experience who served congregations. The job is regarded as low-status because of its low pay. Nevertheless, many able rabbis willingly accept the lower pay because of the greater personal and intellectual freedom the post offers, as well as the challenge of working with young people in a university environment. Silverman was warning me not to rock any boats lest even that avenue of employment be denied to me.

I looked at him coldly. "Sammy," I said, "I will not be threatened. What makes you think that I want further employment within the Jewish community?"

After the meeting, my friends urged me to reconsider. They assured me that they would be able to prevent the Federation people from interfering with me once the agreement was ratified. I thanked them but told them I would neither stand in the way of the Hillel Foundation nor would I want to depend upon my friends to fight my battles.

Betty was behind me all the way. We had no idea of how we would support ourselves. We had almost abandoned hope of finding a suitable academic appointment. We toyed with the idea of becoming expatriates. At the time, we were spending our summer months in Déya, Majorca. We thought that as expatriates we might live cheaply enough so that I could continue to study, write, and lecture. We really did not want to become expatriates. We considered it only as a last resort. I also thought of working on a *kibbutz,* abandoning the intellectual and theological work which had apparently brought me to a dead end professionally. We had no real idea of what we might do, but we were certain that I could no longer honestly serve the Jewish community in a rabbinic capacity. Fortunately, our pessimism about my job situation was unwarranted. By the time the crisis came to a head, three of my books had been published and *After Auschwitz* had been widely adopted for courses in colleges and universities. Academic institutions were beginning to express serious interest in appointing me in spite of opposition from within the Jewish community. The position I took at Florida State University has been as fulfilling in its way as my marriage to Betty has been in its.

The story I have told does not end with some kind of resolution of a plot. In real life there are no such definite resolutions. The same story cannot be told the same way twice. Were I to attempt to retell my story five years hence, it might have a different meaning to me. Today, I see myself as having been a profoundly sick man who turned to the study and practice of religion as a way of achieving his fantasies of omnipotence, but found instead a measure of healing. I cannot say with certainty that the path I have chosen has given me healing. I am, however, convinced that my involvement with religion made it possible for me to apprehend the historical and psychological depths of my own being. Without a serious confrontation with the religious dimension of my identity, I would have been condemned to a kind of truncated existence. Having been formed by forces that had been gathering for millennia, I would have been aware of only a distorted, flattened vision of the present, never apprehending how rich, terrible, and beautiful the present really is when comprehended in its true depth.

Above all, my encounter with religious thought and practice has permitted me to live the life I freely chose, given the limitations of my situation, rather than follow a path others had long ago ordained for me. Only by entering into the world of religion could I appropriate it as my own rather than confront it as a strange and alien inheritance that would have forever exerted its mysterious subterranean influence upon me. I look upon the misery, the passion, the illness, the deluded ambitions, the hopes, opportunities, and joys that have constituted my life and I embrace them all. I am both my memories and my yearnings. I am also the intersecting point of the love, hatred, and fright that have entered into all of my encounters with others. There were people I hated because I feared what they could do to me. They are a part of my life as are the thousands of others whose lives have touched mine. And, I know that I have become a part of all those others. Without them I would have been a blank slate, not a human being. We are each of us private isolated selves, locked up and unreachable. We are at the same time all the men and women whose lives have touched ours. We are also all the men and women to the first generation whose lives have made ours possible.

I want to stress that when I accepted my post at Florida State University, I left the *professional* employ of the organized Jewish community. I did not reject Judaism. However, I will not permit any man, living or dead, to define what Jewish existence ought to mean to me. I have been compelled to reject Yochanan's bargain and the servile consciousness that became its by-product as soon as Yochanan's deep religious faith was lost. His bargain was right for my ancestors. It cannot be mine. Without compromising the integrity of my religious identity, I would embrace rather than exclude. I want to be truly catholic. I cannot reject any man's gods or experience of the holy. I have especially rejected the doctrine of covenant and election, the idea of a chosen people, whether claimed by Jews or Christians, because the sacred is not an object of private property in the exclusive possession of any single individual or group.

Nor will I reject Jesus, his disciples, and most especially Paul of Tarsus. They are a part of my history and my personal story. But, neither

187

will I permit any man or any church to claim them as their exclusive possession and tell me what Jesus must mean to me. I have known in my bones what it means to be the intended sacrificial victim. What Jew does not after Auschwitz?

In the summer and fall of 1972, I was sent by Florida State to teach in its Study Center in Florence, Italy. Betty and I were accompanied by Hannah and Jeremy. We were exceedingly fortunate in our choice of apartment. We rented a terrace apartment overlooking the Arno and the Ponte Vecchio. Every day we looked across the Arno from the terrace and the living room at Filippo Brunelleschi's Cupola over the Duomo, Giotto's Campanile, the Palazzo Vecchio, and the Uffizi Gallery. Day by day we walked the streets of Florence, coming to know the Pitti Palace, the churches of Santa Croce, Santa Maria del Carmine, Santa Maria Novella, San Lorenzo, and a host of other unforgettable sights. We traveled the length and breadth of Italy, beholding in wonder and appreciation the incredible variety of ancient, medieval, and modern treasures that country bestows on those who would but look. At this moment, I can see in my mind's eye Duccio's extraordinary hymn to the Virgin which he composed with his paint brush, the Maesta of the Cathedral of Siena. I can also see the mosaics depicting Justinian and Theodora in Ravenna's Church of San Vitale. I do not know whether I recall Venice's church of Santa Maria de la Salute or Canaletto's painted vision of it. I see Bernini's statue of "Santa Theresa in Ecstasy," in Rome's Church of Santa Maria de la Vittoria. I also behold the Cave of the Sybil of Cumae, north of Naples. It was there that I gave a lecture on archaic Mediterranean religion to my students. According to Virgil, Aeneas is supposed to have come to the cave to inquire of the Sybil after his flight from Troy to Italy at the end of the Trojan War. Most especially do I see the Triumphal Arch of Titus erected in the year 80 C.E. by the Flavian House to commemorate their victory over Jerusalem ten years earlier. Out of respect to my forefathers, I will not walk under that arch, but neither can I reject it, the imperial city, or any of the other treasures of the civilization of the West, pagan, Christian, or humanist with which Italy abounds. No member of my family would be alive today had Titus not been victorious and had my ancestors not been taken captive to the European continent. We are the children of his victory. Nor would I be alive had the Church not triumphed in the West. I am as much the human consequence of that which my ancestors rejected as that which they affirmed.

There was a time when each of the families of mankind could pretend that they were able to close their gates, turn inward and shut out the sacred experience and the history of the other families. In their mutual isolation they could nurture the illusion that theirs alone was the true way. That illusion is no longer possible for me or for many others, no matter what their religious background. As Betty and I traveled from north of Venice to south of Naples, we could dismiss none of the worlds we encountered as foreign to us. The gates can no longer be closed. All of us must find new ways of being true to what is unique in our inheritance while recognizing that the apparently alien worlds have shaped and continue to shape who we are and what we are becoming.

While the family was in Florence the question of Jeremy's bar mitzvah came up. He was fourteen. He had not had a bar mitzvah when he became thirteen, as his brother had a decade earlier. Jeremy had been living in Berkeley, California with his mother and did not prepare himself to have the ceremony. It was decided that Jeremy would train for his bar mitzvah in Florence. The ceremony would later take place in Israel. Fortunately, Rabbi Michael Berenbaum, now Chaplain to Jewish Students at Wesleyan University, and his wife Linda were doctoral students in residence at the Florence center. They volunteered to supervise Jeremy's training.

The date of Jeremy's bar mitzvah was set for the third Sabbath in August. Two weeks before the event, the Berenbaums invited Jeremy to drive to Munich for a brief visit. While in Munich they visited Dachau. Three years before, Jeremy had accompanied me when I had business in Germany. During the earlier visit, we spent a night in Cologne, the place to which the Roman legionnaires had probably brought some of our ancestors immediately after the fall of Jerusalem. On both sides of his family, Jeremy is in all likelihood descended from Jews who had been brought to the Rhineland by the Romans and had dwelt there for well over a thousand years before moving toward Holland and Lithuania respectively. I told Jeremy about the probable significance of Cologne in his family background.

"Daddy," the eleven-year-old-boy interrupted, "tell me about the death camps." Jeremy was my second son to ask me about the death camps for the first time on German soil. Aaron had asked the same question in 1960 when he was eleven and accompanied me on a trip to Düsseldorf, Bonn, and Cologne.

We were standing in front of the towering Kölner Dom, the great Cologne Cathedral, as we spoke of the camps. I tried to give my son as accurate yet unsensational an account as possible. If I erred, it was on the side of cool understatement.

Jeremy listened without saying a word. Finally, he responded:

"Daddy, get me out of this place. I don't want to be near these people."

It was a child's response. He made no distinctions. He did not inquire after causes. His was an unreflecting reaction to a horror far greater than any he had ever imagined. And, he knew how narrowly his mother had escaped that horror.

When Jeremy visited Dachau in 1972 he was better prepared to think about the unthinkable. When he returned to Florence from Munich, he wanted to discuss his experience at length. I asked him to wait until his bar mitzvah ten days hence. Three days before the bar mitzvah, Betty, Jeremy, Aaron, and I got into our Fiat 124 Familiare and took the Autostrada to Rome's Fiumicino Airport to fly to Israel. Aaron lives in Atlanta, Georgia and had flown over for the event. Before boarding the plane for Israel, we went through the stringent inspection that had been necessitated by the recent machine gun attack in Tel Aviv's Lod Airport. Two hours later, we were met at Lod by Lucy, Betty's daughter, and her friend Shalom Goldman. Lucy had been a student at the Hebrew University for several years and had rented a house in Jerusalem's Arab section from a Mr. Bedouin, who owns an antiquities shop on the Via Dolorosa where Lucy worked for a while. The house was only a five minute walk from the Western Wall, all that remained of the ancient Temple of Jerusalem destroyed by the Romans. Lucy and Shalom had arranged for a group of their friends to come to the Wall on the Sabbath morning and to constitute themselves a minyan, a religious quorum of ten men, so that we might celebrate Jeremy's bar mitzvah at the site of the ancient sancturary.

It was at this point that I told Jeremy of the connection between Dachau and the fall of Jerusalem. I told him how Titus had breached the walls of the city and the Temple, forcing his ancestors into their European captivity. I also told him of Yochanan's bargain with Vespasian. I explained that the bargain had kept his ancestors alive, but that it also left them without defenses when the Nazis changed the rules.

"The fires that incinerated the corpses at Dachau were lit by Titus when he placed his torch against this place. The fires burned slowly. At times they were hardly visible, but they were never entirely extinguished. Your ancestors became landless, powerless wanderers when Titus won his

190

victory. Hitler ended what Titus began. Himmler and Eichmann knew how to take advantage of Yochanan's bargain for their own purposes."

A bar mitzvah is a puberty rite that introduces a boy to manhood. I did not have one. I wanted to give Jeremy the initiation into manhood my father had been unable to give me, but I did not want it to be a ceremony such as the heirs of Yochanan ben Zakkai celebrate in American suburbs. I wanted the primal character of the rite to be manifest. It was important that Jeremy return to the place of his ancestral origin—to the very place which, in Jewish mythology, was the first solid spot formed out of the primeval waters at creation. It had to be a movement of return and new birth. There was, however, more to it than that. As Jeremy's father, I was taking my place in the chain of generations, but I also found myself identifying with Jeremy and with what he was going through. It was as if he was entering manhood for both of us and, if only for a brief moment, I had achieved that darkest of all wishes. By identifying with Jeremy I had become father to myself. I have reason to believe that Jeremy's bar mitzvah did what it was meant to do. He understood on that day as he stood in the heat and the dust before the Wall that he was in truth a contemporary of Yochanan ben Zakkai, Eleazar ben Yair, Titus, Vespasian and Bar Kokba.

In the afternoon after the ceremony, I took the family for a drive. We drove first from Jerusalem to Bethlehem. On the day of his bar mitzvah, Jeremy visited the Church of the Holy Nativity which is supposed to have been built over the site where Jesus was born. Jesus is a part of Jeremy's story although Jesus was rejected by many of his own people and made the excuse for two thousand years of assaults against them. I wanted Jeremy to know that Jesus was part of his story. We then drove to Hebron which is not a happy city. There has been bitter enmity between the Jews and the Arabs of Hebron dating back at least to the slaughter and castration in 1948 of the Orthodox Jews who founded a Yeshivah there. They wanted to study the Talmud and keep Yochanan's bargain in the very city where the patriarchs, Abraham, Isaac, and Jacob are alleged to have been buried. Whether or not the biblical tradition is literally true, Hebron is a place where Jeremy's ancestors lived and died in remote antiquity. I wanted him to visit that city on the day of his bar mitzvah. I wanted him to know how old he really was on that day.

The next day Jeremy, Aaron, and I drove down the ancient road from Jerusalem to Jericho. We took a right turn when we came to the northern tip of the Dead Sea and drove southward to the western shores of the sea past Qumrun until we came to the base of the great mountain stronghold of Masada. Today, the ascent has been made easy by the installation of a cable car from the base of the mountain to the fortified encampment eighteen hundred feet above. After we had viewed the excavations, the three of us walked to the northern edge of Masada. We looked down on the desert plain and the Dead Sea beneath us. We looked toward Jericho where the Israelites under Joshua first entered Canaan. At that spot, I told Jeremy and Aaron about the decision of Eleazar ben Yair and his followers to die rather than to surrender to the Romans. As the desert sun beat down upon us with noonday intensity I read Josephus's account of the defender's last hours and Eleazar's final exhortation. When I came to Eleazar's warning that the Romans would have their will of those who surrendered, I thought of Dachau, visited by Jeremy less than two weeks before.

I turned to both my sons and asked, "If you had been in Jerusalem when the Romans besieged it, whom would you have followed, Yochanan or Eleazar ben Yair?"

Jeremy answered for himself and his brother, "Eleazar ben Yair."

"But, don't forget," I replied, "that we stand here today because of Yochanan ben Zakkai."

Yochanan's bargain was no longer possible for us. All that remained was freedom and its risks. Nevertheless, even as we linked ourselves to the men and women of Masada on the very spot where they perished nineteen hundred years before, we had to acknowledge our debt to Yochanan and to all of our ancestors who had chosen his way. Because of their incredible discipline over the centuries, it was possible for us to stand upon Masada as heirs of both Yochanan and Eleazar.

As we stood there, I wondered about the future. Was Israel's return after two thousand years of wandering and misery but the prelude to a final nuclear holocaust? After Auschwitz, it is inconceivable that the Israelis would consent to their own annihilation, whether piecemeal or sudden. Were they convinced that the end had come, there would be no second Jabneh, no second Auschwitz and no second Masada.

There would be no second Jabneh; the first had led to Auschwitz when the Germans changed the rules; nobody could risk the consequences of a second submission. There would be no second Auschwitz; Jewish lives would never again be purchased so cheaply. There would be no second Masada; only Jews died at Masada.

For years there have been persistent rumors of Israeli nuclear weapons. I have no hard facts, but it is inconceivable that the Israelis could have listened to threats of annihilation for twenty-five years without producing their own doomsday weapon. Faced with the destruction of the only political entity they can trust to defend their existence and dignity, the State of Israel, they would unleash their bombs on Cairo, Alexandria, Amman and Damascus in the certain knowledge that the extinction of Haifa, Tel Aviv and Jerusalem would swiftly follow. There is a limit to the pressure the Arabs can exert. Should the Israelis become convinced that, once again, the world will consent to the extermination of Jews, as the European and Japanese response to the oil boycott would indicate, the Israelis will not depart from history alone.

Nor is it likely that the religion of Yochanan's heirs could survive a nuclear apocalypse. What forms of religious consciousness would possess or afflict the Jewish remnant, no man can foretell.

Yet, as I thought of Israel's deadly peril, I was mildly optimistic. Nuclear terror may offer the only credible guarantee of peace. For twenty centuries it has been possible to slaughter Jews at will. More often than not there was gain in the bloody venture for the slaughterers. In the century par excellence of broken promises and broken trust, the dearer it becomes to eliminate Jews, the greater the likelihood that peace will someday come to the Holy Land and all of its peoples.